J. K. LASSER'S

MANAGING YOUR FAMILY FINANCES

(*New Revised Edition*)

J. K. LASSER'S

MANAGING YOUR
FAMILY FINANCES

(New Revised Edition)

J. K. LASSER TAX INSTITUTE

DOUBLEDAY & COMPANY, INC.
Garden City, New York
1973

ISBN: 0-385-03582-9
Library of Congress Catalog Card Number 70–186029
Copyright © 1968, 1973 by J. K. Lasser Tax Institute
All Rights Reserved
Printed in the United States of America

PREFACE TO REVISED EDITION

The 1970s opened on an uncertain note for the economy. For all of us, the major concern is inflation which continues to increase despite steps taken to stem and reverse its tide. Many other economic problems face the nation—and the individual. Some of them will be solved, others will not. But on the balance, we trust that the economy, one in which all can thrive, will stabilize itself during the seventies.

In this context, we believe the updated edition of MANAGING YOUR FAMILY FINANCES provides you material with which you may more advantageously plan your finances in today's economy.

BERNARD GREISMAN, *Director*
J. K. Lasser Tax Institute

PREFACE

J. K. Lasser's MANAGING YOUR FAMILY FINANCES has been planned as a guide for those who want to develop and follow a conscious and intelligent approach to family finances.

Whether you are a young person on your own, newly married, or already established with a family and beset by financial difficulties, you will find methods, advice, and suggestions for dealing with all aspects of money management.

We outline a definite program for the skillful management of income, large or small. Perhaps for you the problem is not lack of money; it is misdirected spending, confusion regarding responsibility, the failure to provide for the future and for emergencies. Or perhaps you, like many others, are caught in the squeeze between inflation and an income that never seems adequate. Whatever your situation may be, the techniques here detailed can be applied to the particular circumstances of every family to promote financial stability and freedom from the constant anxiety that money trouble creates.

MANAGING YOUR FAMILY FINANCES thoroughly explores—

The control of expenses: how realistic plans may be devised to handle present and future commitments, including the spiraling costs of everyday living, of education, of health protection.

Increasing income: how to cut costs, and how people of all ages can embark on personal money-making enterprises; what aspects of the Federal income tax law can be used for your benefit; how and where to save, and how to initiate a sound investment program.

The financial hazards and legal commitments to be faced in buying or selling a home: how to finance purchase of a residence.

The desirability and danger of credit; how to enjoy a state of indebtedness while maintaining complete control.

Protection for the future, for self, dependents, survivors: what you can expect from Social Security and from private insurance; the importance of wills and the effects of joint ownership; the steps to be taken for a secure and healthy retirement.

Your application of the ideas presented in this book can enable you to resolve present financial difficulties and to avoid the many pitfalls faced each day in the use of money.

We gratefully acknowledge here the contribution and editorial supervision of Joyce Clarke, and the sections provided by Helen G. Meyers and Miriam Gelband.

BERNARD GREISMAN, *Director*
J. K. Lasser Tax Institute

CONTENTS

x *Contents*

J. K. LASSER'S
MANAGING YOUR FAMILY FINANCES
(*New Revised Edition*)

Chapter 1

PROGRAMMING YOUR FINANCIAL FUTURE

Today, man can circle the planet in a few hours; he can land men on the moon and bring them back; he has invented computers to give instant answers to questions that people take hours or days to work out. This is a miracle world, but the average person in it continues to worry about a problem as old as civilization—*Money*.

Money should help to answer problems, not to be a worry in itself. Yet quarrels about money continue to be a major cause of divorce, of dissension between parent and child, and of breakdown in family relationships. Managing money wisely may not save every marriage, but it can go a long way toward it.

The management of money is vital in a constantly fluctuating economy. Individuals who are employed and in comfortable circumstances may suddenly find themselves seeking work and needing savings. No time is better than the present to study how to make the most of your money.

FIRST STEPS

This is a work book from which you draw the information and suggestions most suited to your situation. You add to it your own facts and figures, according to your circumstances. We suggest you first read the whole book through, noting the points of particular interest and the ideas it gives you. Then talk over problems and discuss *goals* frankly with the family. The program you develop is your own—not one for the Joneses with whom you may, or may not want to keep up. Your goals will change as one after the other is fulfilled. The steps you take now make each one possible.

When husband and wife sit down together to discuss their financial program, their first step should be to make a pact—to keep emotions in low key. A cool businesslike attitude is absolutely necessary. Let wrangling over past mistakes go. Make a decision to work together to overcome difficulties and to build a more satisfying life through the wiser use of money.

Children should not be left out of financial planning. Their future is involved too. Seek their interest and cooperation early; you will find it a sound investment. The children's part in the family program is discussed more fully in Chapter 3.

DEVELOPING A FINANCIAL PROGRAM

A disciplined financial program can be used to advantage by the person of limited income and by his neighbor who enjoys apparent affluence. The first needs to learn the many ways to make money go further and how to multiply it; the other, to use money to best advantage. Many men and women who are trained to do professional or technical jobs with the utmost efficiency fail dismally as managers of the money they earn. In today's society with its opportunities for travel and entertainment, its tempting advertising and merchandise, money can disappear all too easily without fulfilling any of a family's true objectives.

In Chapter 2, we outline a method for assessing net worth, achieving goals, and establishing financial security. In this chapter, we are concerned with basic planning which can be adapted by young career people, those newly married, and people of all ages who constantly run into financial problems.

When young marrieds set up a plan, they will, of course, change their pattern if a working wife stops working; when they start a family; and if they move from an apartment to a house. They will budget afresh with each change, enlarging their system, and redirecting saving toward new goals. Through frank discussion and planning together, they can build an invaluable bulwark against future inharmony.

WHAT YOUR MONEY MUST DO— AND WHAT YOU WANT IT TO DO

Some of the money the employed person receives is spent before he gets it. Deductions include Federal, state, and city taxes; Social Security (FICA) tax, and perhaps state disability insurance. Your company may also deduct for health insurance and a pension fund. All these deductions are customarily shown on a slip attached to or accompanying the pay check. The deductions cover *liabilities,* such as taxes which you must pay in any event, and *assets,* such as Social Security benefits and company pension, which you will eventually receive. The protection you receive from a group health insurance plan also counts among your assets.

Your money, then, is at work before you receive your pay; this part of your financial planning is already handled for you. You are responsible for the rest. Therefore, *take-home pay* is what we shall discuss here. (The self-employed person will, of course, make the necessary adjustments for his particular case.)

From your check, you now have to cover certain inescapable expenses which we describe as "fixed." Some, such as rent or mortgage, and insurance premiums are set amounts you can forecast easily; some, your additional taxes, for instance, are still uncertain in amount. To get some idea of what you owe, you have to estimate or use last year's figures.

In addition, you have to pay out for what we describe as "everyday" expenses. Among these are food, clothing, repairs, medical bills, and all the little things, such as hair grooming and newspapers. Since you have control over a large part of these expenses they can be described as "flexible."

After your pay check has covered the fixed and the everyday expenses, it has to work for you in achieving certain objectives, mainly to bring improved conditions or opportunities into the family life. This is the *plus* side of money management and the reason for much of it.

DEFINING YOUR SPENDING GOALS

You would do well to start your program by setting down your spending goals on paper. In Chapter 2 and elsewhere we refer again to the setting of goals. They are of paramount importance because, without them, people have a tendency to fritter money away—and then to wonder why they lack what others have. So—define your goals even before you get down to figuring the dollars and dimes. *The vision of what you want the money to do will help you over any difficult patches that may lie ahead.*

If you are heavily in debt, your first goal will certainly be to get out of it (see page 16). A repayment plan, worked out with outside help if necessary, must precede everything else. All members of the family should account for expenditure until the situation is completely overcome.

THE BUDGET

Smart money management starts with a budget or, if you prefer another name, a spending plan. In the home, as well as in business, the budget is a means of controlling expenses and of directing spending wisely. Many people recoil at the very idea. They think a budget is a strait jacket—something that will tie them down and take all the joy out of living. On the contrary, the budget is a means of releasing money to better use, and of putting the budgeter in control of his fortunes. It is a way out of continual financial harassment, and a tool with which to handle rising costs, taxation, sudden sickness, and other emergencies. It means money at work for you, achieving your objectives, present and future.

At this early stage, the new budgeter should settle questions such as who is to keep the records, who is to handle what expenses, and how personal allowances shall be scaled. (See Chapter 3 for detailed discussion.)

Many families, having discovered the value of methodical financial planning, use it to steer a course throughout life. A civil engineer who began budgeting in the early days of his marriage is still using this method twenty years later. He and his wife have raised two children, planned college education, and bought and sold three houses—each time with profit. In the early days when money was needed to finance a home and car, they borrowed from relatives. Each transaction was businesslike, and at current loan rates. Following his financial program, the young man repaid interest and principal promptly on the due dates. Though income is at a modest level, the family enjoys the newest appliances, has a good car, and can take vacations across the ocean or across the country. "Budgeting takes time," the civil engineer conceded. "But the results are well worth while. We'll never give it up."

Managing money wisely is chiefly a habit, and one you can build into your life. Establishing a good habit isn't necessarily easy; you may have to get rid of poor habits of money management at the same time and so will need to discipline yourself. But the result will repay you handsomely, in cash and in satisfaction.

PROGRAMMING THE FAMILY INCOME

The budget plan given below covers two classes of people: Those who earn regular salaries or wages (with or without other sources of income), and those whose income is uncertain and irregular.

While the experienced budgeter usually plans ahead for a calendar year (the period we shall discuss below), the new budgeter may prefer to set up a shorter program. If you wish, start with a three-month trial period. You can enlarge it later.

You may find it helpful to do rough planning on large sheets of paper that will not restrict you. Use unglazed shelf paper if you like, or tape sheets together. Later, when you have decided on your personal setup, you can transfer to a suitable columnar book or pages, or rule up a large notebook.

It is a good idea to pencil in projected figures so you can confirm or change them later. If you use ink or ball point for a whole period you are likely to end up with confusion or else feel you have some inflexible chart that is going to tie you down.

STEP I—THE PATTERN OF YOUR INCOME

If you are steadily employed, you can probably forecast your income for the year. You also know what additional sources you usually have, such as *savings bank interest, dividends, regular gifts, bonuses,* and income from *rentals, profitable hobbies, part-time work,* etc.

Draw up your Step I form into fifteen columns as indicated below:

Source of Cash Funds	Jan.	Feb.	Mar.	(etc. . . . . . . Dec.)	Total	Notes
Take-home pay: Husband Wife Interest Dividends Other... ••• •••						
Total						

Project your figures across the year (or shorter period). If you expect a raise, change the entries *after* you have it. A smart policy in money management is never to spend such money in advance or even to plan on covering essentials with it. Many people get in trouble with credit payments (see Chapter 6), because the money they counted on failed to come through. You play safe when you work on a minimum basis.

You cannot say in advance exactly what your savings bank interest will be. You might pencil in last year's figures as a guide, although with good savings, you may do better this time. However, an emergency withdrawal of savings might mean a drop in interest. Again, it would be wiser not to count on expectations. Other figures may be estimated or based on last year's income, as for instance, profit from a hobby or a rental.

If your employment is irregular, or depends on business profits or commissions, you will probably have to use last year's figures or a reasonable estimate in your projection. The person who receives income in large amounts at irregular intervals is often prone to spending sprees, then has to borrow to meet the inevitable bills. If you are in this category, start now with discipline; be conservative in your plans, basing them on minimum expectations. You may find it helpful to total expected income for the year, divide it by 12, and to allow yourself only one-twelfth for each month. You are then on the same basis as the regular wage and salary earner, but because your total is uncertain till received, you should exercise restraint in spending until you have directed savings into a solid bank account.

Finish up your Step I form now with a line of monthly totals.

STEP II—PROGRAMMING YOUR COMMITMENTS

Draw up a 15-column form similar to that used in Step I.

Fixed Expenses	(January through December)		Total	Notes
Total				

On the left under the main heading of Fixed Expenses, note down this type of obligation:

Additional Federal, state, and city taxes
Mortgage or rent
Repayments of all types of loans and installment purchases
Insurance premiums
Telephone, heat, light, water, etc.
Pledged contributions
Society or union dues
Savings (a *fixed obligation* to yourself and your family) for future
  goals and emergencies.

You know when these fixed expenses have to be paid. Some are certain in amount and you can project them across twelve months. Some are variable, such as the telephone bill. You can use previous bills or estimate this type of upcoming payment.

Note that Step II does not include department store and similar billing, only installment payments, if any. This step is designed to cover your *fixed expenses* of which regular savings should be a part.

SUMMARIZING STEPS I AND II. ADJUSTMENTS

You now have a total line for your income (Step I), and one for your fixed expenses (Step II). In summarizing, you can use a separate paper if you prefer, but if you have room, save copying by running your Step II totals under those of Step I. Deduct one from the other. *The resulting figure shows what you now have available for your everyday expenses.*

	Jan.	Feb.	Mar.	(etc. .... Dec.)	Total
Step I (Total income) Step II (Fixed expenses)					
Available for Step III (Everyday expenses)					

No doubt your Step III line is uneven because you have more heavy expenses one month than another. Perhaps the expenses of some months will be so heavy you are practically in the red for your everyday expenditure. You also see some months show few, if any, fixed expenses.

HERE ARE WAYS TO MAKE AN ADJUSTMENT

Some people make a total of the heavy obligations that only come up about once or twice a year, divide the total by twelve, and bank that sum monthly. By so *averaging,* they prepare for vacations, certain taxes, insurance premiums, and educational expenses.

Example:

> *Total cost*

Taxes
Insurance
Heating
Vacation
Education

————————

Total   ÷ 12 = (amount to be set aside monthly)

However, the experienced budgeter will want to consider each item separately in order to project the figures across the budget form. The civil engineer referred to on page 5, gives the explanation:

"We have averaging in use on several items: heating is one of them. Our total annual cost is budgeted at an equal amount each month, though with hot summers and extremely cold winters the actual bills differ widely. The same idea of equalizing the set-aside amounts is applied to water and electricity costs. Again, we ignore seasonal variation.

"Our local taxes are paid three times a year, but we average them to a monthly figure. Insurance premiums due annually are divided by 12."

People with few such fixed expenses—and a young couple both working may not have many—may prefer to even up their adjustment form simply by raising the *savings* on Step II so that Step III comes out to a more or less even monthly figure. (Goals for savings are discussed on page 15.)

Exactly how the juggling and adjusting is done is your personal affair. *The aim is to arrive at a consistent monthly figure for everyday expenses in line with the budget you draw up in Step III.* As you can see, it will be necessary for you to work backwards and forwards on these steps before you can develop the best plan through which you can reach the objectives you have named. (Page 4.)

Throughout your early budget experiments, remind yourself that you will need at least a full year of record keeping before you can come up with reasonably settled forms and figures. When people read of budget plans, they often assume they can solve their financial difficulties overnight by just filling in the suggested forms. Usually, a personal situation is far too complex for such an easy solution. *The budget works for you when you have worked at it.*

STEP III—THE KEY TO YOUR BUDGET

A period of recording your present rate of expenditure is necessary before you can settle on the most profitable plan for everyday expenses. Only by seeing how much you are presently spending in certain categories can you set up an improved pattern.

A newly married couple will have to set up many aspects of their budget on a tentative and experimental basis, but keeping track of all spending will provide invaluable records. Though it may be annoying to keep noting down all amounts spent, it is absolutely necessary to good money management to find out exactly where the money is going.

Some budgeters, once in the habit of such record keeping, prefer to continue it. Most people find it too constricting and, once they have established a suitable set-aside for a particular category, such as food, will not continue to run the last dime to earth. Plan on at least two months of strict record keeping for all members of the family, and note that if you keep these records in summer your pattern may be different in winter. A budget readjustment may be called for seasonally *within the set figure you arrive at for Step III.*

THE CATEGORIES OF EVERYDAY EXPENDITURE

Base daily accounting on the headings you intend to use when making up your budget. Following is a list of suggested main categories and the types of expenditure which would be entered under each:

Food. In this category, include food bought for meals at home, school lunches, and all meals out. Alcoholic and soft drinks, and candy should be included, also any taxes and tips.

Household Maintenance. Repairs, supplies, paid help or services.

Furnishings and Equipment. This will cover furniture, floor coverings, accessories such as tableware, curtains, and slipcovers, television, radios, etc., cleaning of any items.

Clothing. Dry cleaning, laundry, and charges by tailor and dressmaker would come under this heading as well as garments and the material for making them.

Transportation. Automobile upkeep and operation; commutation expenses, air, train, bus, and taxi fares.

Health Care. Fees for professional services, including hospital; drugs, supplies, and eyeglasses.

Education. Textbooks, supplies, tuition.

Recreation. Entertainment, reading, hobby material, games.

Personal Care. Beauty parlor and barber's charges, toilet items, etc.

Family Allowances. Each person's spend-as-you-please money.

In general, avoid overanalysis. It can prove tiresome and discouraging unless it serves a particular aim. So, separate details only when necessary. The cost of meals out can go in with other food unless you are reporting them as business expenses or you need to track down where the food dollars are going.

Of course, you will need details and receipts of items you may be deducting for income tax, or need to record for inventory or insurance purposes. Too, you may wish to separate cash from check transactions.

METHODS OF KEEPING TRACK

We suggest spending be noted in a small book or pad carried in purse or pocket. Receipts and store tapes should be placed in a prearranged place in the home, such as a box, a drawer, or on a spindle. Enter these outgoing payments on a form drawn up in accordance with your family situation and need of specific details.

Here is a suggestion:

Date	Food		Clothing		Housing			Transportation		Health		Personal		Etc. ....
	At home	Out	Purchases	Cleaning, repairs	Phone	Supplies	Furnishings	Car	Other	Doctor drugs	Dentist	Allowance, hair care	Drinks, tobacco, candy	--
														--
Total														

Refer to the list on page 10 and above, but work out the full form according to your own type of expenses, the number of people in the family, and the need to subdivide (which should not be carried to excess). Note the points on which the suggestion above differs from the list. For example, these headings show the telephone under everyday expenses. Earlier, we showed it on Step II as a fixed expense. You can place it as it best suits you, or split the set rental charge from excess charges, especially if you wish to place a limit on family calls.

Since this record keeping is to account for everyday expenses, we omit the Step II (page 7) items, such as rent, insurance, utilities. Nevertheless, you may well want to record them separately so that at the end of a month you can accurately show:

Total family income for January   _____
Total expenditure for the month   _____
(Money in hand? Good! It can satisfy a goal.)   _____

WEIGHING UP YOUR SPENDING

On page 8 you arrived at Income Less Fixed Expenses Equals Amount Available for Everyday Expenses. By averaging, you found you could even up the Step III line. Now you have been keeping a record of your actual spending. Was it in line with your Step III figure?

If you are fortunately not overspending, you now only have to keep on the same track, perhaps making a few adjustments within certain categories. If, even better, you can draw a line under Income less Expenses for the month above and show a saving, you have money in hand to put in the bank or to satisfy needs on your list of goals (page 4).

But too many people will find themselves overspent. That means they have used money they should have put into savings or have gone to the bank and taken out money already saved or, worse still, they have borrowed to cover expenses. If you are overspent, trim spending for next month. See Chapter 4 on cutting costs. Do not take on more fixed expenses (Step II), such as installment payments. Let the spending goals wait until you have a surplus.

YOUR STEP III BUDGET FORM

After you have been keeping records for a period you can project figures on an annual basis (though you may not find it practical

to plan closely for more than two or three months in advance).
Below, a form is suggested:

	Jan.	Feb.	Mar.	Apr.	(etc. ...... Dec.)	Dec.	Notes
Food Housing Clothes etc. etc.							
Total							

Through this form you control your budget because, if you keep
spending in line with projections here, you are fulfilling your other
objectives, covering the Step II fixed expenses, and the savings
program (page 15).

*If you set up a record of what you actually spent and compare it
with your plan, you will have a useful guide to help you to cut
back—and to maintain a vital reserve fund.*

At times, of course, your control over Step III expenditure may
break down. Unexpected medical bills may roll in, just at the same
time you have to pay the plumber, painter, and roofer. *The only
sound answer to such emergencies is the reserve in your savings
account.*

Until you have that reserve in a substantial condition, set a minimum operational figure for your everyday expenditure, and make
the necessary adjustments *within that figure.*

For example, you see a lot of money going under recreation and
clothing while members of the family complain new furniture is
needed or another car is positively necessary. Here, a family conference may be in order to establish what is essential and what is a
luxury. If plans for large purchases are ahead, the family may have
to agree to a new ceiling on recreation, clothing, entertaining, or
what not. You establish a new budget figure in these categories, and
step up savings to meet outright or installment buying.

As we have noted, it may not be practical to budget daily expenditure for more than two months in advance, and sometimes a

shorter period is desirable. But when your Step III form is fully developed, you should have established a reasonable sum which, each month, will cover your family's daily needs and take care of department store and professional billing.

You may also have to allow for rising costs for food, housing, repairs, etc. if inflation in the economy is not sharply controlled. The cost-of-living index is a regular guide to the current trend.

The point is that, unless you are heavily in debt and need to take the steps outlined on page 17, you need never develop any sense that a budget is a limiting factor in your life. You are simply using this means to foster a realistic attitude toward money among members of the family and to channel that money toward the needs and aspirations of each one.

UPCOMING VARIABLE BILLS

A hurdle which frequently throws the hopeful new budgeter is the charge account (see Chapter 6). Weeks after the purchases are made, the bills arrive. If provision has not been made for their payment, interest charges may be incurred on the accounts.

You should keep a record of credit spending so that you will be ready for the billing. Note the date each department store or other company usually bills you; if one company bills on the sixth of the month and another on the sixteenth and you are paid twice a month you can set aside the money in your checking account from two pay checks.

If you are already working your budget you will be less haphazard in your buying than formerly, and not buying in excess of planned items. But because people do tend to buy on sight (and sometimes it may be wise to do so), a record of what is being charged (from gasoline to garden tools) will help in adjusting next month's plan to meet the expected bills.

THE DEDUCTION METHOD OF KEEPING TRACK

Once people kept their budgeted money in cash in envelopes or jars. These days money allocated to a certain category may be in cash, a checking account, and a savings account. How can you keep track of your spending?

An idea you may find useful is to set up index cards or pages of a notebook which show the budgeted amount in each category and then to deduct from it as purchases are made. For example, the mother of a family knows that the agreed sum for clothing buying this month is $100. She has cash in hand for small purchases, the rest in checking and savings accounts. Carrying a card in her purse, she marks down charged shoes and a dress; her husband reports at night his cash purchase of shirts; a teenage daughter who has been handed cash returns the change and reports the buying of a skirt. Deductions from the budgeted $100 show only a few dollars left. The family can readily see that, except for minor purchases, clothing buying is over for the budgeting period.

A variation of this method is to give each member of the family cards with his portion of the budgeted category on it.

Some budgeters can carry their budget in their heads, but when several members of the family are spending, the deduction method can help to solve problems in money management.

STEP IV—PROGRAMMING YOUR SAVINGS

Saving is not something you do spasmodically—when you find a few extra dollars over on the pay check. It should be an integral part of your program. Putting at least 10 percent of take-home pay into savings each pay day establishes the savings habit. You use accounts at banks, savings and loan associations, and in credit unions to cover such categories as an emergency fund, upcoming commitments scheduled on your Step II form; short term needs—vacations, gifts, Christmas, etc.; plans for college education, aid to an older relative, a summer home, retirement for yourself, anything you like to name.

Chapter 9 will guide you in selecting your savings establishment. Some will allow customers to open several accounts, each for a specific purpose. Most run Christmas Clubs, but not all pay interest on the deposits. You and your family may prefer to earmark a portion of your regular savings as the Christmas Fund, using a day-of-deposit to day-of-withdrawal account. But those who find themselves dipping too freely into special funds may need the safeguard of the old-fashioned Christmas Club Plan that cannot be drawn upon until the holiday season.

Individuals in the family may want to deposit their personal allowances in the savings bank and to draw on it as they wish. A local savings bank also helps safeguard against too much cash in the house.

Whether you open accounts in several savings institutions or have only one, you can work out the application of your funds on a form ruled into a number of columns. Use a column or so for notes and dates of deposits and withdrawals. Then, across the page, run names of your banks or savings institutions and, under them, the various funds you are, in effect, establishing in each one.

You can then note the amount you are channeling from fixed savings into such funds as reserve, college education, vacation, Christmas, etc. You can also run records of savings which cover your Step II obligations. Probably you will be depositing money needed for monthly bills straight into a checking account. But money for annual insurance premiums, or put aside as car depreciation, school fees, and other less frequent payments, might as well earn interest in a savings institution until you need it. With such planning ahead, you are putting your money to work for you.

If additional savings seem necessary to build up certain funds, a family can adopt its own variations of the piggy bank method. Some people save cents, nickels, or dimes, others empty their pockets or purses of small change each night, still others put aside money received for coupons at the supermarket or what they have saved by "do-it-yourself" instead of using a service. Some savers achieve a glow of satisfaction by taking to the bank money they were tempted to spend on an unnecessary purchase. In time, all or any of these plans add up to dollars for some particular objective.

SAVINGS BANK INTEREST

When you noted down your total income (page 6), you will have put down the interest your savings are earning. Usually, this money will be kept at the bank in order to earn more interest for specific items you are saving for. In practice, therefore, the interest is generally part of savings money rather than available to spend.

HANDLING A DEBT PROBLEM

Are you burdened by past debts? If the bills are not too large, and the creditors are not pressing you too hard, you can probably arrange to work out a regular plan of payments from each pay check. Your most considerate creditor might help you to work out a reasonable repayment plan that would be approved by the other creditors. If your creditors understand you are handling your indebtedness systematically, they will probably agree to a certain period of time by which you anticipate clearing the load. A sincere intent to repay and a businesslike plan will usually win respect.

What if the debts are too heavy, the creditors press you, and you cannot handle the problem by spreading payments over several months? Your answer may be to get a "rehabilitation" loan. (See Chapter 6 for advice on where and how you may borrow—and the type of loan establishment to avoid.) A number of banks and also reputable small loan companies offer counseling as well as refinancing. They will work with you in setting up a debt-repayment plan. When you pay off your creditors through a rehabilitation loan, you only have the one debt on your mind. Plan the repayments on your Step II form.

Once your system of regular debt repayment is set up, you can plan to reduce overheads by adopting some of the ideas for smarter buying and cutting costs suggested in Chapter 4. See, too, ways to increase income given in Chapter 5.

A certain amount of indebtedness is usual and even desirable in our credit-oriented society. (*Debts plus prompt payment equals a good credit rating. See Chapter 6.*) But if you are constantly having to cover one loan with another, falling short on payments, or committing a fifth or more of your net income to such payments, you should lose no time in getting rid of the burden. *Set down the extent of your problems on paper* and, if necessary, seek outside assistance. A local social service or county extension worker may be able to give guidance. Too, clergymen are usually in a position to channel people to suitable advisors.

The average family will find their answers in adopting a disciplined program of debt repayment, of making extra money, and of lowering expenses.

Where your family is faced with a dire debt emergency, it may appear that the only solution is bankruptcy. But there may be other ways out. Ask your attorney's advice.

LOOKING TOWARD EXPANDED LIVING

In this chapter we have given methods and forms which demonstrate how you can keep your records, how you can pinpoint the heavy inescapable expenses, how you can conveniently check the difference between income and fixed outgo, and how you can methodically spread savings to take care of commitments and plans for the future.

We have not made any suggestions as to *how* you should spend or save your money. There can be no generalizations, no "average budget." You do the planning, but in the chapters that follow you will find guidance on buying, on credit and installment purchasing, house purchase, insurance, the stock market, and taxes. The application of that advice to your particular situation is your program for sound money management.

Chapter 2

AN AGENDA FOR YOUR FINANCIAL PROGRAM

Financial independence and security are the goals of most individuals and families in our society. Is this twin goal an objective only the fortunate few can reach? Is there some certain way you can achieve it?

It may as well be said—nothing is sure in this world! Nevertheless, the prizes tend to go to the organizers, the people who map out their course of action and pinpoint the targets.

You can build for the future on what might be termed the Foursquare Program for Successful Living. Here are the four squares and their cornerstones:

INSURANCE —The Social Security Program
           Life and Annuity Plans, including pension and
             profit sharing
           Health and Accident Protection
           Home and Property Insurance
SAVINGS   —Banks
           Savings and Loan Associations
           Credit Unions
           Government Bonds
INVESTMENT—Stocks and Corporate Bonds
           Mutual Funds
           Home Ownership
           Business or Professional Enterprises

PERSONAL　　—Budgeting
　　　　　　　　Defined Goals
　　　　　　　　Family Cooperation
　　　　　　　　Factor X

Just what is that last item, Factor X? Let it be defined as what you bring to the program yourself. You need to be alert to trends, to plan intelligently with your family needs in view, to organize each aspect of the plan, and yet to remain flexible and be able to adjust when the economy or your personal situation demands a change in course. Factor X is the key to any successful financial program since without *skill in management,* which is what it amounts to, neither a business nor family can achieve its aims.

ESTABLISHING YOUR NET WORTH

No financial program can be made for the future without finding out where you stand today. Depending on your circumstances, you may or may not have made use of the methodical system of planning and spending described in Chapter 1. But now, as you initiate your plan, and annually thereafter, you need to assess your net worth.

Turn to the forms given on the next two pages. They will help you to make your tabulations. Add and delete headings to suit yourself, but see that you cover all items that add to your total worth and every liability against it.

ANNUAL FINANCIAL STATEMENT FOR THE FAMILY

(Date)

ASSETS

Cash on hand	$_____
Checking accounts	_____
Savings accounts	_____
Money lent to others (repayment expected)	_____
Value of life insurance (Cash surrender value plus dividend accumulations)	_____
Annuities	_____
Retirement funds	_____
U. S. Savings bonds	_____

Investments—
 Stocks, bonds, mutual fund shares   _____
 Real estate   _____
 Profit-sharing plans   _____
Your home—full market value   _____
Other property (List such items as)—
 Automobile   _____
 Household furnishings   _____
 Furs, jewelry   _____
 Sports and hobby items   _____
 Clothing, etc.   _____
  Total Family Assets $_____

ANNUAL FINANCIAL STATEMENT FOR THE FAMILY

(Date)

LIABILITIES

Unpaid Bills
 Charge accounts $_____
 Credit card accounts   _____
 Taxes   _____
 Insurance premiums   _____
 Other   _____
Balances Due on—
 Installment contracts   _____
 Loans (from banks, savings and loan
  associations, insurance companies, etc.)   _____
 Other   _____
Mortgages payable on home and other property (or
 rent)   _____
  Total Family Liabilities $_____

SUMMARY

Assets $_____
Liabilities   _____
  Net Worth of the Family $_____

In completing your statement, you will need to ask questions, do some research. Your insurance agent, your employer, and your bank can give any help you may need in filling in figures on annuities, retirement funds, and U. S. Savings bonds.

Be thoroughly objective when you value property of any kind
—home—automobile—household equipment—personal items. What
would they bring on the market today? Has your neighborhood de-
preciated? What effect have new industries or highways in your area
had on property values? Your local newspaper's real estate section
and advertising are useful sources of information for property prices.
An automobile dealer's Blue Book will help you make a realistic
estimate of your car's worth—*and it may be less than you think.*

Personal property is hard to value. How much would you ask if
you were putting it up for sale? Would you get that price? Clothing
and equipment depreciate as styles change; but antiques, paintings,
and hobby collections may acquire value. Custom mart advertising
and the columns of specialty journals at the library may help you
make your assessment.

The value of your stocks, bonds, mutual shares will be easier to
assess. *Use today's quotations to get your total.* The fact that later
in the year you may take a loss or find your stocks soaring is
immaterial.

With your net worth established, you and your family can look
ahead and plan for the year. You are in a position to set up *a five-
year plan,* as businesses and governments do, and to gear income
and outgo to the fulfillment of your objectives. Note, too, that data
you have now gathered is essential to estate planning (see Chapter
16).

A REVIEW

How do you stand *now* on the Four-square Program? This is the
time to review present status in each category and to define what
changes are necessary. We will check over each item. Note down
points where your own financial program appears to be weak. Refer-
ences are given to later chapters where full discussion is given.

Insurance. Social Security benefits (see Chapter 14). Ascertain
your present standing by requesting the Social Security Administration for a statement. (You may do so once a year.) From your
district Social Security office, you may obtain the official Form OAR-
7004, which is a postcard addressed and ready to mail to Social
Security offices in Baltimore, Maryland.

Check over the benefits your family could receive from Social Security if and when certain eventualities occur—disability, retirement, death. With full information, you are in a better position to consider what additional benefits should be provided for your family through private insurance.

Life insurance and annuities. The head of a family should review his policies, asking such questions as these: What will the family live on in the event of my death? What provision is made for the children's continued education, especially for college? What other sources of income are there within the family group? What other potential earning ability?

How much life insurance is necessary? You provide the answer to your situation by a thorough analysis (see page 152). If you conclude you are underinsured, Chapter 10 offers suggestions for you. Toward retirement, you may contemplate annuities; see page 167. Nevertheless, some breadwinners make themselves and their families "insurance poor" by overprotection. That is why we suggest you view the whole situation at one time and *continue to do so annually.*

Pension and profit-sharing. When weighing up your assets, be sure to include your benefits under your employer's plan for pension or profit-sharing, or any provision made if disability forces early retirement. At the same time, you must consider what would happen if you die before or early in retirement. Would your company bear any responsibility toward your widow or other dependents? *If not, you may find it necessary to step up private insurance or earning possibilities.* (Chapters 10 and 5)

Health and accident protection. The group coverage you have at your place of employment or through a union or other organization may not be sufficient in these days of rising medical and hospital costs. Consider your need for a major medical policy or loss of income insurance. (Chapter 13)

Home, property, and automobile insurance. Wherever you live, your personal assets are vulnerable to loss by fire, theft, vandalism, natural disaster, and civil disorder. Use the list you made to establish net worth as a basis for a household inventory. Keep it up-to-date as you acquire further items of value, or have reappraisals made because of changed market values. The inventory should be stored away from the articles it describes, preferably in a bank safe deposit box. See page 129 for discussion of insurance for home and other possessions. In particular, consider how you stand on automobile insurance. *Are you adequately insured?* Is liability insurance required in your state? If not, wisdom may dictate your obtaining this safeguard against the possibility of burdensome responsibility for very heavy damages.

Savings. In Chapter 1, it is suggested that you separate (at least on paper) your savings into funds, each one aimed to a certain goal. In addition, you will require a standing emergency fund, possibly also ready money for investment purposes. What proportion of your savings should go into so-called "safe" savings (protected by Federal insurance)? What proportion into government bonds, stocks, and mutual funds? While some suggest certain percentages, we believe a categorical statement cannot cover every situation. You, the individual, must decide. (See Chapters 9, 11, and 12.) Nevertheless, you should certainly avoid tying up all your assets in real estate, stocks, and bonds, so that the availability of ready cash depends on a pay check. The emergency fund should be at least the equivalent of one year's salary, and readily accessible at a nearby savings bank in a day-of-deposit to day-of-withdrawal account.

Investment. Chapters 11 and 12 discuss stocks and corporate bonds, and mutual funds. You have an equation to work out: Element of risk in the stock market against loss of dollar value in savings and interest at the bank. Venturing into the market is probably the wrong answer for the young married couple who have yet to establish a full program of regular savings and insurance. In general, fulfill your savings program first.

Home ownership. (Chapters 7 and 8) Your own home is a sound investment which will pay dividends through good maintenance and improvements, but keep a watchful eye on the possibility of declining neighborhood values.

Business and professional enterprises. Investment in some profitable hobby or the development of a small business can be a sound aim, especially with retirement years in view. (See Chapter 5.)

The personal factors are those which we are emphasizing throughout this book, particularly the first three chapters. From the start, we have mentioned cooperation between husband, wife, and family. The overall attitude of you and your family toward money management is far more important than any major or minor event that may throw the budget out of whack. The family who have established *a basic working agreement on money matters* can repair the damage because they understand the elements that go into saving and expanding money to do the work they want it to do.

DEALING WITH INFLATION

Points that are sure to come up in your family discussions are: What will a change of residence, that new car, or an overseas vacation cost when we are ready for it? Will the savings we put aside now decline in value? Will the cost of borrowing rise? Should we buy now—or pay more later?

Those questions are asked by millions of Americans. Inflation, a major problem for government and individuals, is not likely to disappear overnight. All you can do is to watch the trend, look out for the government reports on the cost of living. Decisions on whether to buy or save can only be made in the light of a present situation. When it appears that costs are rising, that new sales taxes are imminent, people do tend to "buy now." At least, if they prove wrong and prices drop, they have the use of the item bought.

In recent years, the economy has not favored the thrifty. People who put money into savings accounts, government bonds, or other forms of investment which gave fixed returns found that their interest dollars bought less and less. On the other hand, people who borrowed money to invest in successful enterprises not only enjoyed that success; they paid back dollars of less value than they borrowed.

You will have the inflation factor in mind when you set aside money for such future needs as education for the children and for retirement. There are everyday steps you can take to counter this trend in the economy; you will find them detailed in Chapter 4. The advice given to the person who needs to cut corners is also designed to fight the battle of inflation.

YOUR FAMILY RECORDS

Calculating your net worth has necessitated your referring to many personal papers. Because many people need to organize in this important area, we discuss it below.

Do you know where all your important family records are now? Your marriage certificate, your will, Social Security card? Your employment record, listing employers, salary earned; your present standing in a profit-sharing or pension plan? And all the documents connected with your home, insurance, investment, or installment buying? If you know exactly where to find such data, you are more methodical—and wiser than many of your neighbors. All too often, when emergencies arise, vital documents cannot be located. Sometimes they are misplaced through neglect or sheer carelessness; sometimes the one person who knows where the papers are is stricken by illness or accident. The problem can be avoided, as shown below.

KEEP A RECORD BOOK

Family records will, of course, differ according to the assets owned, but the whereabouts of all data should be set down. If a loose-leaf notebook is used, it is easy to have extra photocopies made of all or any of the pages. It may be desirable for duplicate information to be in the hands of adult children, or kept at an office. Printed record books are obtainable, but you may prefer to make your own in line with your other financial records and inventories of valuables.

Here are some important items which should be listed with a note of reference about their location:

Certificates of birth; marriage; divorce; death; naturalization. Official documents of life's major events are essential for innumerable purposes, to prove date and place of birth, to obtain American citizenship for the foreign-born, to claim Social Security benefits. If one or other of such important certificates is missing, obtain a certified copy in case it is needed—to collect on insurance, to claim an inheritance, to obtain a passport, or when remarriage takes place. You may not yet know of all the occasions when members of the family will need one or other of these major documents.

If you need a certified copy of a birth or death certificate, inquire at your state or city's central vital statistics office, usually associated with the Department of Health.

Social Security. Members of the family who have cards should make a note of the numbers and where the cards are usually kept. The cards come in two parts, so you may keep the stubs with other important records. Then, if a card is lost, a stub can be mailed to your local Social Security office with a request for a duplicate. Supply name, address, and place of business, in addition to the number, when writing.

Bank accounts. List bank names and addresses with the numbers of savings account books and the names of the members of the family who own each one. Each year banks advertise for missing depositors who have either forgotten their accounts or died without informing their relatives of them. See that the necessary information is available in your family.

Also list the names and addresses of banks where you and any others have checking accounts, and the numbers of those accounts.

United States savings bonds. Maintain a careful record of your bonds, noting full serial numbers, issue dates, and denomination. If the bonds themselves are lost, stolen, or destroyed, send such information at once to the Bureau of the Public Debt, Division of Loans and Currency, 536 South Clark Street, Chicago, Illinois 60605. You will then receive full information on how to get replacements.

Insurance of all types. Record information about each policy, its number, amount payable, and method of settlement. Include information about any personal coverage at place of business, such as participation in group health, pension, or profit-sharing benefits. List names and addresses of all companies involved and state where policies are kept.

Credit cards. Legislation and protective measures taken by issuers of credit cards have cut down on the responsibility of holders for goods and services charged by thieves. Nevertheless, you should list all your account numbers and the names and addresses of the issuing company. Advise loss immediately by phone or wire, *and* in writing.

Inventory. It has already been suggested that you keep a household inventory in a bank safe deposit box. If you do not have one, use a fireproof box at home. If you file at the bank, you might want a duplicate of your inventory in your record book, so you can see when additions and reappraisals are necessary on the original.

YOUR SAFE DEPOSIT BOX

For a very small sum a safe deposit box can be rented at your bank. Here, you can safeguard valuable jewelry, stock certificates, deeds, legal records of all types, passports, bankbooks, personal papers, and the above mentioned inventory. Your will is best left with your attorney, but a copy should go in the box.

You will have to guard the keys to the box, for you are the sole possessor and you should appoint a deputy who can open the box in case you cannot. Check with the bank on its regulations affecting deputies.

You might also discuss with your attorney the legal implications which might arise, particularly at time of death, if you rent the safe deposit box jointly with your spouse.

YOUR AGENDA AND ITS PRIORITIES

You now have before you an assessment of your net worth. It will serve as a guide to what is financially possible for you and the family as you together establish an agenda. The objectives on that agenda, and those you name as priorities, will, of course, reflect your circumstances and what now seems most important to achieve. If you are young, perhaps living in an apartment, home ownership may be the initial goal, together with a sound insurance program. Later, planning for your children's education may be the prior aim. Ultimately, you will be looking toward retirement.

In between come many types of long- and short-term priorities, from new furnishings to vacation travel; automobiles and television, or perhaps dealing with sudden but temporary adversity, such as a job loss, accident, or sickness in the family.

Whatever your targets are, write them down, and then *define exactly how you will finance them.* Out of current income, from the savings, insurance, and investment program? Tie your objectives into your savings funds. Some may come within a one-year program. But as you set up those one-year projects, do not fail to look five years ahead. Will you then have increased education expenses? Or a likely commitment to an elderly member of the family?

Think your objectives through, and do not let too many short-term goals absorb your savings while you fail to take note of middle and long range needs. *Plot out the five- and ten-year objectives* so that, in due time, you are making provision toward retirement. Such planning for many people begins in middle life when they purchase a summer home and so locate a second community where they can establish roots in readiness for full-time residence in later years.

You are planning now with finances as they actually are. If certain objectives seem impossible because of limited means, weigh the budget and decide if some areas could stand trimming. Then see Chapters 4 and 5. They provide ideas for cutting expenses and for expanding income.

It might be added that if money management is to be really sound, it needs to be well seasoned with humor and a certain element of relaxation. The people who frowningly deny themselves and their family a minor joy because "it is not in the budget," and the people who cheerfully dump every resolution for a spending spree need to work toward middle ground. As you set up your Four-square Program, see it is built there—in the middle.

Chapter 3

FAMILY COOPERATION IN
FINANCIAL PLANNING

In putting forward suggestions for your financial program, we have assumed that husband, wife, and family have come to terms, can discuss the situation frankly and can make reasonable, harmonious plans for earning and spending.

This is the ideal situation, but it must be recognized that some families face areas of violent conflict over money. Psychological difficulties may lead to gambling, wildcat investments, or lavish generosity out of all keeping with circumstances. A husband or wife may be a spendthrift or a penny pincher; one may indulge in heedless spending even after agreeing to a plan to pay off debts; another cuts corners and subjects the family to financial squeezing and unwarranted limitation. Such people may well be among those who must eventually have professional advice.

This is a book on money management, not psychological counsel. Where this type of help is necessary it may be found through a Family Service Agency, which can be located through a telephone directory. Where none can be traced, write to Family Service Association of America, 44 East 23rd Street, New York, New York 10010 for names and addresses of agencies in your area.

WORKING TOGETHER ON THE SPENDING PLAN

One of the first decisions to be reached in a family money management program is—who will manage what. If you are only just married, you have a good chance to come to an early understanding on this subject—and so to avoid one of the conflicts that endanger marriage. If you are long-married and the division of responsibility is a source of trouble, decide now to start afresh. The following steps outline a reasonable program:

Begin with a working partnership in handling money. The pay check earned by the husband is not his alone—to be doled out as he pleases. His wife earns her share, and often works a far longer day in the home. On pages 41–44 we discuss the role of the working wife and her earnings. Here, we are concerned with the husband's salary which should be used to cover all major expenses for the family. Responsibility for its distribution belongs to both partners. From a joint checking account (see page 34), the husband can handle items such as rent or mortgage, taxes, insurance, and expenses of the family automobile. From the same account, the wife takes over food and clothing expenses, probably the utility bills, and the cost of entertaining at home. List the type of bills faced in your household and decide which items husband or wife will handle. Often the wife will look after budgeting and keep the records of expenditures. Here, much will depend on personal temperament and ability. In contrast to the man who likes to "be the boss" and keep his wife in the dark on finances is the man who hands over his pay check to his wife and lets her return him his lunch money and transportation expenses. Neither make good team members.

Certainly, adjustments will have to be made where one partner is "plain dumb" at figures and extravagant into the bargain, or where the other invariably spends too much and too wildly. (When the two types combine—outside family counsel is invariably needed!)

ESTABLISHING WORKING HABITS

Help yourself in the job of budgeting and paying bills by setting up of a special area in the home where papers are to be kept. If all members of the household know that a certain drawer or portion of a desk is for bills, financial records, checkbooks, etc., there is little possibility of payments being overlooked. Establish your own "in and out" system of bills, from receipt in the mail to payment. File receipts carefully. You may neeed them at income tax time.

We suggest a monthly basis for budgeting, but you may find it convenient to use pay periods. Whatever system you use, accompany it with a definite set-aside of time to enter figures in your own records and to write checks. If you fail to establish a regular schedule for dealing with your plans, payments, and records, the good management of money is unlikely to happen for you!

HOW SHOULD BILLS BE PAID?

Paying bills with cash and getting a receipt is becoming old-fashioned in our credit-conscious society. It may be possible for you to settle your telephone bill at a local bank, but for the most part payments are made by checks which, when returned from your bank, automatically become your receipts.

If you are a young person or someone living alone who faces few bills, you can perhaps manage with a savings account only. Your savings institution will issue you the few checks you need or you can buy postal money orders, bank money orders, registered or cashier's checks. Such measures should not be used for long since it is desirable to maintain a checking account for credit reference purposes. (See page 86).

YOUR BANK ACCOUNTS

If you have a choice of several banks in your vicinity, visit them all before deciding on which will be your personal bank. Inquire about the types of checking accounts available, the charges, and extra services. Most banks offer folders describing their different accounts so you can make comparisons.

Costs of checks vary. Banks compete not only on services offered but also on such items as handsomely styled checkbooks and checks, plain and fancy. Some highly-colored pictorial checks tend to make accurate reading difficult and forgery easier. Usually, the more conservative checks are less expensive.

Titles given to types of accounts may differ, but in general they offer these facilities:

REGULAR CHECKING ACCOUNTS

The regular account is best suited to customers who will keep a substantial balance each month and be active in making deposits and in writing checks. These accounts are for personal, business, or professional use. Essentially, the balance kept in the bank earns a credit which is applied against maintenance charges and fees for checks and deposits. If a balance is large enough during a statement period, there is only a low fee or none at all for account activity.

Be alert to any new offers by banks. For example, recently several banks in a major Eastern city adopted a policy of "completely free" checking accounts, both regular and special. If you are paying heavy maintenance charges at your bank, you might do well to switch if such an offer appears in your town.

SPECIAL CHECKING ACCOUNTS

The special account is generally favored by people who cannot maintain the minimum balance called for in a regular account and who will only write a few checks each month. Banks usually charge monthly for maintenance and also for the processing of each check.

"No charge" *checking accounts.* A variation on the special account

may be available if you shop around and specifically inquire for it. Some banks offer a "no charge" service in conjunction with a loan application. Once the loan application is approved, the customer has the use of a checking account without service charges. Free un-numbered checks imprinted with the customer's name are available. For a small charge, you may have numbered checks imprinted with both name and address.

The monthly statement sent on the "no charge" account will in-dicate if the customer has used part of his loan, and what interest he owes. The smart customer, of course, does not use the loan at all. He maintains a balance in the account at all times and so has a free account.

The bank customer who has a loan checking account may also be entitled to a check guarantee card—similar to a credit card—which shows that checks up to a specified amount, such as $200, are good for payment.

Joint checking accounts. When you have decided upon the most suitable type of checking account, you may want to set it up at the bank as a joint checking account, whereby checks can be made out by either husband or wife. This works well in that each can handle particular areas of responsibility without reference to the other, and gives a sense of ownership to both. A career girl giving up her own salary upon marriage or shortly after does not feel like an unpaid de-pendent when she handles part of the family finances through a joint checking account.

Note, though, that close cooperation is needed to make the joint checking account a success. Husband and wife must keep each other informed of how the balance stands. Bouncing checks reflect on your credit—and incur bank charges besides.

Caution: Avoid writing checks that exceed your balance and then making a covering deposit at the bank. Under today's electronic processing systems, checks are cleared swiftly. Your deposit may come too late.

PERSONAL ALLOWANCES CONTRIBUTE TO FAMILY HARMONY

A personal do-as-you-please allowance for everyone is a most im-portant factor in family financial plans. No one should have to ac-count for every penny. If one member of the family appears to fritter away his allowance and another hoards it to buy something that seems particularly pointless to everyone else, that is exactly what the personal allowance is for. So—no interference!

What each allowance should be will, of course, depend on family circumstances. This advice only—*even if the budget is very tight, there should still be a little spending money for everyone.* It represents freedom and emotional outlet, which, in the long run, may safeguard other areas of a spending plan.

An affluent family may tend to develop too easy an attitude toward such personal allowances. Because large amounts are available now, it does not say that a widow, a married daughter, or a son who goes his own way will always have such sums to play with. Where the personal allowance can be large, the more reason to study how it can be wisely spent.

HOW MUCH FOR THE CHILDREN?

Not too much, certainly. A too-free handout for Billy and Betty is not going to aid in their mature growth. Though you may have a good income, you do not know what financial problems your children will face. Therefore, a sound training in money values from an early age may well be one of the best gifts you can offer.

But try to follow the happy midcourse between good training and generating anxiety over money. Flexibility may be called for where one child is slower than another in developing understanding on how an allowance may best be spent. Children, even within a family, will differ widely in their perception of money values.

But, although you may avoid the trap of giving a six-year-old a teenager's allowance just because you can afford it, you cannot ignore the cost-of-living rise at the candy and toy store. The youngsters need more than you had at their age. Ten cents in pennies looks like a fortune to the little tot but he soon discovers its true worth at the counter. Best to give raises gradually by nickels, and to train the child to understand the principle of saving for what he wants. When he has chosen to fritter away a quarter instead of saving toward a dollar item, that's his choice, but he should have to take the consequences. He can save—*or he can earn.* Once he understands *how* he can obtain something for himself, he has learned a valuable lesson and gained a personal satisfaction.

An advance against next week's allowance is not good training for Billy (though his parents may well be borrowing the cost of his home!). Nor is it advisable for him to be given money for doing household chores which he should learn to accept as his own—without pay. Extra money should be given for work he does not usually do—a job you might undertake yourself, for instance.

Some parents, it must be said, feel that a child should receive *no allowance at all without earning,* either at home or by doing chores for the neighbors. Certainly the principle is good, and if you institute it in your family, you will do far better than those parents who willingly hand out on demand.

COVERING THE ROUTINE EXPENSES

Will you add the cost of movies, church contributions, or other week-by-week expenses to the allowance? Often parents prefer to give the extra money as needed until the teens are reached. But if a particular child is ready for the experience, he should be allowed to handle his own finances.

HANDLING AN ALLOWANCE

After age nine or ten, the personal allowance will need to rise—so also the money given for specific spending, till you deal with the problems of teenage money management. Your circumstances, the cost of living, and what is customary in your area will influence what you allow. Of course, children will ask for what their friends say they are getting, but parents have to consider what the money has to cover and what raises can be given within the family budget. When a child wants more than parents can afford, ways to earn might be suggested.

If you have been letting the children in on family financial discussions, bringing them up to understand where the income comes from, and how you manage expenses, you may save yourself some of the headaches of handling teenage allowances. The child who has less than his peers will adjust better if he understands the family situation.

The growing Billy or Betty not only want all that their contemporaries have, they are also bait for advertisers, and want to assert their independence by buying what they please. You will need a specific agreement on what the allowance covers. School lunches, club dues, toiletries, and hobby items are expenses the young person should manage. But start the clothing allowance gradually, with responsibility for shirts and skirts, rather than for essential items such as winter outfits. The youngster who has been allowed to exercise a certain freedom of choice while shopping under parental guidance will later on respond with wiser choices than the teenager whose mother has done all the choosing and buying for him. The temptation offered by consumer goods today is so great the children need an early education in sensible buying.

To relieve family expenses—and to provide good training, too, the 16-year-old should try to get after-school and vacation jobs. When a young person can earn, he should be able to cover clothing and other incidentals by the time he reaches age 18.

CHARGE ACCOUNTS?

The experts say charge accounts are definitely not for the teenager. Yet some banks have courted the young people with special credit cards and their charges are welcomed at many stores. The parent has to decide—in the light of family finances at the time and whether or not the son or daughter is able to handle credit with restraint. For the young person who earns, charge accounts may be hard to deny.

The lowering of voting age to 18 opened the way for changes in the law of many states to lower the age of legal majority from 21 to 18. But when parents and others formerly standing surety for young people are not required to do so, banks, credit card concerns, and stores are likely to be particularly careful in their screening of applications for credit.

FINANCING A COLLEGE EDUCATION FOR YOUR CHILDREN

Planning for a child's college expenses can well begin when the infant is born. Expenses are mounting so rapidly that the average family faces a severe financial pinch as soon as the college years arrive. When your teenager begins thinking about choice of a college, he (or she) should be made aware of college costs. No matter how happily you assume the burden, he should anticipate sharing the load. One way will be through inquiries about the various scholarships offered, and the taking of competitive tests.

To counter the astronomical escalation of cost, the sources of aid have increased as have the amounts obtainable. Governments, both Federal and state, the colleges themselves, and various organizations have developed new plans for student aid. As the college years approach, you will need a list of sources so you—and your student—can find out what financial help is currently available from each one.

But, first, set up a savings plan. If you begin to save for college when a child is born, you will have a head start on the parents who think the account can wait till the youngster is at least in grade school. Even if the budget only permits a small amount to be set aside, you establish the fund and can increase the weekly or monthly savings with the child's growth and with improvements in your finances. (See Chapter 9 on banks and the best rates of interest on savings.) Aim to have at least $5,000 in the account by college time for each of the students in your family.

In addition to a savings bank program, you will want to consider the college fund possibilities in savings bonds, insurance, and investment in assets likely to appreciate in value. Government bonds are safe, and you may be able to buy them through a payroll savings plan.

Insurance (Chapter 10) should, of course, cover the risk of the breadwinner not living to fulfill his savings and investment program for his children. Educational endowment policies force savings, but lack the coverage against death obtainable in a straight life policy. The latter offers more protection, plus the cash value. You can then borrow against the policy, or obtain funds by turning it in. If your insurance agent suggests buying juvenile insurance for a college fund, explore the idea, but bear in mind that this is generally more expensive and carries less benefit.

Investment in common stocks has long been considered a hedge against inflation. Gyrations on the market in 1969 and into the '70s made the small investor think twice. Whether or not you invest to meet college costs will depend on current conditions. (See Chapter 11, also Chapter 12.)

Trusts, discussed in Chapter 15, can be set up for financing a child's college education.

These avenues of funds anticipate that college costs lie in the future. The checking up on scholarships and loans comes when the student approaches the senior year in high school. Your state may offer scholarships to qualifying students who attend certain colleges or universities within the state. This should be taken into consideration when filing applications for admission. Counselors at high school and the finance office at the preferred college will give full information. Below are sources of college aid you should investigate:

SOURCES OF FINANCIAL AID

Federal government. Request up-to-date information on all programs of financial aid from the Office of Education, Department of Health, Education, and Welfare, Washington, D.C. 20201, or from a regional office in your area.

State government. Write the Higher Education Office in your state capital to inquire if the state has current plans for aiding college students. Not every state has a major scholarship program.

Local. Loan and scholarship programs are generally set up by high schools, the community, churches, synagogues, service organizations, unions, businesses, and corporations.

The college. All colleges have aid programs but the scope and type will vary considerably. Packaged aid may be in the form of a scholarship (not repayable), loans (repayable), and employment. A plan developed at some universities in 1971 is "deferred tuition," whereby the student defers payments on a portion of tuition costs. Later, when earning, he will pay a percentage of this adjusted gross taxable income to the college. The repayment plan may span as long as 35 years.

Scholarships. For comprehensive listings of scholarships, loans, and combinations of the two, consult such publications as *Lovejoy's Scholarship Guide,* available at libraries, newsdealers, and bookstores. Look for the date of publication on all such reference books because you need the latest.

Commercial loans. Inquire at local banks which may cooperate in low-cost student loan programs. Finance companies make educational loans, but investigate the interest rate and repayment plan thoroughly. Also check on what happens if the student dies, or otherwise fails to fulfill the program.

Veterans Administration. Widows of veterans should make specific inquiries of their local VA office for the latest educational benefits available for the children.

THE PUBLIC COMMUNITY COLLEGE

Where funds for education are a great problem, the junior or community college can offer answers. Class hours at these newer style institutions of learning generally extend into the evening, and over weekends and summer months, thus catering to people who have to work for a living. Courses offered can prepare a student for continued education at a four-year college, give practical training in such fields as electronic data processing and medical technology, and offer opportunities to adults who feel they need new skills or expanded horizons.

The community college, which is tax supported, is not high cost and may even offer some free courses. With the trend toward offering education beyond high school to all who want it, the one-time unpopular "junior college" has new life and is spreading rapidly across the land.

IS COLLEGE ESSENTIAL?

There are many individuals who achieve marked success in business without having attended college—by choice or for economic reasons. Yet parents have continued to make sacrifices to give their children the advantage of a college education. Statistics have shown that the lifetime career earnings of a college graduate may be over $200,000 ahead of an individual who has not gone beyond high school. The graduate-degree student again has a higher lifetime career income than the college student.

Yet in a time of economic reverse, the college graduate has a hard time getting a job in keeping with his education. In fact, the opportunities may be greater for the person who can repair TV sets, be a skilled auto mechanic, or initiate a creative career.

If you are the parents of a son or daughter who is just not interested in what the four-year college offers, and vocational training appears more attractive and fulfilling, do not pressure the young person into pursuing academic studies. Not only will money be wasted; the student will be maladjusted. Vocational training along the line of an interest will cost less and offer more opportunity.

MONEY MANAGEMENT AND THE WORKING WIFE

Here, we are concerned only with the working wife and the money she earns, not with the many other aspects that arise—the psychological effect on her children, her husband's reaction, whether she works from economic necessity or for personal satisfaction. The questions that arise are:

1. If there are small children, does it pay for a wife to work?
2. How should a wife's pay check be used?

DOES IT PAY FOR A WIFE TO WORK?

It depends on the individual situation. Will it be necessary to hire someone to take care of the household or the children while the wife is away from the house? If so, *and the wife is qualified to earn a high salary through her profession or career,* the answer may well be *yes;* the expense, and sometimes the difficulty, of engaging a housekeeper may well be justified. When the wife would earn only an average wage or salary, it may not pay to employ a substitute to care for very young children. When the cost of a mother substitute is added to the wife's commutation, lunch, additional clothing needs (and her taxes!), there is too little left over from a run-of-the-mill job to justify the many difficulties involved.

The question is often examined, too, where a couple have the care of an infirm relative, or in families where there is a mentally or physically handicapped child. In many of these cases, it may be advisable to engage specially qualified home help or to place the dependent in special day or full-time care facilities. Whatever extra money the wife can earn is needed to meet expenses; in some cases, there will also be a psychological need to have the diversion of a job instead of full-time care of the dependent.

Factors to Be Weighed

In your situation, there may be many reasons why you want a working husband/wife partnership. Here, we only point out the factors you must weigh in connection with money. Take pencil and paper, and be prepared to analyze these points:

Taxes. Consider the tax impact of a two-salary income. With unchanged deductions and exemptions, you now have a much higher gross income—and consequent increased Federal, state, and city income taxes. Not only is the tax bill larger; payroll withholding for taxes on husband and wife's incomes may be insufficient even though you ask your employer to withhold greater amounts than required by law. A large lump sum may be due when the mid-April deadline rolls around. You may also have to consider the impact of higher state and city taxes on the double income. However, you may be among those who can claim a deduction for child care. (See Chapter 15.)

Payroll Deductions. The wife's employer will reduce her pay check, not only by Federal and state taxes, but by Social Security, and probably by group health insurance and a pension plan. Consider the effect of that reduction if the wife only wants to work for a short time to cover special financial needs. But, on a long-term basis, a working wife acquires assets for the family by gaining her own Social Security benefits and company pension, and by participating in a health insurance plan.

Other Deductions. Some types of work involve union or club dues. Check this possible expense when seeking new employment.

Child Care Help

Remember that your employment of a mother substitute carries more expense than just the woman's wages. Social Security payments are due from employer as well as employee on cash wages of more than $50 a quarter, and you will probably have to pay carfare for a day worker. You may have to provide uniforms, or work smocks. Your telephone bill may increase. (You had better set a rule about calls, though it may not be observed!) The employee may not buy food, or use household appliances and cleaning products as economically (or wisely) as the wife she replaces. Therefore, running expenses for the household increase. *These points carry weight when the wife is not in a high-pay job.*

If you employ someone regularly for domestic service, ask your state's unemployment insurance bureau if you have to pay unemployment tax as well as Social Security. In New York, householders are liable for this tax if they pay a domestic helper $500 or more in a calendar quarter.

Day Care, Nursery Schools, Summer Camps

Your family may use all three, whether or not the mother works. But when she holds a job, they will certainly be needed. Ascertain the expenses involved for additional child-care hours, or for weeks in the summer.

Household Services

Today, it is recognized that the jobs done by the once taken-for-granted housewife cost a great deal when they must all be handled through outside services. If in your home the wife opts for outside employment, additional cost may develop from such sources as laundry, dry cleaning, rug shampooing, window cleaning, gardening, maintenance.

The working wife who attempts to do all her home jobs in addition to outside employment may run up doctor bills, too.

Food

The working wife does not have time to shop around the various supermarkets for the specials; she may buy more at the expensive but convenient small store. Too, the family may eat out more often. Count on a rise in food costs and on evening or Saturday shopping at the market.

PART-TIME OR TEMPORARY WORK

The housewife may consider this type of work because she thinks that she will also be able to cover most of her usual duties. She should realize that she will still need suitable clothing and that, for only a part-time or short-time salary, she will have the usual deductions from salary and most of the expenses of the full-time worker.

How did you come out after discussing and checking the points we have raised? Can a working wife contribute to your financial program—and at the same time run the household? Weigh the pros and cons of your personal situation, both financial and psychological. If the financial plus is small, but the wife needs the stimulation of outside activity, the decision for her to work may be wise. On the other hand, where the money contribution works out as a definite plus, but the wife is likely to be harried by the combination of job responsibilities and the home, you may be well advised to seek some other way to increase the family income.

THE WIFE'S PAY CHECK

In the average home where there are two pay checks, there are many reasons why husband's and wife's income should be pooled. Mutual confidence is established, and there is none of the "holding out" of "my" earnings—a fruitful source for marital discord.

From her pay check, the wife will certainly have to deduct her additional expenses, such as transportation (perhaps a second car will be needed) and lunches out. Her personal allowance from the check must now cover the type of clothing suited to her job, and all the accessories. She will want money for gifts and contributions, and more for personal spending. Both husband and wife should keep a record of their needs for a while to see just how much a personal expense allowance should add up to.

Where household help is employed specifically because the wife works, the payment is sometimes made directly by the wife before the rest of her money goes into the pool—simply because she prefers to be responsible for her stand-in.

It is certainly desirable that a husband's income should be used to cover the basic expenses—rent or mortgage, utilities, taxes, insurance. When every effort is made to live on the husband's income, the couple are prepared to manage when there is to be a baby, or when, for other reasons, the wife gives up her job. Sometimes, a two-salary income deludes young people into taking on far too heavy a financial commitment; then, when suddenly they are reduced to one salary, they are in trouble.

It is a good idea for the wife's earnings to be directed toward some special purpose. Many wives work specifically to see their children through college; so, after the expense deduction, they put their money into the education fund. In childless families, or after children are grown, the wife's salary can provide the luxury items, special vacations, or be earmarked for the couple's retirement.

FAMILY COOPERATION IS A NECESSITY

In this chapter, we have examined a number of points affecting the family. Cooperation is essential to the successful working-out of these considerations. We emphasize the importance of frequent family discussions to study needs and spending objectives, to reset budget goals, and to get rid of those sore points that fester in too many homes.

Your money management plan can work for you in establishing a genuine partnership in the business of being a family.

Chapter 4

RAISING CASH THROUGH CUTTING COSTS

Mr. and Mrs. Average Consumer want the most value out of each dollar, and rightly so, since the spiral of inflation has eroded the value of 100 cents so drastically over recent years. Your income increases to the extent you cut down on unwise buying and wasteful usage. Cutting costs, in small ways and large, can add up to substantial savings which can be used for the benefit of your family.

Federal, state, and city authorities have all been at work in recent years trying to ensure that the buyer gets the right quality, quantity, and price on his purchases. Publicity about truth-in-packaging, truth-in-advertising, unit pricing, and various investigations by the Federal Trade Commission have sometimes left the impression that the customer now enjoys more protection and can buy with greater confidence. This is not so. Even when Federal or local law has been passed, there may be a time gap between the date of the new regulations and the date of compliance on the part of the manufacturer or retailer. Sometimes there are loopholes in the law that remain unplugged. Careless pricing, if not deceptive, is a problem that may well remain with the buyer even when he can have greater confidence in the claims of advertisements and what he is getting for his dollars. To protect your rights as a consumer, adopt smart buying habits, steer clear of likely gyps, and don't let the pennies get away.

Check yourself on this cost-cutting, wise consumer profile. Do you:

Shop around, compare values, investigate thoroughly before making a major purchase?

List your needs before going to supermarket and sales?

Look for the genuine price markdown?

Buy for the quality of the product rather than the attractiveness of the package?

Avoid waste in use of utilities? Care for home equipment?

Question the cost of services? Explore the possibility of do-it-yourself projects to cut expenses?

Pointers on money-saving buying habits, economies in the home, and the employment of self-service are given below:

BUY WISELY

In food and household items—Watch store advertising, make out lists, and stay with them. Impulse buying is well-known to be the joy of merchants, the downfall of the consumer. Freezer and storage space may permit you to stock up on bargain specials, but when you buy, make sure that you are not splurging on items the family could very well do without. The key to successful shopping and a balanced budget lies in the question "Do I really *need* it?"

Do you read labels to compare products for quantity and grade? By law, labels must provide the buyer with certain information. Read them to see if brand-name products—usually priced higher than those packaged or canned for the supermarkets—really offer better value. Though the price gap between the two has diminished, it has not vanished. Brand-name products "on special" may offer a price bargain.

If you do not know canning standards and grades of meats, fruits, vegetables, and dairy products, you can send ten cents to the U. S. Government Printing Office, Division of Public Documents, Washington, D.C. 20402, for price list No. 86, which names numerous low-cost guides to all phases of consumer interest. A good buy is a kit of nine booklets on "How To Buy Food" (Catalog No. A 88.2: F 73/5). In it, United States Department of Agriculture (USDA) grades are described, as well as thrifty values and best selections.

(When buying government publications, use check or money order, or buy a quantity of five-cent Superintendent of Documents coupons for future use. You may request regular free mailings of new lists of the useful and informative books and leaflets the government puts out on a wide spectrum of subjects—from the Log of Apollo 11 to attractive color guides for vacationers and campers. The interests and needs of all segments of the population are served.)

The government offers advice on the vital subject of nutrition. Write to the Office of Information, U. S. Department of Agriculture, Washington, D.C. 20250, for a list of publications on the subject. This department puts out warnings on the worthless diet fads that take dollars better spent sensibly at the grocery store.

Vitamins are expensive, even when purchased from a discount house or under department store labeling; so are health foods and food supplements. Many physicians say that regular, well-balanced meals give the average person all the vitamins and nutrition necessary to health. Ask your doctor if any member of your family is in need of vitamins or other extras. His specific instructions would save you unnecessary expenditure.

SMART BUYER TACTICS AT THE SUPERMARKET

If you want to be a good money manager, you must adopt a precise approach to trips to the supermarket. Preferably leave the children home. If you can't, they should not be allowed to pick up items and put them in the shopping cart. Men usually run the bills up, too. But when husband and wife are a money management team, they have a better chance to beat the odds at the marketplace —two pairs of watchful eyes being better than one.

The shopper who watches the dollars has to take time to look at can and package labels, and to calculate if the larger size really is more economical than the small one. Even when the large size offers the better buy, it may not be economical for you if you cannot use it before it deteriorates or evaporates.

Know the prices of your regular purchases. If the price leaps up at one store, check at other supermarkets before paying it. The item may continue to be available elsewhere at the old price.

Watch price and quantity. You may see a familiar price and not immediately be aware that you are paying more. The quantity has gone down. Another brand may offer the full measure at a competitive price.

A problem that has long had the attention of the Federal Trade Commission is the advertised special which has not been sale-priced, or is not in stock at the store. To get the bargain, the shopper has to point out the advertised price to the manager or a checker, or demand a "rain check." A store that regularly fails the customer on specials is one to avoid.

OVERPRICING

Greater consumer awareness of shady practices of the marketplace has resulted in far more effort on the part of governmental bodies to exercise control. Until manufacturers and merchants fully comply with legislation, the problem of phony sales will remain. When the so-called original price is inflated, the "sale price" is no bargain. Here, the shopper's general awareness of prices and of quality is a protection; only losers rush in and buy without question.

In some industries, overpricing is the norm. Higher priced cosmetics, for example, are said to attract more buyers than those with a modest tag. Manufacturers and their advertising agents say that a woman would feel "cheated" if the beauty product which she expects to maintain or restore her youth were available at a low price. The truth is that the ingredients of most cosmetics are very inexpensive (some can be picked up at a drug store for a few cents), and mass packaging, however attractive, is not expensive either. A woman with the courage to buy her beauty products at the five-and-ten instead of the elaborate department store counter can save considerably—and at no noticeable effect to her appearance.

Cosmetic preparations of one type or another are marketed under as many deceptive labels as food and household items. For example, the shampoo selling for years at "$1.50, regularly $2.50," may not have sold at the higher price for more than a short period when it was first advertised.

THE TEMPTATION OF ADVERTISING

The advertising trap is one we all tend to fall into. We enjoy some TV commercials more than the show, a magazine advertisement better than the article alongside. We mentally note to look for that product. Probably we buy it. On store shelves and in windows plastic bottles and snappy packaging tempt our eyes and the buying impulse. How often did you buy a well-dressed container and fail to compare its price and value with similar, less noticeable goods? Did you stop to think if you really needed it? Day after day, through all mediums of communication, we are being invited into an all-color, all-persuasive world of gracious living and told it may be ours —at a price. Too often we do not stop to consider whether the price we pay is worth the value we receive, in terms of necessity, use, or pleasure.

Some people can afford to buy on impulse and to splurge on luxury items without a second thought; they are an asset to our consumer-geared economy. We all enjoy the occasional mad buy. But this book is designed for those who want to manage their finances more effectively. If you need to save money, be wise to advertising in all its forms. It can inform and entertain; it can guide you to a new product or a new house, but *do not let it direct your thinking*. Stay in control. Ask yourself such questions as: Is this purchase necessary? Can it be bought elsewhere for less? Is it effective? Durable?

There are publications which show the results of tests and which make disinterested comparisons of consumer goods. Look for *Consumer Reports* and *Consumer Bulletin* at newsdealers and in libraries. Annual paperback guides on the same subject, and on buying from discount stores are also available.

Research pays, particularly where expensive purchases are involved. You can curb impulse buying by cultivating the habit of comparison shopping and reading up on value tests.

CAUTION—IT'S A GYP!

Rackets come in a million varieties and defraud people from the unsophisticated poor to the millionaire taken in by fraudulent "works of art." Keep informed by reading books and magazine articles on the subject so you are better able to spot any situation, approach, contract, or gimmick where fraud may exist; detect the shoddy "dressed-up" item offered for sale; know what to do if you become the victim of a swindle of one type or another.

There are always new rackets, so only caution and general knowledge about the tactics of the smart operator can offer you protection. But each day hundreds of people will fall for widely publicized types of frauds, taken in by a smooth approach, apparent trustworthiness, and usually a subtle appeal to human greed, vanity, and desire for a bargain.

Authorities at Federal, state, and local levels are constantly clamping down on various profitable schemes, some of which involve companies trusted by the general public.

A type of gyp may be the school, correspondence or otherwise, that offers courses which you expect will lead to sales or employment. The courses themselves may be genuine, but the market for sales or jobs is either low or nonexistent. Watch out, too, for the phony agency. An old story still around in various forms is the supposed talent placement bureau to which the victim pays fees for photographs and services never rendered.

In the past, many people have succumbed to high-pressure, door-to-door salesmen, signing up for goods or services on a fine-print contract. That contract would be sold immediately to a bank or finance company which was entitled to extract all terms of payment, even if the goods turned out to be shoddy or the services nonexistent. Here, Federal and local authorities have developed a new plan—a three-day "cooling-off" period. These "grace days" permit second thoughts on the part of the person who signed up under sales pressure. But grace days are not yet offered everywhere in the country and certain limitations may apply when they do. If you sign up in the seller's store or office, for example, you may not be allowed to back out of the contract. Always be cautious before signing installment contracts. Demand time even if the salesman says the offer is due to end or you will not be eligible for some bonus. Pressure tactics on the part of a salesperson should be a warning signal for you to go slow.

"Home improvement" rackets thrive in the suburbs and towns every year despite frequent warnings in the press. Don't be taken in by the "inspector" who says you need a new furnace and, of course, can refer you to the right man to supply and install it. Also call your Better Business Bureau, the Chamber of Commerce, or local authorities before you have your driveway blacktopped by an unknown crew who are "working" the neighborhood, supplying shoddy materials and workmanship at a grossly inflated price.

You can protect yourself, the family, and your finances in the following ways:

Beware the person who calls, telephones, or writes offering *something for nothing*—a prize, just a few moments of your time, nothing to buy . . .

If an "inspector" calls, do not be convinced by a badge. Shut the door on him while you telephone the city office or utility he is supposed to represent. If he is genuine, he will not object to your precautions.

Don't accept the verbal promise of salesmen in or out of stores. (This applies to such items as insurance, too.) See that any payment plan or installment contract offered for your signature *carries the same promises*. Redress may not be possible.

Don't be hustled into signing documents. Read the fine print and if you do not understand it, don't sign. Some checking-up may be in order.

Never sign a document which has blank spaces on it. See that any details that have to be typed or written into a printed form are completed to your satisfaction before you sign.

Telephone or call at a Better Business Bureau when you suspect sharp practice.

If door-to-door solicitation is a trouble, advise your local authorities. In some areas, complaints from residents have resulted in the banning of all such callers who lack a license.

Beware of "bait and switch" tactics. An advertisement for some "fantastic bargain" may be the bait. At the store, the salesman tries to switch you from this particular offer. "It's not so much of a buy. Let me show you something better." He will—and the price will be a gyp.

Here is a variation on "bait and switch." A well-known discount store in a New York suburb advertised at an amazingly low price a blender said to be manufactured by a company known across the country. One woman who went to the sale found a number of disgruntled buyers at the display. Reason: the blender was a substandard product practically guaranteed to fall apart at the first blending. Nearby, she noticed a display of better quality blenders at a much higher price.

While the store did not have a fast-talking salesman at hand to push the switch from the poor-quality advertised product, the effect was the same. The woman, too smart to buy herself, saw several people (not to be disappointed in their purchase of a blender) take a higher priced one to the check-out counter.

You may observe similar "switching" tactics in operation in all stores, not only discounters. Sale goods in short supply or substandard items are frequently set out near an attractive range of their full-priced counterparts.

Sometimes unsolicited items appear in the mail. You didn't order them, but the bills keep coming. The best way to deal with such merchandise is to return it to the Post Office, unopened, "Refused —Return to Sender" marked on it. (Repack opened packages.) Inform your Better Business Bureau and ignore the letters which may follow. If you inquire about state law, you may find that, as in New York, you may regard the unordered item as a free gift.

Children sometimes get involved in unwanted subscriptions or not-so-free offers when they send in coupons. But, since binding contracts cannot be signed by minors, the parents are under no obligation to pay for unsolicited items. Return, as above, unless your state's law frees you from any obligation.

Americans are traditionally charitable, and their willingness to give lines the pockets of swindlers who sometimes even use the names of well-known persons on the letterheads of their "organization." Fund raisers have been known to absorb all but a tiny percentage of offerings running into millions. See that your giving is directed to worthy causes you know something about, probably through your place of worship, your community, your personal work as a volunteer, or because it is nationally known.

SALE TIME

Sales are your dollar-saving friends if you use them to full advantage—and don't let them take advantage of you. Shoppers naturally watch the advertising and many go to stores with list in hand. Then buying fever sets in; bargains may be snapped up without proper consideration of size or color. Mother hopes that if the shirt won't fit Dad it will fit Johnny and that the low-priced rug really is the right buy for the front hall. Because sales often carry a "no return" stipulation, the too-hasty buyer has to put up with the results or just give away the bargain to charity. Many dollars gobbled up by indiscriminate sales buying would have been better spent on full-priced items.

The secret of smart sales buying is to note down what you really need from among the items advertised and then to examine them carefully for size, quality, and suitability. "Seconds" in towels and sheets during the white sales can be a help to the family spending plan: slight irregularities in weave do not affect durability. Clothing buys are available at special sales and when a season has passed the height. At high-class stores quality clothing is marked down regularly—providing real bargains, whereas much cheap clothing supposedly on sale is manufactured for that purpose. The careful buyer will watch for markdowns from earlier prices and will take advantage of manufacturer's sales in lingerie, housewares, and appliances.

BUY AND SELL AT THRIFT STORES

Thrifts shops abound in cities and suburbs, some run commercially, many by charitable organizations. They offer a perpetual sale. Such outlets provide an excellent way to furnish a child's room or a recreation area, though the family may have to do a refinishing job. In many towns, stores are run as "exchanges" for children's outgrown clothing, cleaned and in nice condition. At such exchanges and at some thrift shops, you can leave your family's clothing for sale. Stores take a percentage of profit on goods sold. By buying and selling in such a store, you can cut clothing costs substantially.

BUYING AT THE DISCOUNT STORE

Again, you can save if you are wary and demanding; if you know that *exactly the same article regularly sells elsewhere at a higher price.* A common policy at the discount store is to tempt you in with an advertised "loss leader." This bargain may be genuine, if you are not subjected to the "bait and switch" tactic described on page 52 (but note that other merchandise you may buy at the same time may possibly be substandard or available elsewhere at the same price).

Discount stores, like others, vary. At some you can take away your purchase in factory-sealed cartons; the manufacturer, not the store, stands behind guarantee and service. You get a substantial price reduction on a costly appliance for the trouble of carrying away and installing your buy personally. At one time a strictly cash-and-carry operation, today's large discounters accept bank and other credit cards. Some also have their own charge cards.

If you want some major appliance, decide on the brand, model, and year of the item and check around. You may find the discount store offers a genuine bargain; you may prefer to have a favorite department store stand behind the purchase; you may discover a local store's price compares well. With the major appliance purchase, a main consideration is getting repair service during the guarantee period.

THE TRADE-IN

While you may be well aware of the value of the trade-in when you buy a car, do not overlook smaller items that may be acceptable. Take, for instance, a typewriter. You may see a favorable price quoted at a large store where trade-ins are not acceptable. A reputable small dealer in your town may quote a slightly higher price, but he may allow you a sufficiently good margin on a trade-in to put you ahead—and you got rid of your old machine.

Check on this type of possibility with your vacuum and other equipment.

LET A RENTAL SAVE YOU MONEY

Many families will pay a great deal for certain types of equipment which will rest in attics, basements, and closets most of the year. Before you buy a rug shampooer or camping equipment for a family trip next summer, consider renting.

When the question of buying some expensive item comes up, the family should consider the number of times it is likely to be used and also how soon it is likely to become obsolete. If you can find a reliable renting source for what you want, your pocket may be considerably better off.

If you are a city dweller, you may find car rental far more economical than car ownership. When renting, shop around for the most advantageous rates.

Rental services are multiplying. Check the yellow pages of your telephone book and inquire at your local hardware and department stores. Your friends may be able to name some good sources for rentals.

RANDOM SPENDING

In Chapter 1, we suggested keeping account of your spending for a period, at least. If you have carried out this project faithfully, you will be well aware of the amount of money that has been casually spent by members of the family—especially if teenagers are involved.

People buy readily at the five-and-ten, the newsdealers, and at drug, cosmetic, and toiletry counters. If money isn't doing a good job in your family, there may be much frittering away of cash on small items.

PAY WHAT YOU OWE—AND NO MORE

If you are not careful when you pay cash or sign to have items or services charged, you may lose out. A watchful eye on the cash register when the supermarket purchases are being rung up can save dollars over the year. More particularly, see that sales slips for charges are correctly completed before you sign them.

If you are charging items that will be delivered later, a clerk may offer you the bill to sign, saying you need not wait for the totals to be filled in. Insist on the bill being completed, then check it before you sign. One suburban shopper who took these precautions found a substantial error in the store's favor. This mistaken charge might have been overlooked when the final statement was paid, or, if found, would have been troublesome to straighten out with the computerized billing department.

Sometimes an unwary customer may be charged the regular price for an item instead of the advertised sales price. The clerk's error may well be unintentional; the loss is still the customer's.

SAVING THROUGH HOME ECONOMIES

When you use your household equipment and appliances properly and to full advantage, you are cutting costs. The devices give the service you require; you avoid repair bills. Be sure to follow manufacturers' instructions for use and care—and see that the members of the household understand them, too. Care is an important economy. Overloading breaks down the washing machine, the full dustbag prevents the vacuum cleaner from functioning, the sewing machine needs regular oiling to do its job properly. When saving money is important, you cannot afford to be careless in the little things which, neglected, can build into costly repair jobs.

Do you keep fuel costs low by conserving heat? Fuel is a householder's major single expense, and in building or buying you surely will investigate a house's heating system (and air conditioning) thoroughly and see that the necessary insulation is installed. Perhaps, too, you attend to plastic calking and weather stripping to prevent leaks and drafts from cracks and spaces around doors and window frames. But do you watch the little things as well? See to it that the family closes doors and windows? Or do you leave the damper open in the unused fireplace and never close the entry to the unheated attic? Do members of the family use radiators for stacking magazines so that heat—and money—is lost? Everyone should cooperate to pull draperies and shades so that cold air is kept out; the thermostat setting should be lower at night.

Adopt cost-cutting practices for air conditioning, too. Waste spells cost and you should inform yourself of the simple, everyday actions that will prevent loss on your type of equipment.

Maintaining the Home. A guide to help in cutting repair bills is available for 15 cents from the Small Home Building Research Council, University of Illinois, 1 East St. Mary's Road, Champaign, Illinois 61820. This eight-page guide covers the home, inside and out, including mechanical systems such as heating and cooling, and tells the homeowner how to keep a comprehensive record of repair jobs, their cost, and contractor or serviceman engaged.

Money may be saved by keeping curtains, drapes, and upholstery free of the dust that causes deterioration. One householder who left her synthetic curtains up at the windows too long without washing lost eight out of nine pairs—they fell to pieces in the washer.

CUTTING CLOTHING COSTS

Here is a routine to get the most out of clothing buys, especially with a growing family. Keep a box or drawer space for garment tags that recommend special cleaning methods, note which item each refers to so you can follow manufacturer's instructions when necessary; attend to stains and repairs without delay; hang—and air—clothes after wear, shoulders lined up with the hangers and fasteners closed; avoid overcrowding a closet rail; store only cleaned garments, and protect against moths; provide drawer or box space for woven garments that might drop if they were hung.

If the family can be trained to cooperate, clothes should not only survive longer but may be good for thrift shop sale when outgrown—a double saving.

A DO-IT-YOURSELF PROGRAM FOR THE FAMILY

Today, the time-pressured American pays for services and for things once made at home. He pays substantial sums annually for appliance repair, housepainting and plumbing jobs, and for garden care. But what if money-saving is an essential in your household? Can you and the family cut down on expense-making spare time activities, such as movie-going, the ball game, entertaining, or whatever goes in your household that consumes both time and money? The hours saved can be applied to projects that save money. (And if the children learn to find the work pleasurable, they will not feel "deprived.")

There is no lack of instruction available, in pocketbooks, monthly magazines, in the library, on specific subjects. If you don't know how to build cabinets, refinish furniture, repair chairs, remodel clothes, or raise your own fruits and vegetables, you can obtain "how-to-do-it" information easily and enjoy a new hobby while saving money. Check, too, on classes available in your neighborhood. If you send for the government price list mentioned on page 48, you will find a number of useful booklets available for the handy homeowner.

Comparing Costs

Plans to save money by "do-it-yourself" are valid only if you first compare costs. Is it really cheaper to bake, sew, or make, say, a bookcase? Only through estimating such factors as cost of materials, need for professional finish, your own competence, time, and working space can you learn which types of home jobs pay off in savings.

For example, day or weekend-old bakery goods on sale at a supermarket may be cheaper than baking and may save time for the mother of a large family. But making the draperies and slipcovers could prove a saving. A reasonably handy man or woman can fix leaky faucets and deal with a balky tank or drain. But better call the plumber for the frozen pipes.

FUN FOR FREE

Recreation is often costly to a family who have not explored the many opportunities their area offers for free or low-cost entertainment. City and suburban residents often overlook the many possibilities in their area, ranging from museums, some with special sections for children, to a parade or guided tours of great stores and buildings; in a port such as New York, a visit to liners or to a visiting aircraft carrier. (New Yorkers can contact the Navy Public Affairs Office, Third Naval District, 90 Church Street, New York, New York 10007, regarding fleet vessels.)

The homes of famous men and women are open to visitors. Seeing them, students gain a sense of the real past—not one pictured on a screen.

Across the country, visitors can drop in at the plants of great companies (*though advance notice is preferred*) and watch the production of many of those items familiar from store shelves and television commercials. Check the yellow pages of your telephone book and call up companies whose plants you would like to visit.

Local Chambers of Commerce and state information bureaus issue free brochures and you can always get initial information from a library. Take it from there—and cut down on commercial entertainment costs.

PLAY THE SMART CONSUMER GAME

The investment of your time and effort in the Consumer Game will pay off in sure dividends. Cash gains are yours when you resist impulse buying, and let advertising guide you rather than over-persuade you; when you decide what you want and compare values before you buy; when you consult such publications as *Consumer Bulletin* and *Consumer Reports* before selecting major purchases. The old saying *Money saved is money earned* is still apt when millions of Americans are finding that their incomes and other resources are not keeping up with the cost of living.

Keep up with the Consumer Game by building up your home reference library of buying tips and impartial consumer or government reports. This kind of reading matter will help you to work out a family dollar-saving plan based on your real needs.

Though government is now active in the cause of consumer protection, getting value for your dollar is still very much a personal business. When you demand quality, question price, take care of your property, and are alert to deceptive practices, you will indeed raise cash by cutting costs.

Chapter 5

HOW TO INCREASE THE FAMILY INCOME

Is there a gap between your income and outgo? Do your future needs or special plans call for money you do not presently see in the budget? If so, how can you supplement the family income?

The purpose of this chapter is to suggest ideas to you, mainly for the type of work that can be done from or near home, and possibly may be developed into a personal business. That aspect is further discussed on page 71. Suggestions are also given on outside employment.

IDEAS FOR A SECOND INCOME

You may already have some hobby or interest you can expand into a money-making project; your business training or mechanical ability might earn you extra cash after hours; your home, garden, or special equipment offer dollar-making possibilities. Whatever it is you do, the choice is personal, according to need and ability. There are as many opportunities as there are individuals; you may be one who can touch a commonplace idea with unique creativity and go on to make a substantial income. From small beginnings—*renting a room, commercializing a talent,* or *rendering a needed service in the community,* people have entered into apartment ownership, developed large mail-order business, and become presidents of their own companies.

If you are not immediately sure of the right idea, stimulate your thinking through reading up on profitable hobbies, and along the lines of your particular aptitudes, whether a facility in talking (an asset in *selling* or *lecturing*), or *mechanics,* or just plain *sewing* or *mending.* Fads of the moment, say, for tie-dyeing or for unusual handbags, has brought success to creative people who ride the tide, jump off at the ebb, and, capitalizing on the name they have made, are ready to cater to the next craze. Don't underestimate some skill you may have! It may only need marketing.

Books on money-making projects and sideline businesses are available. Their bibliographies will guide you to further reading, and into action. Your local library, with its informed staff, is invaluable to you. We shall also give some other sources of information, and as you follow up one, you will learn of others. If you are determined to increase income from home, you will surely find the right means.

In this chapter, we can do no more than suggest a very few of the ways people have used to earn extra money. Here are some of them:

Your Part-time Project	*Possible Markets*
Teaching your talent or skill to individuals or classes	Students in the home; leading an adult education class; joining others to form a school
Using your talent (singing, lecturing, entertaining, etc.) in the community	Restaurants, hotels, clubs, groups, churches, local radio and TV stations
Using your training, skill, or interests to render personal services	Various jobs in home or garden; repairs; mothers' or invalids' helper; running children's library; boarding plants or pets; walking dogs; shopping for shut-ins

Raising fruits, flowers, mushrooms, etc.; keeping bees for honey	Direct sales to customers; roadside stands; through local retailers; mail order
Raising and breeding animals, birds, fish	Direct; through classified advertising; pet stores; mail order
Raising for produce (as eggs, goats' milk for invalids), fur, etc.	
Cooking, candy-making, kitchen products of all types	Direct; mail order; retailers. Catering services to individuals, groups, offices, for parties
Products, crafts items, jewelry, woodwork	Direct; mail order; gift shops; boutiques; some department stores

VITAL FACTORS TO KEEP IN MIND

Your object is *to increase the family income*—not just to cover the expenses of some time-consuming project—and certainly not to lose money.

Ask yourself the following questions and give much thought to the answers:

Who needs my talent, product, service or accommodation? To earn, you must offer something others need or will want. You may have to tailor your personal preferences to gain a market.

How can my offer be marketed? Consider classified or other advertising, mailed announcements, posted notices, the telephone, and, of course, that free advertising, word of mouth. Reckon all costs, including those of travel to see potential buyers.

How does location affect my plan? Ideas good in one area court failure in others. Take this factor into full consideration; but because no one offers such an idea in your area may be the very reason that you should. Watch that fine line between venturing where others dare not—and finding a gold mine, and undertaking a project where no market exists.

How much will I make? Be sure to calculate costs of running your enterprise against what you expect to make. *Profit*—and that is what you want—is only the *excess over expenses,* a point too many home-enterprisers forget. Full discussion follows on page 68.

Have I the time needed? Probably, if you are retired, semi-incapacitated, or young and unmarried. The person with a full-time job and the mother with small children must consider if the proposed idea can be scheduled in spare time or if it would prove a burden on health and temper. Of course many busy people find time when they are determined to achieve an objective. But not all can easily forgo socializing or leisure pursuits, especially when the wishes of husband or wife must be considered.

What obstacles do I face? Think these through and list them. Competition is certainly one. You may have to come up with a superior product or service, or cut your profit, even to get a toe in the field. A new slant would help—or maybe you should try a less crowded enterprise. Consider, too, all personal factors, such as lack of cooperation in the home, and if more capital than you have would be required. (In general, the person eager to make extra money is limited to starting in a small way, which is not necessarily an obstacle but rather an opportunity to test market possibilities.)

YOUR PERSONAL ATTITUDE

Only you can decide what you can offer, and *your own attitude may be far more important than actual skill.* Project a modest talent with confidence and enthusiasm; undertake a service with willingness to meet the needs of others, and you open a door to success. Leave a greater ability undeveloped, or a highly original idea unproclaimed; you earn neither dollars nor kudos and confer benefit on no one.

People who have felt short on talent and personal skills have successfully capitalized material assets. Some have *rented rooms* in the home *as offices* for doctors, lawyers, authors, and real estate or insurance agents; some have looked over *junk in the attic* and seen the nucleus of an *antique store;* more than one person has transformed a *collection of old recipes* into a *highly salable cookbook.*

PUTTING MONEY-MAKING IDEAS TO WORK

Here are three real-life examples of people earning successfully through diverse means: A childless housewife runs a typing service from home; a widow who was left with young children operates as a caterer; a retired man sells both commercial and fine art.

Rose Shapiro, whose salesman husband had an uncertain income, decided to operate a *typing service* from their apartment in an outlying suburb of New York City. She culled the names of professional people, small firms, one-man businesses, etc., from the telephone directory and mailed out announcements. She also advertised in local newspapers. At first, she handled the work herself. Now, with a group of women working for her in their own homes, she has, in effect, placed a typing pool at the disposal of her clients. She serves a wide area in the county and her main job is to drive around making pickups and deliveries. Mrs. Shapiro uncovered her profitable market with a modest investment in advertising.

Linda Tracy, a widow left with young children to bring up, recognized a potential market in a well-to-do community where people entertained a great deal. She would offer a catering service for parties, weddings, and gala occasions. Like Rose Shapiro, she began by mailing announcements to potential customers and by advertising in the local paper. Soon, word spread about her skill in cooking and her pleasant and efficient service. Over the years, Mrs. Tracy built up a highly successful small business out of her home kitchen. Now, her children long since grown, she has premises with up-to-date cooking facilities and a gift store in front. Her mobile staff of assistants go out on a variety of catering assignments.

Albert Helwig, who retired after years in an advertising agency art department, found he and his wife needed a supplement to their present income. So, from his home in a city suburb, he developed a number of greeting card designs which he took or mailed to companies that bought from free-lancers; he canvassed small firms in the area for advertising art jobs; he sold his "fine arts" output at local art exhibitions and from displays at a restaurant; he sought assignments to paint pictures of people's homes and landscapes from their favorite photographs.

STEPS TO BE TAKEN

None of these people began with heavy financial outlay. The two women made their initial lists of possible customers by checking social and business news in local papers and by browsing through telephone directories. At stores, Mr. Helwig looked over popular styles of cards. One store owner told him of the Greeting Card Association which would supply him with lists of greeting card companies that buy from free-lancers. Similar information could have been obtained from a magazine such as *The Writer* which lists markets for greeting card verse.

Initiative is your great asset in launching any home enterprise and, like these people, you have to dig for information and your customers. Both may turn up through unexpected channels.

Look for publications covering your interest: *hobbycraft, animal raising, woodworking,* etc. In most reference libraries you can check *The Readers' Guide to Periodical Literature* and *N. W. Ayer & Son's Directory of Newspapers and Periodicals.* Because you should have up-to-date information on your project, be sure to check this source for titles of publications.

Talking to people will put you in touch with information, ideas, and criticism. You will have to distinguish between the pessimistic types who see insurmountable obstacles in every setback, and those who can alert you to factors you may not have taken into consideration. See that your advisor is qualified. Your local Chamber of Commerce will prove helpful. *It is, of course, essential to see your city, town, or village authorities.* Not only can they give you valuable general information, but they will tell you how zoning and other regulations affect your plans. Before plunging into an enterprise, you certainly need to check on the law. For example, control over the preparation of food is exercised not only locally, but by the Federal government through the Food and Drug Administration.

TAKING YOUR IDEA TO MARKET

We have seen how three people went about marketing their diverse wares. What other means are there to *market a skill, service, or product?*

Locally, there is always the *telephone* which is sometimes used to initiate an approach, sometimes to follow up on a mailed announcement. Your area may have a *customer's market type of publication,* made up entirely of classified advertising, through which you can reach the public. Inquire at your newsdealer. The local newspaper may give your project publicity in a news item. You may be able to *post notices* on company, organization, or church bulletin boards, or in stores. If your community has no regulations against *house-to-house selling* you can use this approach.

If you have items for sale, such as *jewelry, fine sewing, workshop products,* or *kitchen products,* ask local stores to buy from you. Some may purchase outright; others will suggest a consignment basis; that is, you share a portion of the price with the seller, or take unsold goods back. Department stores often buy specialty items in quantity. Show samples to a buyer.

Women should look up the address of their nearest "Women's Exchange." (Try the phone book or the Chamber of Commerce.) The exchanges customarily sell "on consignment." In New York State, the Department of Commerce runs a Woman's Program. Information and assistance is available on all aspects of selling a product or service, or in starting a shop. Find out if your state now has such a program.

The Small Business Administration, a branch of the Federal government, has offices in main cities of each state. Write the one nearest you, or to 1310 L Street, N.W., Washington, D.C. 20417, asking for titles and prices of their booklets and guides (many are free). You can get information on licenses and regulations, financing, management, record keeping, pricing, selling, advertising, and other aspects of part-time and small business.

SELLING BY MAIL

Selling goods, services, and information by mail is "big business," but there is room for you, if you are willing to pay for advertising. If you have fine homemade wares for sale in quantity, space in a national homemaking magazine may be worth the investment, especially at the Christmas season. Most people will start with local newspaper advertising and, with suitable enterprises, expand to nearby radio and television stations. Frequently, they can also enjoy the publicity of a news story.

Often, the lone individual will sell through a mail order house which will catalogue novelty and other items and sell by "direct mail" (approaching potential customers through the mails with advertising), or "mail order" (advertising in the press). If your product or service justifies it, you can enter the direct mail field yourself by buying lists of names from brokers.

Read up on all phases of marketing before venturing deep. There are books on retailing, direct mail, and mail order. Here again, the Small Business Administration can provide booklets and advice.

If you are barred from running a mail order business from your apartment or house because of the terms of the lease or local zoning regulations, the use of a Post Office box number may overcome the difficulty.

YOUR OBJECTIVE—PROFIT

Whatever your venture—*repairing toys, television sets,* or *watches; raising animals* or *produce; remodeling furniture,* or *running a telephone answering* or *party helper service*—you are in it *to make a profit,* so do not lose sight of this objective because you like your sideline work. However, you should enjoy whatever you undertake, particularly when you run it as a sideline. Pleasure in the work for itself is a guard against depression when the start is slow, business lags, or you run into personal and outside difficulties. Nevertheless, enthusiasm—that invaluable asset—should not blind you to the question: *Am I making money?*

From the start, maintain accurate records that will prove the point. Set down whatever costs are involved—for materials, for improving facilities, for expert advice. You will need these records for your tax return (see Chapter 15); you need them to be your own cost accountant.

Say the materials you buy for some craft item cost you 50 cents, and you sell for $5. Profit—$4.50? Not if you have mailing or advertising costs, have spent time and money on telephoning, used extra light and power, and spent hours creating the item. Income tax is due also, though you may be entitled to business deductions.

When you have fully considered your own *costs,* you should add a fair hourly or daily rate for your *time.* You should check the price of similar products and services. Will people pay a little extra for yours? Yes, if it is unusual, particularly skillfully made, offered with special personal service, or exceptional in your area. No, if it is commonplace, "homemade," in the worst sense, or something that can be better handled by big business.

With time, experience, and increased volume, you may be able to cut costs and so increase profit on an item or service which rendered small profit in the first place. *Investigate pricing thoroughly* before you start, trying to steer between "cheapness," which devalues your product or service, and a figure no one will pay. (Ask if you would pay it yourself!)

The publications you read may guide you to business associations and councils which give advice on pricing. For instance, a craftsman may inquire of The American Craftsmen's Educational Council, Inc., at 29 West 53rd Street, New York, New York 10019, which will give much helpful information. Check, too, on advertising of products, services, and manufactured items for general guidance on current prices.

A WORD OF WARNING

Before we discuss working for others, a word of caution should be added on fraudulent business opportunities. If you want to earn extra money, yet are undecided on the means, you may be scanning the advertisement columns for ideas. You read of some attractive goods or devices that will earn you substantial sums.

A reply to your inquiry may bring an avalanche of mail or a salesman to your doorstep. You could be asked to invest in some equipment through which you can earn at home; you might be told you need only "refer" some offer to your friends; or a certain franchise will make your fortune. Too, you may learn of certain courses which will teach you to make an income as a writer, artist, or what-not. How do you distinguish genuine business or teaching offers from out-and-out frauds?

Observe certain rules: proceed slowly, refusing to be pressured into action; investigate thoroughly—if necessary seeking the advice of your Better Business Bureau or a lawyer; and, most important of all, *sign nothing,* until inquiries are complete. You may be told of some free offer you will miss by delay, but that "miss" may be well to your advantage. The outfit wants your money; it isn't out to help you earn any.

Genuine correspondence schools rarely *guarantee* sales to their students. Beware of the school that does. Also of the "publisher" who will make your book a best seller if you will only pay the costs. Often he is a printer; certainly he will not have the usual channels of distribution. (If you really do have a best seller, you can be sure a top-notch publisher will pay you for it.)

WORKING FOR OTHERS

From home, you can make money by working part-time for others. Watch classified advertisements (or place your own) to uncover local opportunities for selling insurance, or encyclopedias, or cosmetics. There are party plans for selling kitchenware, gifts, and cosmetics. Women often enjoy this mode of selling. A good way to enter is through the recommendation of a friend in similar work. You learn firsthand about the company and its financial practices, and you get tips on handling your first assignments.

People who work during the day can moonlight as collection agents for delinquent accounts, doing bookkeeping for small businesses, or selling by telephone. Skill in repair work of various types provides the second job for many people, as does taxi-driving and retail selling. Moonlighting can provide a substantial boost to the family income.

Research offers opportunities to the woman who cannot commit herself to long-term employment. Market research firms (listed in the yellow pages of the telephone directory) customarily employ freelancers who work for one day or for several, sometimes for longer periods, gathering information which is used by advertising agencies, manufacturing companies, publishers, and others. The job calls for tact, patience, and legwork and involves interviewing people, often housewives. Some researchers have connections with several survey firms, others work for only one or two. The analysis of surveys often means office jobs for temporary workers.

Both men and women interested in this type of work should check classified advertising under Market Research.

OUTSIDE EMPLOYMENT

Outside jobs with regular wage or salary will, of course, offer the best source of dependable additional income in a family. Classified employment advertisements cover every type of opportunity; some open to teenagers, some to retired people. For the most part, the wife and mother is the person who undertakes to be the second wage or salary earner in the family.

If you are new to business or out of touch with today's requirements, turn to your public library. The librarian will direct you to books on part-time jobs, submitting résumés, and, for the housewife, on successfully managing both home and employment.

Getting a job involves these steps: 1. Assessing ability. 2. Possibly taking classes in learning new or improving old skills. 3. Checking classified advertising and/or visiting an employment agency. 4. Sending out letters or telephoning for an interview.

If local classified advertising does not offer a suitable opportunity, you can do more than advertise in the "Employment Wanted" column. You can write to firms in your vicinity inquiring about upcoming vacancies. State your skills and say whether you want full, temporary, or part-time employment.

If direct efforts fail, both part-time and temporary employment are obtainable through agencies. Some specialize in such opportunities. An agency is entitled to a fee, often one week's salary, but the fee will vary according to the type of job offered. Sometimes, even for temporary jobs, the prospective employer will pay the fee.

When dealing with an agency, check the financial arrangements at the start. Usually, the fees are posted in the office, and in most states they are regulated by law. An agency that does not give a satisfactory answer about charges is best avoided.

ESTABLISHING YOUR OWN BUSINESS

Your own business may develop as the expansion of a part-time home enterprise. Sometimes a husband or wife maintains safe outside employment while the other ventures into the personal business. If it expands successfully it will provide the family living or retirement sideline.

Whatever your reason for wanting to start your own store, shop, plant, or other business, make sure that you are first well acquainted with the type of responsibility you are acquiring. While much of the information we give for the part-time enterpriser applies to you, you will want to delve deeper. For example, in addition to reading the printed information supplied by the Small Business Administration office nearest you (see page 67), find out if workshops where the specific problems of the business owner are thoroughly analyzed are currently being offered.

Acquaint yourself with the law regarding the sole proprietorship of a small business. You are personally responsible for all business losses and liabilities (including those incurred by your employees); this means that your property, savings, and monies from other sources may be reached by your creditors for settlement of business debts. You must consider, too, that your illness or death might end operations. Would your family be protected financially? Check, also, on the change in your Social Security status.

In a partnership, where you and one or more partners contribute skills or capital, all share losses and profits, both of which are reported on personal income tax returns. Advantages and disadvantages of a partnership are similar to those of a sole proprietorship. In addition, however, business debts incurred by partners endanger your personal assets unless you insure against the eventuality.

You can organize a corporation and so protect your personal assets, but such a venture is more complicated and costly. Thoroughly explore all the aspects of establishing a business through inquiries, reading, and in consultation with a lawyer or certified public accountant before you take any irrevocable steps.

You may, of course, invest in a franchise, *after the most thorough investigation.* Phony franchise opportunities have claimed many victims. Some are "pyramid" operations, similar to chain letters, whereby one investor obtains others, who, in turn, recruit more gullible people to put money into the scheme. Whether purporting to sell goods or services, this type of operation only guarantees loss of money. Caution and a lawyer's advice are essential. You can start your exploration by picking up a free booklet from the Small Business Administration. When you operate under a reliable franchise you gain the advantage of a "company name," its advertising, and services. You will still have to put up capital, carry many of the responsibilities of a proprietor, and work long hours.

RAISING CAPITAL

We will assume you have a certain amount of capital and a sound project. To raise additional funds, see your local banker first; probably he knows you and if your reputation in the community is good, he will give you a favorable hearing.

But you shop for money as for other commodities and you want the most favorable rates. A large bank outside the community may have a department that specializes in loans to the small businessman.

The Small Business Administration, an agency of the Federal government, may provide you with a direct or immediate participation loan if you can satisfy their office that you have an eligible enterprise. You must first endeavor to raise money privately. Send first to the SBA for their guides on sources of capital. Their free and low-priced publications are invaluable to the small businessman or woman seeking advice on management and financing.

If you approach some private company for a loan, you may find some offering reasonably priced credit, others which are undoubtedly "loan sharks." Do not enter into any contract without legal advice.

If you are a veteran—or the unmarried widow of one—inquire of the Veterans Administration if you can qualify for a loan.

See, too, the section of Chapter 6 dealing with borrowing. Books specifically written about the establishment of small businesses are available and will guide you with complete details on sources of capital.

Your best friend, however, is your own good standing and ability to raise money from personal sources. But if friends and business connections become your backers, you will still need the services of a lawyer to ensure that proper agreements are drawn up.

Chapter 6

BUY NOW—AND BE READY TO
PAY LATER

Today, it is the rare person who does not use credit in some form or another. Credit for the consumer, a pleasant-sounding term for a state of debt, is so readily available now it can be ruin or boon depending on how it is used.

As long as you recognize that credit represents a debt you have to pay, and you are prepared through your financial planning to pay within the stated time, you can enjoy immediate possession of department store goods, plane tickets, gasoline, rental of a car, accommodation in a motel, and countless goods and services merely by showing a card and signing a bill.

Credit cards, department store charge accounts, and installment buying are a convenience—for which you pay even if you avoid the service charges levied on unpaid bills. Pricing takes into account the cost of operating all delayed payment systems, and you, the credit customer, and your neighbor who pays cash for everything, pay the extra hidden cost.

In return, established department stores and many local merchants give credit customers certain privileges; returned goods are accepted more readily for credit than for cash, first announcements of special sales are sent, and the prompt payer gets a good credit bureau reference.

Credit, of course, represents trouble if you lose sight of your obligation to pay. With so many desirable things available, people from all walks of life are tempted to buy now and worry later—and they do. Families in suburban communities with more than average incomes are as vulnerable to serious debt involvement as the disadvantaged city dwellers who sign up for time payments they are unable to meet.

When you start to incur interest charges—in addition to that hidden cost which all pay—stop and think. Is it really necessary for you to delay your payments? Perhaps you only need to work out your problems with the aid of the forms in Chapter 1, spreading savings ahead to enable you to meet bills promptly. Consider the true interest rate—perhaps as much as 18 percent a year; it can mount up alarmingly. What you save by paying promptly could add up to a useful sum in an education or vacation fund.

YOUR CREDIT RATING

Your standing as a good credit risk is a major asset, and you protect it by the prompt payment of your bills. You build up your standing over the years and take it with you across the country. From coast to coast, credit bureaus pass along information and confirm—or deny—your ability to meet your obligations.

Your place in the credit system is established by your use of it. You may have felt that the use of credit cards and charge accounts should be avoided; that you could manage money better and stay out of debt if you established an "I always pay cash" policy. In today's society, this principle unfortunately carries a rebound. The cash payers may have failed to establish credit, and when a loan is needed, they are as disadvantaged as their constantly indebted neighbors who are tagged poor risks.

Once your credit is established as good, there will be less investigation when you apply for new types of credit. At the outset, the department store, the bank, or finance company will require you to fill out a form and to satisfy an interviewer as to your character, your financial resources, and your capacity to pay. You will be called upon to give the name of employers, past and present, to state your salary and other income, and to give details about home mortgages or rent, bank accounts, and your charge or credit cards.

See to it that your answers to questions will stand investigation. If you fail to give full or truthful information, you will damage your credit record—and that is a fatal step in financial mismanagement.

THE CREDIT BUREAU

Not surprisingly, information on file at a credit bureau may be out-of-date or inaccurate. One bureau alone may have as many as 70 million dossiers; another of these privately owned concerns may be a noncomputerized agency that is run as a small business. For years, people found that they were denied credit when, in fact, their record was good. Moreover, they were unable to set the matter straight. Others who had established good credit after earlier trouble were denied jobs or loans because the records remained unchanged.

To right this situation, the Fair Credit Reporting Act took effect on April 25, 1971. While errors will still occur, the individual is empowered to do something about them. When he is denied credit, he may ask which bureau supplied the negative data. This credit agency must then tell the complainer what information is on file about him and who supplied it. Where error is alleged, an investigation must be made. When data is found to be inaccurate or cannot be verified, it cannot remain on file.

Even if your credit rating remains unchallenged, you are permitted to review your file. A nominal fee may be charged. You may inquire about your rights under the new law by writing to the Industry Relations Director, Associated Credit Bureaus, Inc., 6767 Southwest Freeway, Houston, Texas 77036.

CREDIT CARDS

The credit card is designed as a tempter. In the store you will charge merchandise you might have done without if cash were demanded; in the restaurant you think "why not?" and order a particularly expensive meal. After all, payment will not be due until next month.

The person concerned about the good management of his finances will treat his numerous cards as the convenience they are—and keep some account of how much he is charging, where, and when. If his wife does the same, the couple know how much will be needed to cover the inevitable billing. Those whose bills are running too high should preset their credit card buying at a specific level each month.

If you do not know just how and when you are going to pay for the merchandise, gasoline, services, entertainment, or travel charged, you should get yourself on a strictly cash basis until you can bring better order into your financial affairs.

Some invitations to use credit are, in effect, invitations to take a loan at a high interest rate. Do you need this type of advance? Many people enjoy the apparent status of card flashing and easy credit. The purveyors of cards cater to that weakness. Since discipline and control are part of your money management program you can afford to pass up "status" for security.

Plainly, the smart money manager uses credit cards instead of paying cash. *But he does so knowing that he could have paid cash if he so wished;* he is ready to pay bills when due; and he does not charge items or services he would not otherwise have bought.

We do not list all types of credit cards; they are too numerous to mention, besides being well known through advertising. Billing is either through a specific company, as when you charge at a department store or buy gasoline, or may be consolidated, as when you use a bank or club card for services or purchases of a widely varied nature.

Some organizations issuing credit cards do so on payment of an annual fee; they add a service charge on overdue accounts. Your need for such a club card in the course of your business or social life will dictate whether or not you apply for membership. If and when you do so, weigh the specific charges made by the particular organization or club against the benefits you expect from membership. There is no membership fee for bank cards which are accepted by many good restaurants, hotels, and motels.

There is now a trend toward department stores accepting bank and club credit cards in addition to their own charge plates.

DISCOUNT FOR CASH

Businesses must pay a percentage of each credit card sale to the credit card issuer. Consequently, old-fashioned cash can look good over the counter. Several years ago, a reverse of the credit card system came into being and spread in sections of California, Ohio, and Pennsylvania. Merchants and consumers signed up with organizations which issued cards and provided listings of participating dealers. A discount is given for cash payment when a consumer presents his cards at one of the merchants' stores.

The proponents of the discount-for-cash programs believe the plan can challenge the credit card system. But whether it does or not, you may find local merchants willing to give you a personal discount for handing over a cash payment. Merchants who accept credit cards are under no obligation to give a discount to the customer who pays cash, but the person who asks often enough may be happily surprised—and save a useful percentage on his purchase.

CHARGE AT YOUR LOCAL MERCHANT

When bank credit cards proliferated from 5 million to 50 million in less than five years, shopping at the local stores became similar to shopping at the department stores. The trend continues as more and more merchants and services sign up with the charge systems.

For the percentage paid, a merchant is relieved of billing and collection responsibilities. The customer no longer has to bother with cash or writing personal checks, and by delaying payment of the bank's statement until the last moment can hold on to his own money.

In addition to accepting bank and other major credit cards, many merchants still send out their own monthly billings to regular customers, a useful service to the local buyer who does not want to run up a bank or club card account. However, some stores now warn their customers that, like the credit card operators, they will impose a percentage charge on overdue accounts.

CREDIT CARD MISUSE

Dishonest clerks or merchants can misuse your credit card without your being aware of fraud. If the card is taken from view during the billing, the clerk might make additional copies of your plate on blank sales slips. A cash purchase is later billed on one of the slips, and your signature forged. The clerk steals the cash; you get the item on your statement. Always compare your duplicate sales slips with the charges on the statement to make sure they are correct.

At the time of transaction, you should see that the sales slip is accurate. A storeowner who raises the figures unnoticed by the customer can do very well for himself.

On the other side of the counter, new technology is coming to the protection of the credit card companies and banks. One system tested in 1971 enables a merchant to insert a credit card with a magnetic stripe into a terminal linked to a computer at a central authorization center. If the card is reported stolen or the holder has already exceeded his credit, no approval of the new charge will be given. As variations of such point-of-sale tests of credit spread across the nation and better checking systems are developed, losses through fraudulent and misapplied use of cards will be substantially curbed.

LOSS OF CREDIT CARDS

What if you lose credit cards? You may have read that since January 1971 the customer whose card has been misused need not even pay the $50 liability limit if the company has not informed him of the new law and provided an addressed, postage-paid envelope for notification of a lost card. Also that after January 24, 1972, a credit card must bear the holder's photograph, fingerprint, or signature. Without such identification, the holder is not held responsible for misuse of his card. These credit card provisions of the Truth in Lending Act should not lull a cardholder into a false sense of security. A number of cards lost or stolen might still represent a sizable bill at $50 each.

Protect yourself and the issuing banks or companies by guarding your credit cards as carefully as cash. When loss does occur, report the facts immediately—whether or not you have been provided with an addressed envelope. Follow up a phone call or wire with a letter. As noted in Chapter 2 (page 27), you should keep a list of credit card numbers and company addresses in a safe place.

If after reporting a loss you find the missing cards were only misplaced, also notify the companies immediately. Your cards' numbers will be on an alarm list and using them could place you in an embarrassing situation.

INSURANCE

Credit card coverage may be bought separately or, in some cases, added to personal policies such as homeowners or casualty policies. You may at the same time acquire other benefits, such as insurance against loss on altered checks, but you may also have to prove that you handled your cards with due care and immediately reported loss. Inquire about company rates and requirements, which vary widely.

YOUR CHARGE ACCOUNT AT DEPARTMENT STORES

Stores use different types of accounts, according to their class of business. With the *Open or Regular Account* you buy from stores in person, by mail, or by telephone without down payment or service charge. But the statement which you receive is invariably marked "Payable within 10 days of receipt of statement." In practice, this works out as a 30-day period, and some stores will—protestingly— carry unpaid balances forward for several months for the customer with a good credit rating. Ultimately, of course, they will threaten to sue—and you should certainly settle the account in a hurry to avoid such proceedings. In the meantime, you are likely to have been labeled a poor risk at the central credit bureau.

The above type of account is being superseded by a variety of accounts, all of which carry some form of service charge on the past-due balance, depending on the type of contract you entered into. Penalties are usually incurred for not paying by a specified time after receipt of the monthly statement.

Titles of accounts vary from store to store and it is not always possible to say which title fits which method. Some retailers combine different forms of payment into their installment contract. For example, one national company's *Revolving Charge Account* contract permits the customer three choices. He may pay within 30 days, no penalty, or, if he fails to so pay, he automatically becomes liable for a 1½ percent charge on his outstanding balance. He then remits whatever installment payment is due according to a set schedule. That is, if he owes $50, he may have to pay $10 a month, but if he runs his account to $200, he pays $20. He can also pay in advance.

Another form often described as the *Revolving Credit Account* works this way: The customer agrees with the store credit department on an amount to be paid monthly. The store then sets a limit on what he is allowed to buy, so that the amount outstanding will not exceed the original set level. This type of account is helpful to those who are too easily carried away by the array of merchandise in the store and the magic-wand effect of the words *"Charge it!"* Debts above the agreed amount must be paid *immediately*.

The *Retail Installment Credit* agreement of a famous coast-to-coast store operates as a Regular Charge when the bill is paid before the next statement date. Otherwise, the customer has to pay a service charge of 1½ percent per month and at least ⅙ of his current balance. Ten dollars is the minimum monthly payment.

A well-known discount department store has been operating *Regular and Budget Accounts* for some years. At one time, such stores worked only on a cash basis. Now, the store offers a three-way option account: You pay the entire balance; you pay the current minimum amount due, according to schedule; or you pay any amount in excess of that minimum. The finance charges vary slightly over the five Eastern states served by the store, according to local law.

The *Optional Account* of a well-known Western store also can be used as a Regular Account, or the customer pays according to the current extent of his debt. When his balance is $50, he pays $5; when he owes $200, he pays $10. He, of course, pays the 1½ percent per month charge.

The 1½ percent charge has been common in the retail business on bills to $500 with a reduction to 1 percent a month on larger amounts. Some states impose restrictions which reduce the annual percentage that may be charged. You should ascertain the current rate allowed in your state. An eventual uniformity seems likely.

Many companies as well as department stores set up "Easy Payment Plans," which do not have the optional regular account feature. The customer pays a presettled amount each month until the specific merchandise is paid for. The time periods of installment contracts (also see page 83) will vary and the "carrying charges" also. You must also keep well in mind the percentage you would actually be paying. Your pocket might be better served if you get a loan (see pages 85–94) in order to buy the goods outright.

PAYMENT OF CREDIT ACCOUNTS

A problem with the payment of various types of credit accounts has been the imposition of service charges on amounts the customer had already paid. Sometimes the trouble arises because the payment has not reached the company's accounting department before the next billing period. But some stores deliberately use this type of billing, especially on revolving charge accounts. Under this "previous balance" system, the customer's partial payments are not deducted when interest is computed. If the store used the "adjusted balance" system, taking payments and credits into consideration before computing interest, the customer would pay less interest.

Some states have rules against the use of the previous balance system, but allow companies to use the "average daily balance" in computing bills. Under this plan, the customer does get credit for his payments, but he is charged interest in proportion to the time his balance was not reduced by the payment.

If you have a complaint about a store's billing practices and can get no redress, make your complaint known. Some local newspapers and radio stations handle such consumer grievances. You can write to the Federal Trade Commission, your state attorney general, and your representatives in the national and state capital. Even if Federal law still does not cover the situation, your state's law may require the adjusted balance system. Where new regulations are issued, certain stores may be slow to fall into line and customers will find it necessary to draw attention to the fact.

INSTALLMENT BUYING

One of the most important points about your savings program is that it enables you to pay cash for the goods you want instead of paying someone else additional money for a loan or time plan. This is where your planned goals serve you. You decide that next year you will have a new car, or a refrigerator-freezer. You could go out and obtain the desired goods now at the cost of installment payments, or you could save the money at interest in a day-of-deposit to day-of-withdrawal savings account until you had the purchase price. Here, you would have to weigh your actual need of the item—essential now or desirable sometime; the pace at which you can save (your work on Chapter 1 provides an answer here), the interest rate at the savings bank weighed against installment charges—and the possibility of a rise in price. You should be aware of the economic factors currently obtaining so that if, say, the price of certain appliances is rising, a good installment contract is worth more than saving against a rising tide of costs. An alternative is to get a bank loan for major purchases (see page 89).

THE INSTALLMENT CONTRACT

We give some warnings about installment contracts here and in Chapter 4 in order to alert readers to the possibility of fraud and of becoming involved in deliberately inflated but legal commitments.

We hope, of course, that you will be doing business with ethical establishments. But even when you are so doing, you still have to be alert and to bear in mind such points as:

Your ability to make a substantial down payment. A large initial payment will reduce the spread of payments and the charges you would be paying. If you do not have the means to make that large down payment, should you be undertaking the installment payments?

What will your other commitments be during the period you would be paying on time? Have you left yourself a cash margin for emergency? Certainly it is not possible to safeguard against all eventualities, but it is the too heavy load assumed for too long a period that drives many families to seek Family Service advice.

The repayment period. Interest charges mount up during the spread-out paying period. Such advertising as "Easy terms! No down

payment, three years to pay" may involve you in a prolonged and
inflated debt. Choose to pay as quickly as you can. The shorter the
period of repayment the lower the overall cost.

SIGNING AN INSTALLMENT CONTRACT

Whether a contract is offered to you by a ready-money lender, or
by a store where you wish to buy "on time," or by a door-to-door
salesman, you should know that this person or his company is likely
to sell the installment contract to a third party.

That third party may be a bank or a sales finance company and
the matter may well be in order. You pay on time; no trouble, no
comeback. But when you do not pay, *the buyer of the contract has
the legal rights set out in that contract*—he may repossess the property, take over your security, have your wages garnisheed, or take
you to court. You have signed; unless a "cooling-off" period is
operative (see page 51), you are definitely committed to whatever terms you so accepted. It behooves you, therefore, *to know
what you are signing for, to know what will happen if you fail in
payment*.

Since your legal commitment will be *what the contract says* and
not what the salesman or lender says (unless those statements are
written into the contract), your first step is to read the fine print
of the contract before you sign it and to see that full information is
given. Examine these points:

Does the contract spell out in detail what you are buying? The
price of the merchandise or the amount of cash lent? What your
allowance is from trade-in (see page 55) or the sum of the down
payment? The total of your debt and how payments have been divided? The number of your installments and when they occur? Im-
portantly, what are the credit charges?

What happens if you cannot pay? Are the goods repossessed? If
so, are there terms under which you can redeem them? What are the
details on nonpayment penalties? *Note that repossession of the goods
may not relieve you of commitment to pay.*

Can your pay be attached if you fail to meet installments? Does
the contract include an assignment of part of your wages? Garnish-
ment of wages is now curtailed in many states, but not in all.

Has the salesman or lender filled out all the spaces in your contract? Sign nothing till blanks are satisfactorily completed or you

may become liable for charges or goods you did not consent to accept.

To whom are you to make your payments? You may suppose your contract to be with a certain store or dealer when, in fact, you will be dealing with the bank, finance corporation, or central organization who has bought up the contract or acts for your merchant or lender.

These third parties, known as "holders-in-due-course," have been able to repossess the item bought, yet the debtor would still owe his installments. Some states have now limited the scope of the holder-in-due-course doctrine. But because a consumer is still vulnerable if payments have not been kept up, you should inform yourself fully on the law in your state. If you are buying on the installment system and the merchandise proves faulty, you may only have a limited time in which to lodge a complaint. Once that time is passed, you have no redress; you still owe installments on a faulty or useless item.

Will the monthly payments completely cover your indebtedness for the goods or loan, and interest? If not, you might find a lump-sum balance still has to be paid, and without delay. This type of provision is being eliminated by merchants and lenders of good standing, but may still occur and prove a trap for the unwary and ill-prepared customer. Check for it.

Credit laws vary considerably from state to state. Inquire if your state's Banking Department issues information for the consumer. The position in New York is defined in the booklet "Know Your Rights *when you buy on time*," obtainable from the New York State Banking Department, 100 Church Street, New York, New York 10007.

When you have signed your contract, make sure you have a copy and that you keep it safely for reference.

Changes designed to protect the consumer are taking place at both Federal and state levels. Be alert for these developments and see that in your credit dealings you receive all the protection the law affords.

YOU NEED A LOAN

Don't buy at the first stall is still good advice when you want *to buy the use* of someone else's money to meet an emergency; to purchase a house, a business, a car; to finance education, or to replace a pile of small bills by one large one.

If you are not presently wanting to buy—i.e., borrow—money, don't think this section isn't for you. Sometimes money is needed in a great hurry and if you are reasonably well informed on lending establishments and their terms, you can hasten to the one most likely to meet your need.

The uninformed, worried, and hurried borrower is the most likely person to buy himself more financial trouble in the shape of an unnecessarily expensive loan. In his fear, he may even fall into the hands of a "loan shark."

First, we will examine the preferred attributes of the borrower, then the types of lending institutions and their practices.

CREDIT RATINGS AND LOANS

Your personal credit status (see page 76) is what enables you to borrow at the most reliable establishments at the most favorable rates. A person whose credit record is blotted by slow payments or nonpayments knows he is unlikely to get a favorable reception at the personal loan department of the neighborhood bank.

What people do not always realize are the other factors which weigh for or against them. You are rated on such factors as:

Your job and how long you have held it
Your home-ownership, or standing as a tenant; your neighborhood
Your marital status and the number of your dependents
Your present (and possibly your future) financial obligations
The usual state of your bank balance
Your reasons for seeking the loan

The ubiquitous credit cards may give you the feeling that you have unlimited credit, but you will find that a prospective lender will analyze you, your current situation, and your prospects before he agrees to lend you money. Expect to be questioned by a reputable lender. A loan too easily extended may well mean that you are about to be bound by excessive interest charges. Protect yourself by enhancing your credit rating and by shopping around before you buy a loan.

However, a reliable and well-intentioned borrower through no fault of his own may not find it possible to "buy" at the most reasonable source. He may be young, only shortly settled in a job, and unsettled in his living quarters. He may have paid cash too long; he might be a new arrival in this country. Though he may have to borrow from a small loan company, he can choose a reputable one (see page 93) and begin a good credit rating by fulfilling his obligations promptly.

INSURANCE LOANS

Life insurance policies differ as fund-raising vehicles; the type of policy you own may make a ready loan available to you. Read up on your policy; cash value and loan rate will be stated.

If you want the money briefly, this can be a quick, low-rate, true interest method of obtaining money. Write your company, giving your policy number, and state how much you want. (You can borrow most of the cash value.) Usually, a check will be sent within a few days, no questions asked, and you can repay on a system convenient to you. There are no extras on an insurance loan. You may appear to have a bargain.

But—of course, there is a BUT—you reduce your family's protection against your death by the amount of the loan and the interest charges. The very lack of pressure to repay an insurance loan is not in its favor on a long-term basis. By constantly postponing full discharge of the loan, you shoulder the burdens of a running debt and heighten the risk of being underinsured. You also lack that cushion of financial assurance your insurance policies offer should you have to meet an even greater emergency.

COMAKER OR COSIGNER LOANS

If you, through no fault of your own, do not have an established credit rating, raising a loan may be difficult. Here, your resource may be a person who has the required financial standing. If you can find such a friend or relative to *cosign* a note or finance company, you get your loan. Your *comaker,* who personally believes in your integrity and ability to repay, has taken equal responsibility for settling with the lender if you should fail to do so.

It might be added here that if you are asked to cosign a loan, do so only if the borrower is a relative or friend you know well, and in whom you have complete confidence. People take a risk when they cosign for neighbors, boarders, fellow workers, and others who are really mere acquaintances. Even a cosigner's credit rating may be in jeopardy if the borrower defaults.

INSURANCE OF LOANS

With many types of loans you automatically acquire life insurance —for which you may or may not pay directly, according to your source. The life insurance buys protection for the lender against your death and consequent inability to pay the debt. It may sometimes appear that you are getting a particularly good deal—a competitive rate of interest plus insurance. A closer look at the terms of the contract may prove otherwise. You and your family would derive no personal benefit from the insurance—except for the coverage of the debt in case of death, and taking full cost into consideration, the overall contract is no bargain.

You may be offered "free insurance," which is part of the deal, but the cost may be built into the interest charge you will pay. Sometimes, in addition, you will be offered the benefits of accident and health insurance for "pennies a day." Should you protect your responsibility for the loan to this additional degree? Before doing so, check on whatever coverage you already have in case of accident or disability and what the general state of your finances would be in such an eventuality. If your loan is heavy and your overall situation would be weak in case of health breakdown, the insurance may be well worthwhile.

LOANS AT THE SIGN OF THE GOLDEN BALLS

The sign of the three golden balls, hanging over dingy stores on back streets and in run-down neighborhoods, has denoted the local pawnbroker to generations of borrowers throughout the Western world.

In twentieth-century America, the dusty little shop has, in many places, blossomed into handsome establishments run by corporations. The principle of lending remains the same. The customer takes security, in the form of jewelry, furs, a camera, a musical instrument, etc., to the pawnbroker; in return, he receives a loan and a receipt. If he is unable to pay back the loan, plus interest, he will never return to redeem his pledge. In time, the article will be sold and the pawnbroker gets his money back.

We hope that you will never need the pawnbroker, but if you ever use such services, seek out the reputable man who allows you to seal your pledge of jewelry in a bag or to write the serial number of equipment on your receipt. When you make a pledge of this kind, you have to guard against substitutions by a dishonest employee.

Interest rates vary locally, and may be affected from time to time by new laws. Before dealing with a pawnbroker, check on interest rates at your bureau of consumer affairs, or similar agency. "No questions asked" is still the rule at the pawnbroker's and he may charge more than other lenders. But when cash is needed short-term, the establishment still has a place in the complex society of today.

BANKS

Once chiefly interested in lending money for business purposes, the commercial bank today is a prime source of personal loans, generally given at advantageous rates. In general, when you need a loan, you should approach a bank first to check on its terms and your eligibility. Depending on your area and requirements, the interest rates will vary, but you will get the more favorable terms when you put up collateral, such as stocks, bonds, insurance policies, a savings bank passbook, or execute a chattel mortgage on your car. (Passbook loans on your savings account are discussed on page 92.)

You do well to deal with your bank for loans. When you meet their repayment terms, which are rigid, you establish a good credit relationship. The bank has, of course, checked your credit record and established the good purposes of your loan.

Banks vary in their interest rates for different categories of loans. In the New York City area "signature" (unsecured) loans of up to $5,000 are obtainable for emergencies, including hospital and dental expenses; vacations and Christmas shopping; hobby equipment and debt consolidation, etc. The scope is wide, and you can apply for the loan by mail or even by telephone.

Automobile or boat loans are offered up to $5,000 with three years to pay. Property improvement loans (also see page 129) range from $100 to $15,000 and terms may be spread over as long as seven years. Education loans, which are insured, are available from $300 to $15,000.

Business loans, of course, continue to be big bank business. With a sound commercial or professional purpose, you can approach a bank for a loan—perhaps $100,000 or more, and you might have five years in which to repay.

If a veteran, you may be eligible for a G.I. Business Loan. While your first approach would go to the local office of the Veterans Administration, you would probably find the bank makes your loan through its participation in the G.I. Bill lending program. Terms are better than those offered to other borrowers.

Once again, it must be said that because of the variation in terms offered, you should shop several banks for the specific loan you want.

USING STOCKS AND BONDS AS COLLATERAL

If you own stocks and bonds and you need a loan you have ready security for a bank loan. The bank holds your stocks against cash, and you sign a "time note." This note may become due before you are ready to repay, but if your securities still have high market value, you will probably be able to have your note renewed. You only pay interest.

You should be alert, however, to several factors in this type of loan. You do not get the current market value of your securities as a loan. The bank will offer less, a protection for both against possible decline in value. You will not be asked to put up additional security or have your note recalled unless the stock drops to below the actual amount of the loan.

Say you cannot pay the loan, but the market is good. The value of your stock soars. You are in luck. The bank will sell all or part; it collects the debt, you collect some profit.

Your pledged stocks and bonds still bring in your usual dividends, and these may help to offset the cost of your loan.

Of course, when you repay a secured loan your stocks and bonds are returned to you.

BANK CREDIT PLANS

Currently, bank credit plans blossom overnight. They vary in detail, but not in substance—the people who use them will pay interest, and that adds up to good business for the banks.

One plan establishes the borrower's right to credit of up to $5,000. The borrower does not actually receive any money. He makes use of the available credit whenever he pays his bills with the special checks issued to him. He pays a monthly interest charge on the amount of credit he actually uses, and for the checks. As he repays the amount borrowed plus interest, he establishes his right to use the credit again.

Another system does not require special checks. A borrower of good standing may write a check for more than he currently has in his account. But, because he has arranged for the bank to set up a credit reserve of between $400 to $5,000, his check is met. In *multiples of $100*, the bank will move money into his otherwise overdrawn account. The borrower repays on a 12- or a 24-month basis, plus a monthly interest charge of 1 percent *on the daily unpaid* balance. If he repays in less than a month, the interest is proportionately reduced. If he does not call upon the reserve by overdrawing his account, he incurs no liability for interest charges. (He pays the regular bank charges the bank imposes for checks and service.)

In both of these credit plans the borrower must meet standards of credit eligibility similar to those required by a bank in making conventional type loans. The loan proceeds are not turned over to the borrower under either of these plans. Instead, the loan comes into existence when the arranged-for credit is used—by the writing of a check.

The loan application can be dispensed with because the bank customer has had to fill out a detailed application form in the first place. In reality, he is processed like any other type of borrower although he does not get a loan as such. With a regular bank loan the borrower describes his purpose, which must be approved. Under these plans he uses the credit as he pleases.

Details may differ from one area of the country to another, but variations of these plans are widespread today and new developments may be expected in the computerized society.

CREDIT UNIONS

Membership in a credit union is discussed on page 136. Members are able to secure loans at varying rates of interest. State and Federal law sets the limit of interest rate but some credit unions charge below that limit. A credit union's rates may vary for the class of loan; say, a maximum of 12 percent per annum for furniture and similar consumer items, nine percent for loans for the purchase of an automobile, boat, or trailer. The rate on secured loans might be even less.

The solvency of a credit union may be affected when a large number of members fail on their loan repayments. A Federal insurance plan and other safeguards are not taking effect, and credit unions are better able to make the loans for the "provident and productive purposes" for which the organizations were established. These purposes include loans for medical bills and funeral expenses, weddings and home purchases, household repairs, starting a business, and taking vacations.

THE SAVINGS BANK

When the need for a loan arises—for an emergency or an important purchase, the person who saves regularly at a bank or savings and loan association has an advantage. If he has a day-of-deposit to day-of-withdrawal savings account, he can draw on it for the needed funds—and the only cost is the interest he loses while the money is gone. The good money manager will arrange to repay his account on a regular basis as if he had borrowed from an outside source.

But you may have a regular savings account where withdrawals can only be made at the end of a quarter without loss of all interest for the period. You need money right away. Here, your best plan would probably be a loan on your passbook. The savings bank will advance you the sum you need at a comparatively reasonable rate and, at the same time, you do not lose the interest accumulated on your savings. All the time you are repaying the bank for your loan, your regular savings bank interest will be paid by the bank and, in some part, this will reduce the actual cost of the loan. See the section at the end of this chapter on true annual interest rates.

You are required to repay your loan in monthly installments over one to three years at some banks. Other banks leave the manner of repayment largely to the discretion of the borrower. Self-discipline is important here lest the interest charges mount up.

SMALL LOAN COMPANIES

Here, we discuss licensed small loan companies, which probably means that they are reputable and operating within state law. (Most, but not all, states provide some protection for the borrower.)

You will, no doubt, find it easier to walk into your friendly small loan company—open long after the banks close and on Saturdays, too—and to walk out with a $500 loan than you would to get the same money from a bank.

But in return for speed and lack of intensive questioning, you will pay their high interest rates. These may vary. The true interest rate of, say, 3 percent a month, comes to 36 percent a year; this is an expensive loan. A larger financing company may offer a better rate than it did a few years ago. One giant corporation currently charges only 19.8 percent per annum on the average loan.

The small loan company can assist the person without a credit background to consolidate debts and thereby to improve his future standing. Some will provide competent budgeting and counseling services which are of real benefit to people who cannot see their way through a difficult financial situation.

In general, go to the small loan company only if you cannot get a loan from a lower-rate source. If you do so, check on the company first. This can be done through the local Better Business Bureau.

THE LOAN SHARK

You already know that the reputable loan company operates under state license, which gives varying degrees of protection to the borrower. The loan shark operates for his own benefit, or possibly for that of a larger and altogether sinister organization. In these days he may set up shop in attractive surroundings which are likely to lull the borrower's suspicions.

Since we cannot list every device an unscrupulous lender might use, we can only urge the prior checkup as above, and be aware of the following possibilities:

You may be asked to sign papers in which there are blank spaces.

You may not be given copies of all the papers.

You may not get a chance to read the fine print; an additional document you did not see may be among the carbon copies.

The amount of the loan may be overstated.

The date of the loan may be incorrect.

The charges may be exorbitant—and they may skyrocket further in mysterious ways if you get yourself involved.

The person who has become involved with a loan shark does not get free easily. Some who have borrowed have accepted lifelong shackles. They fear to go to the District Attorney lest strong-arm tactics be used against them—and sometimes these fears are realized. The threat alone is a burden no one should carry.

Our suggestion—manage your money so that, when you need to borrow, your credit is good at reputable sources. Intelligent handling of finances is your best protection against involvement with a shady loan shark.

CREDITS COSTS AND TRUE RATE OF INTEREST

Credit is available from various sources, banks, finance companies, credit unions, and retail stores, to name the most common. If you decide to buy on credit or to borrow money, you will want to know how much it is costing you to use the lender's money—both in terms of dollars and rate of interest. Then you can compare the varying prices of credit and be able to buy and borrow at the lowest cost. Or you might find that you cannot afford to use credit—the price may be beyond your means.

The complex nature of contract terms and credit charges have long confused the average buyer or borrower. He does not fully understand what he is actually paying for his installment purchase or loan in terms of true annual interest. Like other merchants, those who extend credit advertise their wares in the most favorable terms. When the merchandise is money, this means showing as low a cost as possible to potential consumers of credit. One way to make the interest rate appear low is to state the monthly rather than the annual rate. Another method is by advertising only the dollar cost of a loan with no indication of the true annual interest.

If a person making a loan realized that a loan quoted as $6 per $100 per year would actually cost him 12.5 percent annual interest, he might reconsider his need for the loan. He might decide to borrow for a shorter period or he might shop around for credit from a cheaper source. If it was stated clearly that a purchase on a revolving credit plan could add an additional 18 percent to the price of the merchandise, a purchaser might well postpone the purchase until he himself had saved the price to pay cash.

The Federal Consumer Credit Protection Act of 1969, generally called the Truth-in-Lending Law, was designed to assist the consumer and make actual credit cost clear to him. Many foggy areas still exist, necessitating new law at Federal and state levels. Because the consumer may need guidance for some time to come, we include here several pages of reference material. Rates of interest may go up or down, but by substituting current figures for our examples you will be able to clarify a credit offer that may be puzzling you.

TYPES OF LOANS AND WAYS OF STATING INTEREST

When you "buy now, pay later," "charge it," buy "on time," "use a 'payment plan' " and whenever you take out a loan—you are using someone else's money—and usually paying for the use of it. How much it costs depends on the terms of the credit agreement.

Simple interest. A loan at simple interest at 6 percent a year means that you pay six cents a year for each dollar you borrow. If you borrow $100 at 6 percent for a full year and do not have to make monthly installments, you would have the full use of the money until the end of the year. At the end of the year, you would repay $106. You would then be paying a true annual interest of 6 percent. If you repaid the loan in six months, the interest would be half, or $3. Six percent simple interest comes to ½ percent a month.

A simple interest loan is available from few sources, and usually requires good collateral in the form of a savings passbook, life insurance policy, real estate, etc. The most economical loans you can make will probably be a first mortgage loan or one against your life insurance or bank account.

Unpaid balance—monthly interest. Credit unions and small loan companies, as well as retail merchants and banks on certain types of charge plans, quote charges as a percentage of the balance unpaid each month. Multiply the monthly interest by 12 to arrive at annual interest.

Monthly rate	True annual rate is
¾ of 1%	9%
⅚ of 1%	10%
1 %	12%
1¼%	15%
1½%	18%
2 %	24%
2¼%	27%
2½%	30%
2¾%	33%
3 %	36%
3¼%	39%
3½%	42%

As you repay the amount borrowed, the size of the loan decreases. For example, say your unpaid balance is $120 and is repayable in 12 monthly installments at 1 percent per month. Figure your interest charge on the unpaid balance at the end of the month as follows:

Divide $120 by 12 to find the amount of principal you must repay each month:

$$\$120 \div 12 = \$10$$

Determine the 1 percent a month interest charge payable on $120, your unpaid balance at the end of the first month:

$$\$120 \times 1 \text{ percent} = \$1.20$$

Your first payment is $11.20; $10 principal and $1.20 interest. Subtract your monthly principal payment from the balance:

$$\$120 - \$10 = \$110$$

The second month you would repay $10 of principal and 1 percent interest on your remaining balance of $110 or $1.10. The second month you pay $11.10.

Figure your payments of principal and interest this way each month. Remember, your principal payment remains the same; the interest charge decreases as your unpaid balance gets lower. Your final payment of the loan will be $10.10.

This $120, 1 percent a month loan, actually costs 12 percent per year in interest; in dollars it costs $7.80.

Add-on loan. On an add-on loan, the interest charge is added to your loan or purchase. On a 6 percent per $100 loan for a year you have to repay $106. If you make monthly repayments, as is usual, you do not have the full use of the money for the entire year. Month by month, you have less, but you are still paying on $100 at 6 percent a year. If you repay the $100 plus 6 percent interest in 12 monthly installments of $8.83 each for a total of $106, your true annual interest is 11.1 percent, almost double what you thought you were paying. If your repayments are scheduled over 18 months, you would be repaying $109 (6 percent per year for 1½ years). Your monthly payments would be lower, $6.05 per month; your true rate of interest would be higher, 11.4 percent.

Discount loan. On a discounted loan, the bank discounts or *deducts* the interest in advance. On a $100 discounted loan, instead of $100, you are handed only $94. On a loan for a year quoted as 6 percent per $100 you have to repay $100. Each monthly installment comes to $8.33. Your true annual interest is 11.8 percent. If you repaid a $100 discounted loan over an 18-month period, the true annual interest would jump to 12.5 percent.

The discount method actually works out to a higher rate of interest than the add-on loan. The reason: the same $6 of interest is a larger share of $94 than it is of $100. Roughly, true annual interest on such a loan to be paid back in monthly installments over a year is about double the amount stated.

You can determine true annual interest by applying the following formula:

$$
\text{True Annual Interest} = \frac{2 \times \text{number of installments in year} \times \$ \text{ cost of loan}}{\text{Amount of loan actually received} \times \text{Total number of installments} + 1}
$$

Say you take out a loan of $1,000, quoted at 6 percent per $100, discounted, to be repaid monthly over two years. This means you receive only $880. $120 is the cost of the loan. You figure the true annual interest by applying the above formula as follows:

$$\text{True Annual Interest} = \frac{2 \times 12 \times \$120}{\$880 \times (24 + 1)}$$

This works out to 13.1 percent true annual interest.

Or, say you plan to purchase a washing machine costing $300. The dealer offers you $25 for your old one as a trade-in and quotes you a price of $36 to cover carrying charges to finance the purchase over an 18-month period. You can determine the true annual rate of interest you would be paying by applying the formula:

$$\text{True Annual Interest} = \frac{2 \times 12 \times \$36}{\$275 \times (18 + 1)}$$

The finance charges on the washing machine would come to 16.5 percent in true annual interest.

The following table shows the true annual interest rate for a $100 loan at various rates. You can compare the higher cost of a discounted loan as against the add-on loan. You can also see how the length of the period of debt and frequency of installments increases the rate of interest.

TABLE OF TRUE ANNUAL INTEREST
ADD-ON LOAN

Amount of Loan Proceeds	Rate per $100 per Year	Cost of Loan in Dollars	Number of Monthly Installments	True Annual Interest Rate
$100	$6.00	$9.00	18	11.4%
100	6.00	6.00	12	11.1
100	6.00	5.00	10	9.1
100	5.00	7.50	18	9.5
100	5.00	5.00	12	9.2
100	5.00	4.17	10	7.6
100	4.00	6.00	18	7.6
100	4.00	4.00	12	7.4
100	4.00	3.33	10	6.5
100	3.00	4.50	18	5.6
100	3.00	3.00	12	5.5
100	3.00	2.50	10	4.5

DISCOUNT LOAN

Amount of Loan Proceeds	Rate per $100 per Year	Cost of Loan in Dollars	Number of Monthly Installments	True Annual Interest Rate
$91.00	$6.00	$9.00	18	12.5%
94.00	6.00	6.00	12	11.8
95.00	6.00	5.00	10	9.6
92.50	5.00	7.50	18	10.2
95.00	5.00	5.00	12	9.7
95.83	5.00	4.17	10	7.9
94.00	4.00	6.00	18	8.1
96.00	4.00	4.00	12	7.7
96.67	4.00	3.33	10	6.3
95.50	3.00	4.50	18	6.0
97.00	3.00	3.00	12	5.7
97.50	3.00	2.50	10	4.7

Chapter 7

WHEN YOU RENT, BUY, OR SELL
YOUR RESIDENCE

A family looking for a place to live generally has a decision to make on the location: city, suburb or outlying area; type of house or apartment; type of financing, purchase or rental. Before the search is begun, serious thought should be given first to the needs, interests and convenience of family members; then to capital in hand and prospective income and earnings for future years.

If your family is young and growing, an area within safe walking distance to good schools, safe play areas, and a place of worship should be preferred. Try to find out something about the people in the community. An area where most of the residents have grown children, different interests and attitudes from yours and incomes in a much higher or much lower range could be an unhappy choice. Investigate accessibility to shopping, job location, costs of transportation, travel time for work and whether a car is essential to get around.

CITY OR SUBURB

The past ten years have brought about a marked increase in the number of families who have settled outside of city areas. Economic prosperity enjoyed by more and more American families has fostered the urge to seek the "better living" of suburbia. City noises, congestion, traffic, increasing dangers to person and property, increasing costs of insurance against theft, polluted air, high rentals, expense, restrictions, and inconvenience connected with owning or operating a car in the city, extra sales taxes, and city income taxes have contributed to the exodus from metropolitan areas.

Families look to suburbia for more living space at very little if any extra cost. Generally, areas outside the city have cleaner air, are nearer to beaches, lakes, golf courses and tennis courts, and offer a bit of nature and greenery at the doorstep. For the family with young children, the suburbs offer less crowded schools, generally with higher educational standards, more protected play and recreation areas for children, and a wider opportunity for adult members to make friends and take an active role in community and civic affairs.

On the other hand, living in a city better suits the needs and interests of other families. If family members are all adult, they will generally prefer the city. They can get to a theater, concert, museum, art exhibit, and other places of interest with less time, effort, and expense from a city home than from one in a suburb. Working members may even be able to get to work on foot. At least, they will be able to get there by bus or rapid transit and avoid the inconveniences and expense of commuting. Families living in the city find that owning a car is not necessary. It may even be a nuisance. Taxis, buses, and other public transportation are generally adequate. You do not have to meet railroad time schedules or frustrating parking and highway traffic problems to get into the city. You do not have to be driven to or from the train every day for work.

Many families who moved to a suburb for the advantages it

offered their children while they were growing up return to the city
after the children leave the family home and establish themselves
elsewhere. Senior and soon-to-be senior citizens whose children have
left the family home find they can more conveniently enjoy in the
city the interests they developed over their years in the suburbs.
They relieve themselves of burdensome high taxes for schools they
no longer require, of commuting pressures and responsibilities of
home ownership. Most find that the general inflation in the real
estate market gives them a profit when they sell their home. Investing the proceeds in a city cooperative or condominium avoids tax
on at least part of this gain.

RENTING AN APARTMENT

When you rent an apartment, either in the city or a suburb, you
are generally relieved of responsibilities for most repairs and maintenance expenses. You can go away for as long as you please without
concern, by merely turning the key in your door lock. You have no
worries about whether the water pipes will freeze or the furnace will
break down. Your major and only responsibility for the apartment is
to pay the rent when due. (Under many landlord-conceived leases,
paying the rent is about the only thing you can do without violating
some provision of your lease!)

If you decide to rent an apartment, either in the city or an outlying area, keep these points in mind in your search: Is the building
located in a suitable neighborhood for the activities of the members
of your family? Would you feel safe in taking a walk or coming
home after dark? Will the floor plan necessitate buying more carpeting or additional furnishings, or will you have to get rid of some
furnishings, perhaps at a loss, because the space is smaller? Is the
building soundproof? What appliances go with the apartment, and
are they in good working order? Are gas and electricity included in
the rent? Is there garage space for your car, and is it included in the
rent? Does the owner give you the right to storage space in the
basement, and how much? What security does the owner provide
at the main entrance? Is there a superintendent or porter in the
building, and is he regularly available to tenants for necessary repairs?

When you rent the place you live in, you have more flexibility
than when you own it. You can leave when your rental term is up.

Your responsibility is definitely ascertainable in advance and is a fixed amount each month. With your landlord's consent, you can even give up your tenancy during its term with no further liability. However, this depends on your agreement with your landlord. You may continue to be liable for rent until the expiration of your term if the apartment remains unoccupied or your successor defaults.

If you are in a community where rent is controlled and you are in a rent-controlled building, you are protected against rent increases at the landlord's will. Generally, you will occupy your apartment as a month-to-month tenant after your lease expires. You can terminate your tenancy without further obligation by complying with the local law provisions relating to termination. But your landlord cannot force you to get out except as local law may provide for particular situations.

RENTING A HOUSE

In renting a house you should consider many of the same points we mentioned above in choosing an apartment. But a house generally means greater responsibility for maintenance than renting an apartment. You will probably have more space to live in, a front lawn and backyard. But you may have to take care of the grounds, pay the cost of heating and garbage removal (where this is not offered as a public service). However, this is a matter of agreement between you and your absentee-owner. The limits and extent of your responsibilities should be negotiated in advance and clearly set out in writing.

Local laws may require that leases for more than a certain period of time must be in writing. Even if local law does not require your agreement to be in writing, you should insist on this course. It will avoid future misunderstandings of the term, your rights and responsibilities and those of your landlord.

WHAT A LEASE SHOULD INCLUDE

Before you sign a residence lease, see that the following provisions are included:

The term of the lease, with specific beginnings and termination dates.

A description of the property rented (including garage, if any).

Responsibilities of each party for repairs, replacements, alterations, and maintenance.

Services to be provided by the landlord (heat, gas, electricity, if included in rent, elevator service, storage space).

Equipment to be furnished by the landlord (stove, refrigerator, air-conditioning units, etc.).

Amount of rent payable, and when it is to be paid.

Rights of tenant regarding installation of electric or mechanical equipment (air conditioner, humidifier, connecting TV aerial to outside antenna).

Rights of tenant to make changes in decor.

Rights of tenant to assign or sublet lease.

Conditions under which security deposited is to be returned or credited.

Rules and regulations regarding tenants' use of the apartment and building. For example, restrictions against keeping pets, uses of elevators, halls, or other communal areas, if any, for baby carriages, children's bicycles, etc.

If you are a month-to-month tenant under operation of local law, be sure to check what notice, if any, you are required to give your landlord before vacating your apartment so that you will be relieved of further responsibility for rent. In areas where there is no rent control, your landlord can generally ask you to vacate or pay an increased rental when your lease expires.

BUYING A HOUSE

Say that in your search for a home, you have to decide between an attractive apartment and a small house. Both offer adequate room space, but the house offers a garage, front lawn, and backyard as well. You compare the apartment rent, plus rent for garaging your car, with taxes, heating costs, mortgage payments, insurance, and general upkeep of the house. You should include an estimate for repairs and redecoration. Take into account the cash payment you will have to make on buying and expenses of closing title and moving into the house. The house appears more costly, but you get more for your money. And, under a long-range analysis, the house will probably turn out to be less expensive because of the economic advantages home ownership offers. These are (1) tax deductions, (2) build-up of equity, and (3) possible increase in value.

Tax deductions. When you pay interest to a mortgagee, and taxes on real property, you become entitled to a tax deduction for the amounts paid in arriving at your income tax liability.

If you have cash for a down payment on a small home, figure out what the net cost of carrying it would be over a five-year period, as compared with the rental you would have to pay for comparable quarters. You will probably find, as many others have found when they get a 20- or 25-year mortgage, that, after considering the income tax reduction for mortgage interest and taxes paid, the home actually costs less than the apartment. Moreover, in most instances, you will then own an asset of considerable value. On the other hand, you have nothing at the end of a rental term.

(If you are a veteran, local law may provide you with a partial exemption from property taxes. This will provide a reduction in the amount of monthly payments you will have to make to the mortgagee.)

Build-up of equity. Each payment you make to the mortgagee includes amortization. This is an amount which reduces your indebtedness under the mortgage, and in effect amounts to a form of savings. Many a homeowner has financed his child's college education by refinancing the home in which he has, over the years, built up an equity.

Increase in value. If real estate values continue to rise as they have in the past, and there is no indication of a reverse trend, your investment could be further enhanced.

CHECK LIST ON BUYING FAMILY HOME

You usually will find two or three houses in the right price range, each of which may meet most of your requirements. However, none may meet all of them. You must make a comparison of the good and bad features of each and resolve your decision by a compromise. Here is a check list of some of the points you should weigh:

Size and expansion possibilities. If the number of rooms is adequate now but might not be after a few years, is there room for expansion? Will zoning laws permit you to expand the house?

Topography of the lot. Is there sufficient level ground for the play area you require? Will abutting property make necessary a retaining wall? Is drainage adequate?

Public utilities. Will you have to maintain a well, or does the public authority supply water? Is garbage and trash removal a public service? Are the public roads near the house kept clear of snow and ice by a public service? What are the zoning laws in the immediate and neighboring vicinity? A home near an area zoned for commercial or industrial use will not be as desirable on a resale, and will depreciate more quickly in value.

Is the house near a traffic center, a main highway, or a transportation center? Traffic noises may make a home less desirable on a resale. But it must be weighed against the advantages of easy travel to work. Is the cost high for public transportation to work, shopping areas, places of entertainment and recreation, etc.?

Will you need a car to get yourself and your family to daily pursuits?

Is the house within walking distance of schools, place of worship, playgrounds, and shopping areas?

Are there sidewalks for children who walk to school?

Do zoning laws protect the neighborhood from deteriorating?

Are the schools crowded? If they are, you can be sure your taxes will be increased to provide for new schools.

Will your children be bused to schools at a distance from your home?

Are there sewers, or other public improvements in the area for which your house is likely to be assessed?

Have you gone into and around the house on rainy as well as dry days to look for water seepage, cracks in masonry around window sills and in the basement?

Will your car fit into the driveway or garage?

Is the electricity amperage adequate for the electric dryer, air conditioner, and other equipment you may wish to install?

Is the water pressure adequate?

Is the heating and hot water system a costly type? Is it in good condition?

What about other houses in the neighborhood? Are they maintained with pride of ownership or are they run down? You will not enjoy your home or obtain a good resale price if it is the only well-kept house in a neighborhood of rundown houses.

Is the neighborhood stabilized or improving?

Is industry creeping toward the neighborhood?

Do the grounds require immediate planting, a lawn or landscaping, a retaining wall?

Is the price comparable to sales prices of similar homes in the area?

Is the type of house one that is readily salable?

BUYING A MOBILE HOME

If your family is young, you may want to live away from the hubbub of an urban area, and perhaps want time to save for the permanent family home you hope ultimately to buy. Consider buying a mobile home. There are two primary forms of housing in the mobile home industry that you can buy ready-made: The "mobile home" and the "modular home."

The mobile home generally measures from 12 to 14 feet in width, and from 40 to 65 feet in length. The complete, furnished home, containing five or six rooms with bath, can be transported over the road by a regular tractor and set up in a trailer park. The wheels are never removed from the home, no matter how long it stays in one location. (They are generally hidden under some decorative material.) Although the term "mobile" indicates the home is easily moved, this is not in fact always so. The various states have local laws restricting the size of vehicles that can move on their roads, and may restrict the hours of the day when travel for oversized vehicles is permissible. The average move of a mobile home is once in about five years, which is the same for families living in houses.

A mobile homeowner, well-settled in one place, could enlarge living space by adding a second mobile home alongside. With the aid of some carpentry, two living rooms become one; kitchen space is increased; there can be larger or extra bedrooms, and two bathrooms.

The mobile home is generally not considered as real estate. Thus, you cannot get a mortgage on it. You can finance it like an automobile, with monthly payments for as long as 84 months. Therefore, a low-cost mobile-home unit can provide an inexpensive form of housing for a young family. A unit that contains a living room, dinette, kitchen, two or three bedrooms, and bath with shower might cost anywhere from $3,500 upward, furnished. At a modest monthly rental, the mobile-home park provides the pad on which you set the home, with connections for sewage, electricity, telephone, etc.

Some local tax authorities have placed mobile homes in the category of real estate and imposed real estate taxes accordingly. In California, litigation has been instituted to determine in the courts if such taxation is legal—in view of the license fees mobile home-owners have to pay to the Department of Motor Vehicles on the same property.

If mobile homes should be considered housing for tax purposes, they ultimately should be financed as homes—over 20-year periods and on easier terms than the current shorter period.

The Modular Home. The modular home is usually manufactured in two equal sections, like two halves of a house. Each half has the same dimensions as a mobile home, but is really built as half a house. The units do not have their own chassis and are not classified as vehicles. They are placed by the distributor on a flat-bed type of truck and transported to the site of your land. At this site, they are set up on a previously cast, permanent foundation. The two halves are then fastened together and covered at the central peak of the roof. The house then looks like any house built on land. It is now real estate and you can obtain a mortgage on it from a lending institution. The FHA gives mortgages on modular homes for periods comparable to those it gives on regular houses.

If you qualify as a low-income family living in a rural area, the Farm Administration can give you a low-interest mortgage on your purchase of a modular home.

If you should decide to buy a piece of land on which to set up your mobile home, you must first find out if the local zoning regulations permit you to use the land for that purpose.

If you move your mobile home to a park site, your rent will usually depend on the location of the park, location of the particular site you rent in the park, and the quality and quantity of services the park furnishes to its tenants, and the utilities that go with the rental.

Before renting any park site and locating your mobile home, you should find out about schools, churches, recreation, shopping, etc. —all those points you would check if you were buying a permanent home. In addition, it is important to investigate the park thoroughly, and know how it operates. Find out exactly what service the park owner will provide. Does the park have police and fire protection? What about garbage collection? Will you be able to get all the water and electric power you require? Is telephone service available? What are the rules and regulations with which all tenants are expected to comply? Insofar as the choice of a site is concerned, be wary of any location that is low and vulnerable to the flow of water from higher ground. Be sure to check drainage and sewage facilities.

In reaching a decision on whether to buy a mobile home, a modular unit or regular house, keep this in mind: The mobile home depreciates rapidly in value. You will probably not be able to recover your cost if you decide to move after, say, seven years. On the other hand, real estate values have been rising consistently and show no adverse trend. The regular house, or even one brought to your land in modular-unit form, will probably be worth more than you paid for it seven years hence.

BUYING A COOPERATIVE APARTMENT OR CONDOMINIUM

When you buy an apartment in a cooperative building, you pay your proportionate share of mortgage payments, taxes, and maintenance and operating costs of the entire building monthly, like rent. The amount is therefore dependent to a large extent on the size of the unpaid balance on the building mortgage, and the general condition of the building. If the mortgage is low and the building modern and in good condition when you buy, your monthly carrying charges will be lower.

What you get when you buy a cooperative apartment is stock in the owner-corporation. If you want to sell your apartment and the shares of stock, your buyer must generally be approved by the co-op's board of directors which undertakes responsibility for management of the building. Demand for co-ops has increased materially in and near large cities. The risk of tenants defaulting, and of increased costs to remaining owners, is very low.

One of the major advantages of owning a condominium over ownership of a cooperative apartment is that you can generally finance part of your purchase of a condominium through a mortgage from a lending institution. On the other hand, banks have not been making a general practice of lending an individual funds for the purchase of a cooperative apartment since he cannot offer title to the property as collateral, but only his stock interest. Local laws in some states, as for example, New York, now permit banks to lend the owner of stock in a cooperative corporation up to 75 percent of the appraised value of his shares if he assigns his shares and his lease as collateral security for the loan. There are some basic costs involved in such a loan which you should be aware of at the outset. One bank requires the apartment buyer to carry group life insurance for the benefit of the bank. The lending bank will probably want a credit report from you, its own appraisal, and a title search at your expense. A fee will also be charged for the bank's attorney's services, usually depending on the amount of the loan.

In comparing the cost of carrying a co-op apartment with rent, remember that the co-op gives you tax benefits, like home ownership. You are entitled to deduct the amount you pay for your share of real estate taxes and interest on the building's mortgage.

When you buy a condominium you get legal title to an apartment in the building and an interest in the land and all improvements which you hold in common with the other apartment owners. The condominium is a cross between owning a home and a cooperative apartment. You are free to put your own mortgage on your apartment. If there is a blanket mortgage on the whole project, you assume a proportionate part of that mortgage up to the unpaid part of your purchase price. You pay the proportionate share of real estate taxes allocable to your apartment. Like a home or cooperative apartment owner, you can deduct mortgage interest and taxes on your income tax return. But unlike cooperative ownership, you are generally free to sell or lease at any price to anyone—subject in some instances to first offering the unit to the other owners at your asking price.

The tax deductions allowable to owners of cooperative apartments and condominiums, like home ownership, may enable you to buy an apartment for less overall cost than rental of a comparable one. The facts and figures should be analyzed carefully. Too, ownership of a co-op or condominium, like a home, allows for a build-up of equity as a form of saving.

YOU NEED A LAWYER

You should retain a lawyer as soon as your offer for the house of your choice is accepted. The purchase of a house generally represents the most expensive buy of your lifetime. It is economically unsound to "do it yourself" to save a lawyer's fee.

Many brokers ask buyers for a nominal cash payment as a "binder." Such binders are often construed as contracts without giving the protection a contract provides. It is better practice to sign nothing and make no payment. The seller's lawyer can get a contract up in a very short time. Tell the seller to have his lawyer get in touch with yours, and the contract can be signed within a few days. At that time you will make your down payment, usually 10 percent of the purchase price.

Your lawyer will see that all the terms and conditions of the sale are included in the written agreement. If you cannot complete your purchase unless you are to secure a satisfactory loan or mortgage, your lawyer will try to get such condition stated in your contract. If the seller offers such items as carpeting, curtains, appliances, garden equipment, etc. with the house, your lawyer will see that you get title to this personal property at the closing. A seller rarely gives anything not specifically provided for in the contract.

Some home buyers are under the illusion that the attorney representing the mortgagee will look out for their interests as well, and that a lawyer is an unnecessary expense. This is not so. The lawyer for the mortgagee is there to protect the lending institution, not you. If there is an encroachment or easement turned up on the title examination, such fact will affect your interest as owner but will not deter the mortgagee's lawyer from going ahead to give you the mortgage. The mortgagee's interest for the amount it advances will be adequately secured despite this encroachment. But this might affect the marketability of your title. If there is an open assessment against the property, the attorney for the mortgagee will not concern himself about who pays it, or if it is paid. But your lawyer will try to get the seller to pay at least a part.

If the seller has failed to complete certain work called for by the contract as of the closing date, the attorney for the mortgagee may not be concerned. But your lawyer will, for your protection. He will

try either to get a part of the purchase price put "in escrow" pending the seller's performance or make some other arrangement for
your protection. He might get an agreement that the seller can have
the balance that is in escrow provided he completes the work on or
before a certain date. On his default, the money would go to you
for you to have the work done. If the seller has made representations
as to construction your lawyer will try to get them in writing, for
your protection in your investment.

Your attorney can also find out whether the house you are buying
is protected by FHA or VA rules obligating the builder to correct
structural defects, or to make allowances for the costs of repairs.

THE ROLE OF A REAL ESTATE BROKER

You do not incur any liability for broker's commissions when you
consult a broker about buying a house. His sales commissions are
payable by the owner who makes him his agent to sell his house.
Consulting a local broker, who generally knows most of the houses
that are on the market in his area, will save you a lot of wear and
tear and expedite your search for a home. An active real estate
broker generally knows the actual sales prices of homes comparable
to the one you seek. A reputable broker will tell you these prices
to guide you in your offer. He knows what lending institutions will
finance the purchase of the house you choose, what the lending
institutions look for in issuing credit on mortgages, how much an
institution is likely to lend, and where you can get an FHA or VA
mortgage, if you qualify. Brokers are generally more expert than a
layman in the art of negotiating between a buyer and seller, and
know how to keep open negotiations after a buyer's offer of less
than asking price is rejected by the seller.

On the other hand, don't rely implicitly in a broker's sales talk or
enthusiasm for the house he wants to sell. There are some things you
should check. Have an independent expert examine the property.
Check for yourself the location of the school your children will be
eligible to attend. You may choose a house because of the educational standards of the nearby schools—only to find out a child at
your address has to attend another school. Check also at the school
on the availability of transportation. You may be just outside the
one-mile or other distance limit. Your neighbor's child may be en-

titled to transportation, while yours may have to walk or be driven to school.

GET AN EXPERT'S OPINION

After you find the house you prefer above others, and the price is in the right range, get a building expert to examine it for you. His fee will probably be upward of $25 but will be worth it. He will check construction, insulation, the roof, the water pipes, the volume of electric current for appliances, the heating system, and tell you whether there is any evidence of termite infestation—a hidden danger in every house. He will give you an idea of annual heating costs and what repair and maintenance costs you should anticipate. He might recommend additional insulation for savings in heating costs, or other work on the house that will insure years of low maintenance charges. If any costs are to be incurred along these lines, you should take them into account in financing your purchase.

OLD VS. NEW

When you buy and move into a new house you find everything bright, fresh, clean, and modern. You may even have had the opportunity to choose some of its features, such as wallpaper, flooring, fixtures, etc., but only up to the amount the builder has allowed for these. This is generally so when you buy a home from a builder who shows you a "sample" house and then finishes your house accordingly. Anything you want that costs more than the amount the builder has allowed will be put in at your expense.

Builders of new houses usually provide a bare lawn and no landscaping. They do not put in storm or screen windows or doors. You will have to take these items of expense into consideration over and above the down payment for the house. You will also have to weather the frustrations resulting from "bugs" in construction. When a house is new, and until it is "broken in," doors and windows may stick, outside steps may crack, heating and hot water systems may need constant adjustment, and the settling of the house may mean repainting or papering of walls and tile repairs in bathrooms. However, you will be able to finance the purchase of a new house more easily than an older house. You can get a 25-year mortgage more easily on a new house than on an older one, and on a smaller down payment.

On the other hand, an older house has other advantages. It usually has a warmth, charm, and at least appearance of, if not actual, sturdiness not found in new homes offered at comparable prices. The older home will probably save you the expense of lawn, landscaping, screen and storm windows and doors. If the house is in a well-established neighborhood, the schools are not as likely to become overcrowded or inadequate as quickly as in the new development areas. Property taxes will probably not increase as quickly as in new communities. There may be an existing mortgage you can take over, and so save some financing costs. But an older house may need modernization, particularly in the kitchen. It might need a wall knocked down to make way for a "family room." You may have to repaint or redecorate even before you can move in. You may require rewiring to accommodate all your electric appliances. You will need capital to do this. If this will make the cost of the old house more than a comparable new one, and you do not have the ready cash for modernization, it would not be wise for you to buy an older house.

In your search for a family home, you may find a house that meets all your requirements—except that it has no family room, and you also wanted an additional bedroom and bathroom. The price is right, low enough to allow you to add the three rooms. The land appears ample enough to accommodate the expanded house. Nevertheless, before you bind yourself to any purchase, make sure that the enlargement will not cause the house to encroach beyond the building line and will meet legal limits. Also, that the necessary permits for construction of the proposed addition will be granted by the local authorities. Ask the present owner to let you see his survey, showing the limits of the property he is selling. Consult the local zoning and building authorities. Get their advice as to whether you would be allowed to proceed with your project.

When you get title and are ready to proceed with the expansion of the house, you will need an architect, plans, a contractor, etc., just as if you were building the custom-built house discussed below.

One other consideration you should not overlook in choosing between a new and an old house: make certain the older house is in a neighborhood that is not deteriorating or becoming commercial in character. If it is, your chances of getting your investment back will not be as good as from a new house that is comparable in cost.

THE CUSTOM-BUILT HOUSE

Few houses are perfect for every family. You might find the right house, but the location may not please. The custom-built house is the answer for the family that wants a modern home, designed to their wishes, desires, and specifications, in the neighborhood they choose and on the lot they select.

Steps to take. The first step you take as a prospective builder of a custom-built house is to buy the land. Check zoning laws before buying to make sure you can build a residence on the size lot you are planning to buy. Local law may require that building lots be a minimum area. Make sure yours is at least that size. Check also to make sure nearby property is not zoned for commercial use or any use that would reduce the value of your property.

Have a lawyer represent you on the purchase of the land to make sure your title is good and marketable before you go ahead with building plans.

Your next steps should be taken only after a long period of thought, study, and inquiry into experiences of others who have built custom homes. Examine books, pamphlets, magazines, and newspaper articles on home-building. Attend home-construction shows and exhibits. In every way you can, learn about new ideas in home-building, new time- and labor-saving devices. Look into ideas for built-in lighting that is functional and attractive, in place of traditional lamps, fixtures, and chandeliers. Look into ideas of built-in furniture, particularly adaptable for children's rooms. Look into modern wall-oven units, revolving kitchen shelves that disappear within the wall, mirrored closet doors in bedrooms, different types of heating and air-conditioning units, sliding walls, ramps instead of stairs, and possibilities for expansion of the basic house to be built.

RETAINING AN ARCHITECT

Your next step should be to retain an architect to guide you with design and to oversee construction. His fee is usually a percentage of building costs. This may seem high, but what you pay for his services could be offset by savings he effects for you in design or construction, or in both areas.

Expert advice in the blueprint stage of building can help avoid the disappointment many homeowners feel in their finished homes because they visualized something different. And changes, the prerogative of every individual who builds, can be made at far lower cost in the blueprint stage. The same changes can be prohibitively expensive if made later on, during construction.

An architect is like good insurance. He has the techniques and knowledge required to deal with contractors. The average man does not have this, and cannot tell, as work progresses on his house, whether his plans are being carried out as he anticipated.

YOUR GENERAL CONTRACTOR

After your plans are crystallized with your architect, your next step is to hire a general contractor. He carries out your plans and specifications as drawn by the architect and undertakes to give you a completed house. The contract price can be fixed at a stated amount, in which event you will be liable over and above that figure only for extras you request, or consent to at his suggestion. Or, in the alternative, you could enter into a "cost-plus" contract. In this case you assume the cost of all materials, labor, and other services the contractor provides, plus a stated fee. The fee can be either a lump sum or a percentage of building costs (10 to 20 percent).

You could be your own contractor. But to undertake this without being thoroughly familiar with building codes, regulations, permits, and insurance required would be a foolhardy venture. You would probably end up spending more than you anticipated saving. If your budget does not allow for an architect, you could find a standard plan in a magazine, at a home show or a building supply company for a house that meets your requirements within the applicable building codes and regulations.

If you want the contractor to guarantee fulfillment of his contract he will generally do so by posting a bond, for which you are expected to pay. If you know the contractor's reputation to be good, the bond is probably not necessary.

SELLING YOUR HOME

When you list your home for sale with a real estate broker or a local Real Estate Board you have to pay the broker a commission if he finds a buyer who is ready, willing, and able to buy the house on the terms and conditions you offer. Sales commissions vary with localities. Find out what the rate of commissions is before you list your house for sale. If you are able to sell without the services of a broker, you save this commission and can take this into consideration in fixing your price. A word of caution here. Be sure your agreement with a broker does not make you liable for commissions if the house is sold without his services; if, for example, you give one broker an "exclusive" and a friend of yours wants to buy the house, you may be obligated to the broker for commissions nonetheless.

An active broker can help a seller in many ways. He knows what a fair price is for the house, on the basis of other sales of comparable houses in the locality. He has a good idea of how much local lending institutions will advance on mortgages, and the prevailing terms offered. He can be helpful in getting the mortgage commitment for your buyer from local lending institutions.

He is better versed in the art of negotiation than a layman. He is in a better position than the seller is to keep negotiations open even after a prospective buyer's offer of less than asking price has been turned down—in case you have a change of heart and want to reduce the price.

INCOME TAX CONSEQUENCES OF
RESIDENCE SALES

If you sell your principal residence at a profit after owning it for more than six months, you can defer capital gains tax on your profit if you meet certain Treasury tests. You must buy and use a new principal residence purchased with the sales proceeds within one year before or after the sale of the old residence, or, if you build a new residence, within one year before or 18 months after the sale of the former residence.

If you are over 65 when you sell at a profit, you can avoid payment of tax on your gain completely if the adjusted sales price of the house is not over $20,000. If over $20,000, a proportionate part of the gain can be tax-free. The house must have been your principal residence for five out of the eight years preceding the sale.

MOVING TO THE NEW HOME

Start your moving plans early; bookings are heavy, especially from May through September. Check among your friends for the name of a recommended mover, or call your Better Business Bureau. If your move is local or within the state, your mover will probably base charges on men employed on the job and the hours they work, or state a fixed price. If you move out of state, charges are regulated by the Interstate Commerce Commission and governed by weight and distance.

Though governmental regulations affect the cost of an interstate move, do not assume that all carriers will make the same charges. Get quotations from several responsible movers and compare the type of service and protection you will get for each charge.

Carriers are required to carry insurance based upon poundage for claims of loss or damage to property. But the statutory amount is so small that you may not even be covered adequately for the loss of a kitchen utensil. Therefore, most carriers offer several options in their contracts covering their liability. You can pay for *increased protection*. Be sure that your moving contract clearly indicates exactly what you are getting in your agreement. Read all fine print before signing the contract.

Check for damage when your goods are unloaded and see that it is noted on the inventory. On signing the receipt you can add a note, "subject to concealed loss or damage," which may assist you in lodging a later claim.

Allow as much time leeway as possible in your planning. On an interstate move, the carrier must notify you of delay in pickup or delivery. Arrange to have the load received at the new residence because the van will wait only a stipulated number of hours. A non-deliverable load is stored—at the customer's expense.

You must be ready to pay your moving bill upon delivery at the other end. Have a certified check or money order ready for the estimated cost and enough cash to cover a last-minute excess charge. (On a local move, a carrier might accept a personal check for any excess.)

On an interstate move, you can request a written estimate showing approximately what your shipment will weigh and how much you should be prepared to pay at the other end—that is, the estimated amount, plus 10 percent excess. You may request the mover to deliver your goods upon payment of this money, even though the *actual cost* exceeds the estimate plus 10 percent. He must comply, and you have fifteen business days in which to pay the balance you owe.

Your carrier should give you the useful booklet *Summary of Information for Shippers of Household Goods;* or you may obtain it by writing to the Interstate Commerce Commission, Twelfth Street and Constitution Avenue, N.W., Washington, D.C. 20423, or the American Movers Conference (Consumers Service Department), O Street, N.W., Washington, D.C. 20036. Regarding statewide moving, contact your state public service agency; within a city, the municipal consumer affairs department may be able to advise you on any special rules in effect.

If you are moving to a new home not far distant, you might consider a do-it-yourself project. If this is feasible, check your telephone directory's yellow pages under "Truck Renting and Leasing." You can hire small trucks, station wagons, trailers, as well as such equipment as pads and dollies. You may also be able to charge the rental on your major credit card. Large companies in the business often provide free guides to do-it-yourself movers.

Chapter 8

FINANCING YOUR HOME

There are a number of yardsticks or guides offered by economists to help you determine how much you should pay for a house on the basis of your income. One is that your monthly payments for interest, taxes, insurance, and mortgage payments should not be more than your net weekly take-home pay. Another is that you can usually afford to pay 2½ times your family's gross annual income for a family home. If you have small children or dependent parents, you may have to keep under these guides. On the other hand, if your outlook for additional earnings or income is promising, or you have savings into which you can dip for a larger cash payment (to reduce monthly mortgage payments) or for improvements you anticipate you will have to make to the house, you probably could afford to pay more.

INITIAL EXPENSES ON BUYING A HOUSE

There are certain items of expense connected to the purchase of a house in addition to the cash payment on the purchase price.

First, there are moving expenses. In addition, you must consider the cost of cleaning furniture and drapes, or redoing or buying new furnishings, disposing of excess furnishings at sacrifice, or remodeling that might be necessary to suit your needed space, and cost of appliances, garden equipment, or outdoor furniture you will need.

Then there are closing costs, the expenses connected with obtaining a mortgage and title to the house. These costs can be and should be looked into in advance. They will include the following items:

Home inspection. An inspection of a house you are about to buy by a qualified individual or home inspection company is generally recommended. You will be told if there is evidence of termites, and about the condition of the roof, water system, sewage, and general construction. You will be made aware of major repair expenses you may have to assume, if any, after you buy the house. The cost of a home inspection varies, but you can shop around for a reliable inspection at a reasonable price.

Survey. Most lending institutions insist that the buyer provide it with a survey. The survey shows up encroachments against the boundary lines of the land sold. For example, if a neighbor had put up a fence that goes over on your property line, an up-to-date survey made by a qualified surveyor will show this up. If the property has recently been surveyed, the title company that insures the mortgage or title may, on an inspection, bring it up to date at little charge. If, however, the previous survey was made many years ago, or the inspection shows that a fence, a garage, or even shrubbery was added after it was made, a new survey will be required. Cost depends on the size of the area to be surveyed and the character of the community. It can vary from $100 upward for property on one building lot.

Title Company Insurance. The lending institutions generally insist on title insurance before they will advance mortgage money. This is paid for by the buyer. It certifies the title of the seller for the mortgagee. If you, as buyer, want similar insurance for yourself, the title company will issue an owner's policy to you. The cost of title and mortgage insurance depends primarily on the amount of insurance involved. However, rates vary also with the locale of the property. For example, the title companies charge higher rates for insurance on property in metropolitan and suburban areas than in rural areas.

Homeowner Insurance. One of the items of expense you should count on in buying a home is fire and/or homeowner insurance. At the very least, you will have to provide your mortgagee with a standard fire insurance policy to protect its investment in your property. The standard policy covers against loss to the building by fire and lightning. The mortgagee may insist on additional coverage for windstorm or other casualties. (Fire insurance does not extend to the land.)

A homeowner's policy is the type of policy most commonly in use. It is designed to provide insurance for the mortgagee and full protection for the homeowner in one contract, at lower cost than a series of separate contracts. But be aware that there are several types of homeowners' policies and that premium costs will vary according to the location of the property, and the extent and type of coverage. For example, a homeowner's comprehensive policy can protect you against loss from more than fire, floods, storms, or other casualties that may damage or destroy your home. It can include insurance for household effects lost, stolen, or destroyed both in and away from the house; protection against claims for personal and property injuries, and losses for vandalism, water damage, etc. A "deductible" feature may be included, insuring for loss only in excess of the first $50.

Homeowner policies can generally be bought for one year, three years, or five years. The longer term protects the owner against an increase in insurance rates during the term and premium rates are lower. Ask your broker to list separately the cost of the basic policy you have to provide for the mortgagee, and the cost of additional or extended coverage available to you under the various "comprehensive" policies available. Premiums for these policies are high and continuing to increase. Compare costs of a comprehensive policy with the cost of the policy the mortgage requires and with separate insurance for the other risks you want to cover for yourself. See page 130 for further discussion.

Mortgage Expenses. Although the bank or other lending company may not charge you a specific fee for giving the mortgage, you will nevertheless have certain expenses in connection with obtaining it. You will probably have to pay the mortgagee an appraisal fee. You will have to pay its attorney a fee for drawing the mortgage and other legal papers. You will have to pay the recording fee for putting the mortgage on record. And if local law has a mortgage tax, you will have to pay that tax. These expenses are in addition to the cost of survey and title insurance.

Lawyers' Fees. When you retain a lawyer to represent you on making the contract of sale, ask him what his fee will be for that and for the closing of title. In most areas, an attorney's fee is about 1 percent of the purchase price of the house. However, this is variable.

Advance Payments on Adjustments. On the closing of title, certain adjustments are made on taxes, insurance premiums, etc. If you buy subject to an existing mortgage, interest must be adjusted. Generally, as buyer, you will have to be prepared to pay in advance up to six months' real estate taxes and, to protect the mortgagee, insurance premiums up to three years.

A buyer of a moderate-priced house should figure on about $750 in closing costs. When you buy a house on which there already stands an existing mortgage, a part of the closing costs are saved. Moreover, the mortgage interest rate is probably lower than the rate you have to pay for a new mortgage.

Ask about all these items in advance. The appraisal and legal fees for the attorney who draws the mortgage may be included in a flat fee charged by the lending institution for giving the mortgage. You should know exactly what your expenses will be and what they are before you commit yourself.

FINANCING YOUR PURCHASE

The purchase price of your house, over and above the cash payment, generally is financed by a mortgage. The lender is the mortgagee. In consideration for the money advanced to you to enable you to pay the balance of the seller's price, you pledge the house and land as security for repayment of your loan with interest. A mortgage is payable in regular installments, monthly or otherwise, over a stated period of years. Most mortgages are payable over 15, 20, or 25 years, but the term could be more, or less. You will be required to maintain adequate fire insurance, pay taxes promptly, and keep the house in good repair for the protection of the mortgagee's interest.

The monthly payment you agree to make to the mortgagee will include interest on the unpaid balance of your loan and a payment in reduction (amortization) of the loan. It may also include an amount to be held in escrow for payment of real property taxes as due. Although your unpaid balance is reduced by each payment, your monthly payments do not change. But the way your payment is allocated does change. As your balance is decreased, the interest due from you is proportionately reduced. This allows for a larger portion of each payment to be applied toward reduction of the loan. In the first years of a mortgage a greater part of each payment goes for interest. In the later years the greater part goes toward amortization.

OBTAINING A MORTGAGE

Mortgage money can be obtained from commercial or savings banks, savings and loan associations, life insurance companies, and other lenders, including individuals.

The amount of money you can obtain depends on such factors as the availability of money in the market, your credit, the age and condition of the house and its current market value, the number of years over which the loan is to be repaid, and the rate of interest called for.

Points. In periods when the cost of money is high, lenders generally charge "points" to home buyers. Points serve to push rates for borrowing on mortgages above the state's maximum interest charges. In this way, lenders get around local laws limiting interest rates legally chargeable on loans to individuals. For example, you may be charged four points on getting a 20-year mortgage of $10,000 at a 7½ percent interest rate. From the amount loaned to you, $400 will be deducted. You will actually receive only $9,600, but you will have to pay off the mortgage of $10,000. The effect is that you will be paying off the mortgage at a greater than 7½ percent rate (actually, 8.043 percent).

For income tax purposes, points are deductible as interest in the year paid so long as they represent a charge for the use of the lender's money.

TERMS OF PAYMENT

The longer the period over which your mortgage has to run, the more total interest you will have to pay. Your monthly payments will be less if repayment is spread over a longer period. This may better suit your budget.

Say you can get a $10,000 mortgage at 7 percent interest to be paid off over 10 years. Monthly payments to amortize the loan will be $116. If the term of the mortgage is 20 years, payments will be $78; if 25 years, $71. These amounts will include interest on the unpaid part of your mortgage loan until the debt is fully paid off.

Rates of interest vary in different localities and on the availability of money in the general market. You will generally find, however, that most major lenders in a given area offer home mortgages at similar rates. Nevertheless, a difference of a fraction of a percent can mean an overall saving of several hundred or more dollars. For example, compare the monthly payments you would have to pay to amortize a 7 percent mortgage with a 7½ percent and 8 percent mortgage similar in term and amount.

Monthly payments required to amortize $10,000 mortgage:

	10 Years	20 Years	25 Years
7% rate	$116	$78	$71
7½% rate	118	81	74
8% rate	121	83	78

Note that the figures above are for interest and amortization only. The mortgagee may require you to pay a stated amount each month toward real property taxes into an "escrow account," from which taxes will be paid by the mortgagee. This monthly payment is subject to change in amount if taxes are increased. In any event, you must count on this, too, as a carrying charge of owning your home.

Lending institutions in some sections of the country have begun to make mortgages with a "variable" interest clause. This is a provision that the owner might be asked to pay a higher rate if mortgage rates go up (in periods when money is not generally available because of economic conditions). A homeowner who obtains a mortgage with a variable interest clause should see that the variation is clearly fixed and that it should go in two directions—down as well as up—if the money market warrants.

The larger your cash payment, the smaller your mortgage loan will have to be, and the less its cost. The average cash payment to the seller is 30 percent; 10 percent down on signing the contract and an additional 20 percent on closing title. The average mortgage loan is for 70 percent of the price of the house. However, you should not be influenced or misled by the averages. Shop for the lowest interest rate you can get. Make the largest down payment you can afford. And if your goal is to reduce monthly carrying charges as rapidly as possible, get as low a mortgage as is necessary and repay it in the shortest possible time. (See below on your rights to prepayments.)

Keep in mind always that the interest you pay on a mortgage loan is deductible for income tax purposes. The actual cost of a higher interest rate may be less than appears at first when you take into account this tax deduction over the mortgage term. It is only the *interest* portion of each installment that gets this treatment.

OPEN-END MORTGAGE

An open-end mortgage is one that provides that, during its term, the owner can ask for an additional advance to increase the unpaid balance for an extended period under the terms of the original agreement. This provision can be of great value in the later years of a mortgage, when the additional money might be needed to finance a child's education, to make major improvements, or for other purposes. The original face amount of the mortgage is generally the ceiling for the total of new and old loans. The mortgagor usually grants the additional loan if the value of the property, the owner's credit, and other circumstances warrant it. Even if an increased rate of interest was a condition for the extension, it would be less costly for the homeowner than refinancing through a new mortgage.

PREPAYMENT

When negotiating for a mortgage, it is a good idea to get the privilege of prepaying it, preferably without a penalty. Some lending institutions may not allow you to prepay a mortgage. Some will allow prepayment on payment of a percentage penalty of the unpaid balance due. If you have surplus cash over your family needs and want to cut monthly living costs, it might be to your advantage to prepay the mortgage even on payment of the penalty. If you can, get the right to prepay, on defined terms, when you obtain the mortgage. In times when mortgage money is tight, the mortgagee might waive the penalty and gladly accept your prepayment without it.

MORTGAGE-REDEMPTION INSURANCE POLICIES

It is possible to buy an insurance policy that is specially designed to pay the unpaid balance due on your home mortgage on your death. Payment of a mortgage on a family home will eliminate a major expense for those surviving, and might even enable them to remain in the house indefinitely. In any event, the surviving family would not be under pressure to sell at a forced price. If they decide to sell, the entire sales proceeds would be retained, since the property would be free and clear of the mortgage.

SECOND MORTGAGES

Where you do not have the cash necessary to pay the difference between the amount of the primary mortgage and the purchase price, you may be able to get the cash by obtaining a second mortgage on the property. A seller may take a second mortgage to help you buy his house, but he will generally want you to pay it off within a relatively few years. Second mortgages generally bear higher than normal interest rates and other charges that may continue to be burdensome. Except in special circumstances, a second mortgage should not be resorted to by a buyer unless his earnings clearly allow for these payments in addition to all other carrying charges projected.

Interest paid to a second mortgagee is also deductible for income tax purposes.

VETERANS

If you are a veteran, check with your local Veterans Administration about your eligibility and opportunity to get a VA mortgage, or a VA insured mortgage. Such a mortgage will generally run for a longer term, may have lower interest rates, and require smaller down payments.

FHA MORTGAGES

An FHA mortgage is not a loan from the Federal Housing Administration. It is a mortgage obtained from a private lending institution, but this government agency insures the lender against loss in case of the homeowner's failure to repay it. Some lenders are willing to accept smaller down payments and a lower interest rate, and to lend their money over longer periods because of this guarantee. FHA charges a low insurance premium on the unpaid balance, included in the monthly payments the mortgage calls for. There is a dollar limitation on the value of the homes for which it will provide mortgage insurance.

When you buy a home and plan for an FHA-insured mortgage, the FHA will make a complete review of your ability to meet the mortgage obligation. This credit review is made after the bank or other lending institution willing to make the loan submits your application to the FHA. In addition to appraising the property, the FHA will consider your estimated continuing, dependable income, estimated prospective monthly housing expenses, and estimated living costs, debts, and other financial obligations.

Although government agencies are trying to process applications for home loans more expeditiously, these applications necessarily involve a great deal of paperwork. It takes longer to get a government-insured loan.

An FHA mortgage provides the homeowner with a certain feeling of security not usually associated with bank or other corporate mortgages. FHA's policy is to see that every effort is made to avoid foreclosure of insured mortgages where the owner is suffering a hardship because of unfortunate circumstances beyond his control. Lenders are encouraged to wait as long as a year from default before beginning foreclosure, to suspend payments or reduce the amounts temporarily, or to modify the terms for payment of the unpaid balance within the owner's ability to meet them. If the lender is unwilling to enter into an appropriate "forbearance" arrangement with the homeowner, the FHA can ask it to assign the mortgage to it, so that it can work out relief provisions suitable to the homeowner's circumstances.

FHA regulations also include special relief provisions for military personnel.

FHA HOME IMPROVEMENT LOANS

The Federal Housing Administration offers several insurance programs in financing home improvements. In addition to interest there is the FHA insurance premium, similar to that payable on mortgage loans. Here, too, the loan is obtained from a private lending institution and is insured by the FHA. The lender may impose a closing charge, inspection fee, and other fees and charges that will vary from one locality to another. The bank or other lending institution which makes the loan will give you these charges. You should have the figures before you commit yourself to the loan.

INSURING YOURSELF FROM PROPERTY LOSSES AND CLAIMS OF OTHERS

A host of mishaps may occur to you over the years. Fires, storms, floods, or other casualties may damage or destroy your home. You may be struck by a car, or you may strike someone. A burglar may steal valuables from your house or vandals may ransack your home while you are away. A guest may trip on a rug in your living room. Any one of these accidents may involve you in costly litigation and damage claims. Insurance is the best financial protection against these potential losses and liabilities.

You can buy separate policies to meet the risks to which you are prone. You can buy separate policies protecting against fire, burglary, theft, and personal liability in case you injure someone. There are "floater" policies to insure against loss of such property as jewelry and furs. There are various types of comprehensive policies that combine insurance for fire loss, burglary and theft (even away from home), and personal liability. There are also, of course, separate automobile insurance policies which the law of your state may compel you to carry. You should compare the cost and all the features of a comprehensive insurance policy with those of separate policies insuring the risks against which you seek protection. Sometimes the elimination of coverage for an obscure risk, or the increase of the "deductible" amount in a policy will mean a substantial reduction in cost. On the other hand, for but a few dollars more each year, you may increase the amount of protection by a substantial amount.

Various types of policies are available. A competent, well-informed and reliable insurance broker can give you all the information necessary when you describe your needs. But what we want to underscore is the advice to carry adequate insurance on your home. Your largest single property investment subject to loss is your home. According to insurance men, homeowners are negligent in insuring their homes. They fail to increase their coverage as property values increase. Home insurance should be evaluated every few years to see that you are adequately covered for current market value. Ask about an inflation guard provision in your policy. Do not overlook home improvements in estimating the value of the home. Otherwise, when a loss occurs, you will discover that you must pay a substantial part of the loss yourself.

Although the insurance should reflect market value, an estimate of market value may be inadequate if it does not also reflect replacement costs. Here, it is advisable to see that your policy provides an 80 percent clause, even if your state does not require such a clause. Under this clause, claims for partial losses are paid in full, provided the amount of your insurance is at least 80 percent of the total replacement value of the property. If you are underinsured, only a proportionate part of your loss is paid, less depreciation. The depreciation reduction could cut your insurance award to a minimum. The extra cost of this feature is not expensive, considering the protection it gives you.

If you took out insurance when placing a mortgage, the bank required you only to take insurance to protect its loan. Check to see that you have additional insurance that protects your investment or "equity" in the property. On the other hand, do not overinsure your house; do not include the value of the land, the foundation, and underground installations.

Keep an inventory of all your furnishings and household property. In case of a loss, it will provide you an excellent basis on which to claim your reimbursement. As you add new property to your house, increase your insurance coverage.

If, unfortunately, a loss does occur, take steps to reduce the damage. Do not sign any document offered by an adjuster until you are convinced that it accurately reflects your loss. Bring in your own appraiser. The adjuster works for the insurance company, not for you. Do not be rushed into a settlement. If you meet a deadlock, perhaps your agent can help you settle the case or request a special review.

Chapter 9

HOW AND WHERE TO SAVE YOUR MONEY

Money, its value and availability, is at the forefront of much of the world's attention. So, too, is it a center of attention for the individual and the family unit. Where shall the saver place the funds that are being set aside from wage or salary? Advertised interest rates are sometimes confusing; it is not always easy to pick the savings institution that will give the best return.

In deciding where to place your money, you can choose between savings banks, savings and loan associations, commercial banks, and credit unions. In addition, your savings may go into savings bonds or certificates sold by banks. Other forms of investment such as United States savings bonds also offer a secure return.

COMMERCIAL BANKS

Many commercial banks maintain savings, time deposit, thrift or special interest accounts and are the largest holders of savings in this country. In some communities, a commercial bank may be the only institution in the area that accepts savings.

Interest paid by commercial banks on savings accounts varies; it is usually lower than the rate offered by other savings institutions. But commercial banks offer many banking services as yet not available at savings institutions. Of these, checking accounts are the most popular. Checking accounts earn no interest; rather, the owner of the account usually pays a monthly maintenance fee in addition to charges for checks drawn and deposits made to the account. Christmas Club accounts are available at commercial banks as well as at other banking institutions. Traditionally, these earn no interest. Recently, some banks have begun to pay interest on Christmas Club accounts; the rate, however, may be lower than that paid on regular savings accounts. It is, therefore, necessary to ascertain the precise arrangement and nature of the account you open.

Commercial banks commonly pay a lower rate of interest on passbook savings accounts than mutual savings banks and savings and loan associations. On their time deposit accounts—called term savings, certificates of deposit, or other title chosen by a bank, interest rates are also generally less advantageous to the customer. When monetary and economic conditions take a downward path, the rates of interest paid at commercial banks usually drop before those paid at the other savings institutions.

In short, where you have a choice of banks in town, you can probably do better than place your savings account at a commercial bank though you may use their checking and other services.

SAVINGS AND LOAN ASSOCIATIONS

Savings and loan associations are an old American institution dating back to 1831. They may go under other names, such as savings association or building and loan association. A depositor of savings is really a shareholder since these institutions are actually groups of people who use the deposited funds for loans to others. You may go to your friendly savings and loan association for the mortgage on your house, for example.

In essence, these institutions operate in the same way as the mutual savings banks. They are subject to similar ceilings on the rates of interest they can pay savers. At times, certain states may offer advantageous rates and accept mail deposits from other areas.

When you wish to pay bills, you may request checks made out to your payees from the savings and loan association. This type of institution may eventually be permitted by law to offer regular checking services such as those available at commercial banks.

MUTUAL SAVINGS BANKS

Although mutual savings banks have been in existence in this country for more than 150 years, they operate in a limited number of states, mainly in the Northeast, a few scattered elsewhere. They are similar to savings and loan associations in that their loans are customarily for mortgages and home improvements. Some offer loans also for cooperative apartments and for education. A variety of savings accounts are offered: regular accounts with interest compounded and paid quarterly, day-of-deposit to day-of-withdrawal accounts, and investment or term savings accounts which pay a higher rate of interest on money left from two to five years. One bank alone may offer several types of accounts to suit different purposes.

The mutual bank customer need never see his mutual savings bank since these institutions usually feature free bank-by-mail services. In addition, they offer Christmas and Chanukah clubs, and sell travelers' checks. The larger banks may have safe deposit boxes, handle foreign remittances, and sell United States savings bonds. In certain states, they also sell life insurance.

Some banks offer packaged savings plans, which combine a savings account with life insurance and purchase of United States savings bonds. Under a triple package plan, all three are obtainable through regularly made deposits in the bank.

One bank, calling their plan a "triple thrift superhighway to financial security" illustrates the results of regular deposits for ten years:

$5 A WEEK

Starting Age	Cash in Bank	Savings Bonds (Face Value)	Decreasing Term Insurance (Initial Amount)
20	$1,910	$500	$10,000
25	1,880	500	10,000
30	1,830	500	10,000
35	1,740	500	10,000
40	1,570	500	10,000
45	1,500	500	10,000
50	1,070	500	10,000

$10 A WEEK

20	$3,900	$500	$30,000
25	3,820	500	30,000
30	3,670	500	30,000
35	3,370	500	30,000
40	2,870	500	30,000
45	3,000	500	20,000
50	2,150	500	20,000

The cash in bank figures do not include the interest that the savings earn.

The term insurance decreases in coverage to 90 percent in fifth year, 70 percent in tenth year. However, the policy pays cash dividends and can be converted to permanent insurance without medical checkup or may be kept in force 10 additional years at the same premium.

A packaged plan can be worked out calling for deposits at other intervals, such as monthly or semimonthly. Instead of term insurance, a plan can be arranged with straight life or 20-payment life insurance. Or, a savings plan may include only two of the elements, omitting either the insurance or the savings bonds.

CREDIT UNIONS

Credit unions are a special type of institution for savings. They are private organizations, owned and operated by the members, persons in a closely knit group, such as teachers, employees of companies, and members of labor unions, fraternal or social lodges, etc. These cooperative credit societies encourage the members to save systematically and offer free life insurance and low-cost unsecured loans to shareholders.

Traditionally, membership in a credit union has been restricted to persons having a common bond. The bond could be a common occupation such as acting, or even residence within a well-defined neighborhood, community, or rural district; it could be membership in a church, society, farm organization. Or a credit union might be made up of residents in a natural trade area of a rural community or rural district. There are now pressures to change the rules of membership eligibility so that more people could be admitted or allowed to form credit unions.

A significant factor in favor of more credit union activity is a Federal insurance plan that went into effect on January 1, 1971. Federal credit unions—about half the number in the country—now come within this plan which insures members' savings up to $20,-000. State-chartered credit unions have the option to join the plan. These institutions which are fewer in number may have insurance from another source. Coverage for members' savings is essential. In the past, some credit unions have gone under in times of stress, such as the liquidation of a company whose employees were in a credit union. Strikes, lay-offs, mergers, and location removals have also been potential hazards to the members' money.

The first credit union in the United States was organized in 1909. Today, there are more than 24,000 credit unions across the country, serving over 22 million members. Further expansion is to be expected, especially as young people are interested. Students are among those now forming groups. Also, new services may be available. The state-chartered credit unions in Rhode Island may now offer checking accounts. Other states may eventually permit such activity in the credit unions under their jurisdiction.

For further information on credit unions, you can write to:
    National Association of Federal Credit Unions
    1156 Fifteenth Street, N.W.—Suite 315
    Washington, D.C. 20005

    National Credit Union Administration
    1325 K Street, N.W.
    Washington, D.C. 20456

YOUR CHOICE OF BANK

The interest rate alone is not the sole criterion for people in their choice of where to maintain a savings account. Convenience banking near one's home or office, using one bank for checking and for savings are factors that often determine one's choice.

These important points should be checked before opening an account.

Safety of your savings. How will you be protected against loss of your savings? Membership of a bank in either the Federal Savings and Loan Insurance Corporation (FSLIC) or the Federal Deposit Insurance Corporation (FDIC) guarantees the safety of your savings. Each is an instrumentality of the United States Government and insures up to $20,000 of your savings in an account. An individual may have only one account insured up to $20,000 in a single institution.

However, where state laws permit, two or more persons may have individual insured accounts of $20,000 each and, in addition, have an insured joint account. In this way, a husband and wife may have insured accounts in one bank totaling $60,000:

$20,000 insurance protection on wife's individual account;

$20,000 insurance protection on husband's individual account;

$20,000 insurance protection on joint account of husband and wife.

It is also possible to have additional insurance protection when savings accounts are owned in conjunction with one's children or other relatives.

If your funds exceed the insurance limit, you should maintain accounts at more than one savings institution to assure complete insurance protection for all your savings. If your bank or savings and loan association fails, through mismanagement or serious embezzlement, you may incur a delay in getting at your funds, but insurance will reimburse you. Bank closings are by no means uncommon, so you should always check that an institution is protected by FSLIC or FDIC before opening an account. Banks usually carry such notices in their windows, on counters, and in advertising.

There is no cost to the individual saver for this insurance protection. Rather, each member bank pays premiums directly to the insuring corporation. In some states, savings are protected by state insurance agencies.

Compounding of interest. Two banks may pay the same rate of interest. Nevertheless, your savings might earn more money in one bank than they would in the other. The reason: Some banks compound interest more frequently than do others.

Many banks compound and pay interest four times a year. At a 5 percent interest rate, for example, it would take 14 years for money to double.

Regular monthly deposits in a savings account paying 5 percent interest, compounded quarterly, would grow as follows:

If you deposit monthly	*$25*	*$50*	*$100*	*$200*
In 5 years you deposit	$ 1,500	$ 3,000	$ 6,000	$ 12,000
With interest you have	1,706	3,412	6,825	13,650
In 10 years you deposit	3,000	6,000	12,000	24,000
With interest you have	3,893	7,787	15,575	31,151
In 20 years you deposit	6,000	12,000	24,000	48,000
With interest you have	10,292	20,585	41,175	82,351
In 30 years you deposit	9,000	18,000	36,000	72,000
With interest you have	20,809	41,621	83,250	166,504
In 40 years you deposit	12,000	24,000	48,000	96,000
With interest you have	38,095	76,196	152,407	304,819

Daily compounding, featured by many savings institutions, does not give the saver as much more in dividends as advertising sometimes implies. The following table shows comparative annual yield on different rates and frequency of compounding:

Where the nominal rate is:	Compounding yields: Quarterly	Daily
4.0%	4.06%	4.08%
4.1	4.16	4.18
4.2	4.27	4.28
4.3	4.37	4.39
4.4	4.48	4.49
4.5	4.58	4.59
4.6	4.68	4.70
4.7	4.78	4.81
4.8	4.89	4.92
4.9	4.99	5.02
5.0	5.09	5.13
5.1	5.20	5.23
5.2	5.30	5.34
5.3	5.41	5.45
5.4	5.51	5.55
5.5	5.62	5.66
5.6	5.72	5.76
5.7	5.83	5.87
5.8	5.93	5.97
5.9	6.04	6.08
6.0	6.15	6.18

Crediting of interest. Even when a bank compounds interest daily, it may only credit the amount to the depositor's passbook twice or four times a year. The more frequent crediting is more favorable to you.

Difference in the computation of interest. Savings institutions differ in their systems of computing interest even though they may advertise the same rates of interest and periods of crediting to accounts. Now, by government directive, banks are supposed to give new customers full information on interest computation and to advise any change of system later adopted. In practice, a bank may not describe the method used unless a new customer specifically asks for it.

Some banks pay interest only on the lowest balance in an account during an interest period. Others operate complicated systems of offsetting withdrawals against deposits in such a way as to deny the customer the full benefit of interest he thought the account was earning. When an account is used actively—that is, you regularly make a number of deposits and withdrawals—you should seek out a bank with a day-of-deposit to day-of-withdrawal type of account.

Grace periods. Ascertain your bank's timetable for paying interest so your deposits will earn maximum interest. Some banks offer grace periods on certain accounts at the beginning and sometimes at the end of the month also or quarterly. You can utilize grace days to increase your interest yield by making deposits that will earn interest from the first of the month even though you actually deposit late in the grace period of three, seven, or ten days. A grace period of three business days at the end of an interest period will enable you to make withdrawals without loss of interest. Be sure you know your bank's plan on grace days.

Locality of bank. Interest rates vary, depending on where the bank is located. California savings institutions often offer higher interest rates than Eastern establishments; city savings banks are likely to post more attractive rates than a local bank in a rural area. To gain a better return, you can always use the prepaid bank-by-mail envelopes available from many savings banks. But you should be certain your distant mutual savings bank or savings and loan association has the Federal insurance protection described above.

Withdrawals. Before opening a savings account, find out the bank's rules on withdrawals. Is prior notice required? Are any service charges imposed if withdrawals exceed a prescribed number? Unless you are being compensated at a particularly good rate of interest, try to avoid the savings institution which imposes restrictions or penalties on withdrawals.

The giving of premiums by banks for new or increased accounts has been somewhat curtailed by regulations. But funds which you have deposited in return for a gift are usually held for a specific time. You may not be free to withdraw them without penalty.

If you withdraw before the end of the interest period, usually quarterly or semiannually, you stand to lose interest for the entire period.

Sometimes when people move away from their area, as is common in today's mobile society, they close out their savings accounts before the end of the interest period, thereby losing interest. It is wise to find out on opening the account if the bank will honor a request for withdrawal of funds by mail. Then, if the depositor leaves town, a request can be sent to the bank to mail a check closing out the account after the interest has been compounded and credited.

CHOOSING THE RIGHT TYPE OF ACCOUNT

You may require several types of accounts. Generally available are *regular accounts* on which interest is credited quarterly or semi-annually; *day-of-deposit to day-of-withdrawal* accounts which are generally the most convenient and, where rates are the same as for regular accounts, bring in the best returns; and *term savings accounts,* sometimes called certificates of deposit, described below. Some savings banks offer all types of accounts.

In the term savings account, sometimes called time or certificate of deposit account, you agree to tie up a portion on your savings for a specific period in return for a higher rate of interest. The law established the maximum that may apply. Not all banks offer this type of account, and some have lower rates for shorter periods of commitment. In general, we discuss the term savings account available at mutual savings banks and many savings and loan associations. These may differ considerably as you may discover upon investigation.

The plan calls for depositing a round sum, usually $500, $1,000, $5,000 or more, which in an agreed-upon time will "mature." At that time you can withdraw the principal and accumulated interest. If you need your money before the date of maturity you will suffer a penalty loss.

When you open such an account, make sure that you may purchase more "certificates" from time to time through entries in one savings book. One large New York bank requires a new application form for each certificate of deposit, so that the customer could end up with a number of separate "investment" savings books. The computerized system of other savings institutions in the same area enables them to issue only one such book to a customer and enter on separate pages each new term deposit, its maturity date, and its accumulated interest.

Some banks compute interest on term deposits daily, rather than quarterly. This gives a slightly higher rate. "Continuous" compounding, sometimes advertised, does not really increase annual interest appreciably.

When you set up a term savings account, make sure that the bank will leave the interest in the account and compound thereon. A bank may give you a choice of leaving interest in the term account or of having it transferred to a regular account. Anyone who mistakenly makes the latter choice loses the compounding of interest at the higher rate. At maturity, the bank will transfer the account to a regular lower paying one unless the customer requests a renewal. If you have a number of term accounts, as many people do, watch the maturity dates and instruct the savings institution on the disposition of the account.

Income tax on the interest earned on term savings accounts is not deferred even though you have to wait for your money. At the beginning of each year, the bank will send you a report of interest just as it does with your regular account. This total you have to show on your Form 1040.

If you have no savings bank in your area offering term accounts, you can bank by mail.

YOUR BANK ACCOUNT CARRIES CERTAIN RESPONSIBILITIES

Do not be misled into thinking that a bank passbook is sufficient and perpetual proof of your ownership of funds on deposit at the bank. It is not. Every state, to some extent, practices escheat, that is, seizure of property with no apparent owner. One of the most common forms of escheat is acquisition by the state of unclaimed bank deposits.

Depending upon the state in which the bank is located, an account that has been dormant for a number of years becomes vulnerable to the laws of escheat. In New York, the time is 10 years. If a bank fails to reach a depositor through the mails at his last known address and through advertisements and public notices, it must turn the funds over to the state after 10 years, in accordance with state law. Once the money has been handed over to the state, securing its return is quite costly.

To safeguard your savings, you should keep a record of all your accounts, the numbers, banks, and locations (see page 26). At least once a year, have the bank enter interest in each passbook you own. If you move, notify every bank in which you have an account of your new address.

Another little publicized fact is that savings accounts dormant for a number of years may cease earning interest. In addition, a bank may, under its rules, pay no interest on balances below a set minimum, which minimum can change without a depositor's knowledge.

WHAT YOU SHOULD KNOW ABOUT
UNITED STATES SAVINGS BONDS

Savings bonds backed by the credit of the United States Government continue to play a role in the financial security programs of millions of American families; more than $50 billion worth of these securities are currently outstanding. In addition to patriotic reasons, people have been attracted to investing in savings bonds for one or more of these reasons:

1. United States savings bonds can be redeemed at a stated value on demand after two months from the issue date.

2. They are a "liquid" reserve, quickly and easily translated into dollars and cents when needed.

3. They are not subject to market fluctuations; they are never redeemed for less than the amount invested.

4. Interest on savings bonds is not subject to state or local income or personal property taxes.

5. The Federal income tax on Series E bond interest can be deferred, and the annual increases in value need not be reported on the Federal tax return until the bond is cashed.

6. If savings bonds are lost, stolen, or destroyed, they can be replaced without cost.

7. Savings bonds are easy and convenient to buy. They are sold at neighborhood banks. Also, many corporations have established payroll savings plans; an employee can buy bonds regularly merely by authorizing his employer to make automatic deductions from his pay check.

On the other hand, there are certain disadvantages to savings bonds as a form of investment:

1. Although the Treasury has several times raised the interest rate for savings bonds, bond rates generally lagged behind savings bank rates.

2. Savings bonds cannot be used as collateral and cannot be pledged. If the money is needed, the bonds must be cashed and an

immediate tax incurred not only on the current, but also on any accumulated interest on which tax has been deferred.

3. Compared to other investments, such as securities or real estate, savings bonds offer neither growth potential nor capital gain possibility. The lack of growth potential, coupled with inflation, is considered the greatest disadvantage of savings bonds as an investment.

TYPES OF SAVINGS BONDS

There are two types of savings bonds currently being sold by the Treasury: Series E bonds and Series H bonds. The effective interest rate for both types of bonds is 5½ percent if the bond is held to maturity.

The Series E bond. The Series E bond is the type most widely held. It is sold at 75 percent of face value; thus you pay for bonds as follows:

Face Value	Price Paid
$25	$18.75
50	37.50
75	56.25
100	75.00
200	150.00
500	375.00
1,000	750.00
10,000	7,500.00

Series E bonds mature five years and ten months from their issue date. Beginning June 1, 1970, E bonds pay 5½ percent interest if held to maturity; they yield less if redeemed earlier. At maturity, a $25 bond is redeemed for $25.73, a $50 bond, $51.46, a $100 bond, $102.92.

Series E bonds can be cashed in at most banks prior to maturity if they are at least two months old. Generally, no notice is required. These bonds are not negotiable and cannot be used as collateral for loans. They must be in registered form. Registration may be in the name of a single owner, adult or minor, with or without beneficiary, or in co-ownership form. Series E bonds may be held beyond maturity and continue to earn interest.

The Series H bond. The H bond is a current income bond, on which interest is paid by check semiannually. It is sold in denominations of $500, $1,000, $5,000, and $10,000, and matures 10 years from its issue date. The Series H bond is priced at par or face value and is redeemable at par. While the interest on the E bond accrues to maturity, H bond interest is paid every six months by check. The smallest denomination H bond is $500 as compared to $25 for the E bond.

Beginning June 1, 1970, Series H bonds earn about 5.12 percent interest in the first five years and 6 percent for the remaining five years, averaging about 5½ percent if held to maturity. You can redeem the H bond for cash at par on one month's notice at any Federal Reserve bank or branch or at the United States Treasury after it has been held for at least six months. The H bond is not negotiable and cannot be used as collateral for loans. It must be in registered form, and may be registered in the name of a single owner, adult or minor, with or without beneficiary, or in co-ownership form.

Series H bonds can be held beyond their original maturity date and continue to earn interest.

Freedom shares. The United States savings notes known as Freedom shares, which first went on sale May 1, 1967, are no longer being sold by the Treasury. They have a four-and-a-half-year maturity and will earn no interest after they mature. Like the Series E bonds, Freedom shares were sold at a discount. They can be redeemed for the price paid plus accumulated interest after one year from their date of issue.

If you are holding Freedom shares, keep track of their maturity dates and, at the time they mature, inquire if the Treasury has made some special provision regarding them.

TAX ASPECTS OF SAVINGS BONDS

There is flexibility with respect to the reporting of E bond interest on the Federal tax return. Either you report the fixed increase in value on your return each year, or you may defer the reporting of interest until you cash the bond or until the bond finally matures, whichever is earlier. If you own bonds which have increased in value in prior years and you make an election to report the annual increases this year, you must report the total of all these increases in value. That is, you must include all accumulated interest on all the Series E bonds you hold on which tax has been postponed. And, once you make the election to report annual increases, you must continue to do so unless you get Treasury approval to change your method of reporting.

Interest earned on Freedom shares must be reported according to the method used for reporting E bond interest. If you report E bond interest annually you will also report the interest on Freedom shares on your yearly return. Similarly, if you have deferred the reporting of E bond interest, you will likewise defer the reporting of Freedom share interest.

Tax deferral of savings bond interest can be advantageous if payment of tax on accrued interest is postponed to a low income (low tax-bracket) year, such as after retirement. Since future tax rates and circumstances cannot be accurately predicted, tax deferral of E bond interest can prove to be disadvantageous.

Income tax can be saved in this way:

E bonds can be bought and registered in the name of a minor child. The child files his own tax return and lists the increase in bond value as income. If the child's entire income is under $1,700, he owes no tax.

CHECK YOUR OLD BONDS

In an advertisement, a large investment firm once pointed out the amazing fact that American investors at that time were holding almost half a billion dollars' worth of government securities on which they were earning no money whatsoever. This points up the importance of checking old savings bonds, such as A to D, F and G, J and K bonds which are no longer on sale.

Series J bonds that are presented not later than six months after maturity may be exchanged for H bonds without incurring a tax liability at the time of the exchange. The tax liability on any accrued interest on such J bonds can continue to be deferred. The proceeds of other matured bonds, Series F, G, J, or K, can be reinvested in either E or H bonds, but no income tax deferral privilege applies.

All Series E and Series H bonds now outstanding continue to pay interest. A holder may exchange E bonds for H bonds with continued tax deferral on accrued E bond interest.

Chapter 10

YOUR LIFE INSURANCE PROGRAM;
ANNUITIES

For the man or woman with dependents, life insurance is a key-stone in a money management program. Its major objective is to protect the family at time of the breadwinner's death; it can also provide a basis for loans, either as collateral or in borrowing from the insurance company (page 87); too, it may be used in financing retirement (page 256).

Life insurance is tax protected. The face amount payable on death can be received by a beneficiary free of income tax. If the insured person had no incidents of ownership in the policy such as the right to name beneficiaries or take a loan on its cash surrender value, the proceeds are also freed of estate tax.

FIRST STEPS IN YOUR PROGRAM

You should buy insurance with the same caution and comparison that you would employ in buying any other major asset such as a house. When you buy property you will probably approach several real estate agents; you will view a number of houses before making your choice. Why buy life insurance differently?

Many people, indeed the majority, play a passive role and let themselves be selected as " prospects" by a neighborhood insurance representative; by a relative who has recently become an insurance agent or broker; or by a company advertisement which has hooked them into coupon-signing without too much—or any—forethought.

You can decide to practice your smart consumer tactics instead. Begin by quizzing your friends. From them, you obtain the names of companies and some firsthand experiences of their dealings. But, while you make a note of recommended companies, remember that you are not likely to buy the same types of policies your friends have bought; your situation is different and you want general guid-ance only.

You will also note the names of advertised companies and those which have agencies in your neighborhood. Preferably, drop in at the offices to get an impression of how the organization does business and to obtain some information. Undoubtedly you will be bombarded by agents, but you should certainly resist pressure to sign up until you have compared the life insurance plans offered by several companies.

Moreover, when you have decided on a particular policy, you

should not sign until you have thoroughly examined all the clauses and made sure that you understand what is contained in the fine print. If the agent from whom you propose to buy the policy will not provide you with a sample copy, go to another agent.

THE INSURANCE COMPANIES AND THE POLICIES THEY SELL

For your own protection you will want to do business with a well-established company and to avoid those which have yet to prove themselves. The giants of the insurance industry do not necessarily offer the most reasonably priced insurance. In fact, a small company may offer you a better deal, but you should check on the company's background. Make sure it is not a newcomer with a similar name to one well known. See remarks on page 162 regarding mail order insurance.

Basically, two types of policies are available through two types of company, though there is some overlapping. A *stock company* customarily issues nonparticipating policies though some may issue participating policies. With such a nonparticipating policy you do not pay as much as you would for a similar policy issued by a *mutual company* (usually identifiable by the word "mutual" in its title). The company has set the rate of the nonparticipating policy *at what it expects the insurance to cost.* In advance, you know exactly what you will pay for your coverage.

In the case of the participating policy, the company has fixed premium rates *in excess of what it expects the insurance to cost.* Why then should you consider this type of policy? In the long run it may prove less costly than a nonparticipating policy because you will receive dividends after the first two or three years. The dividends are not taxable; they are refunds on your premiums made when the company's actual operating costs are known. The amount of your annual dividends will, of course, vary with company decision and profit. In prosperous times, your company's participating policy may pay good dividends, but an economic slump might mean small, or even no, dividends.

Company policies differ on payment of dividends, some tending to increase them in the later years, thus benefiting the long-lived, long-paying insured person. If you have a participating policy, you can accept dividends in a number of ways, from cash payment (which would enable you to build your regular savings account) to buying additional insurance. *Be sure dividends are paid to you as you want* and not automatically applied by the company to the purchase of extra insurance you may not need.

THE INSURANCE AGENT

As noted on page 162, savings bank life insurance is available in certain states on a come-and-get-it basis, but the vast bulk of life insurance is sold by agents. These men are sometimes employees of a company and may or may not receive a salary in addition to commission. Usually, they are self-employed and work only for commission. (Bear this factor well in mind and ask yourself if the insurance the agent is advising for you is the protection your family requires, or if it just pays him better.)

When you consider the great importance of life insurance to the security of your family, and the amount of money you will invest, you certainly want to be personally satisfied with the individual who will be making far-reaching recommendations to you and to have some background information on him.

If you can interview several company representatives and let them suggest certain life insurance planning for you without committing yourself definitely to any one, you will be in a favorable position to judge both the variations on basic policies offered and the men who describe them to you.

If an agent has been advising and selling to your friends for some years, you know he is no fledgling, but if you are dealing with a man unknown to you, find out how long he has been in the business. While it may be agreeable to give some young fellow a start, let him practice on the less knowledgeable; you prefer to know that your man is experienced, at least four to five years as an agent, and if he can add "C.L.U." after his name, you can be assured he is a Chartered Life Underwriter, having successfully completed examinations and other requirements set by the American College of Life Underwriters.

Beware the man who insists that only some high-priced combination policy will suit your family's needs. It might make you "insurance-poor" the rest of your life, while he gains good commission. Beware, too, the man who wants you to drop some other company's policy to take his. This unethical gambit, known as "twisting," has resulted in loss for many people who allowed themselves to be persuaded into dropping policies they had for years. If you meet with this ploy, take the opportunity to review thoroughly what your original company offered and, if changes seem justified, see what they can suggest to meet your present needs. Only if careful investigation proves that the agent had a valid point should you let a former policy lapse in favor of a new one.

It should be recognized that an agent may be perfectly sincere in his recommendations to you since he himself is likely to be very well indoctrinated by his company, but what he offers is not necessarily right for you. Provide your own clear-cut ideas on the insurance you should have.

WHAT TYPE OF INSURANCE DO YOU NEED— AND WHEN?

In general, your need begins with your financial responsibilities to others. When a young couple first marry, they may live in an apartment and both have jobs. Their money is better directed toward the savings bank than into life insurance unless either must contribute toward a dependent.

The real need for life insurance usually begins when the first child is expected. Soon, the wife will give up her job; the young husband wants to provide for her and for his child's upbringing in case of his death. At this point he may take out *convertible term insurance* (page 154). If his wife has reasonably good earning potential of her own, his main concern will be for the child's care and education.

The need for life insurance becomes greater as the family increases. The wife is less likely to return to work while the children are young; the couple probably decide they need a house of their own. Now the husband must cover his responsibilities as homeowner in addition to the needs of his family. He can combine straight life with decreasing term under a *combination family income policy* (page 159) to protect wife, children, and the mortgage. At this point, the breadwinner will probably find he needs certain supplementary contracts (or riders). Of particular importance and value is the *waiver of premium* rider. Should the husband suffer total and permanent disability, the insurance premiums themselves are protected; the company will pay them.

A desirable and necessary rider is *guaranteed insurability;* here, the insured protects his right to buy more insurance when he most needs it—*regardless of the state of his health at that time.* (Term policies lacking a *renewability* clause should be avoided.)

While a couple may not really need life insurance when first married, the husband might have taken his straight life policy then. He would have gained a more favorable premium rate at the earlier age, and that rate would continue all his life. Also, if he had a participating policy earning dividends, he would be that much better off.

When buying insurance, you should note that the agent receives less commission on term insurance than on the more expensive cash value policies. You may therefore expect him to emphasize the latter. But if you think your needs could best be served by term insurance, *plus your own savings and investment program,* you should not allow yourself to be persuaded into taking other policies.

HOW MUCH INSURANCE DO YOU NEED?

You don't know the true answer, because the actual date of death is unknown and even the fatally ill have been known to outwit the prognosticators. It is well to sit down with paper and pencil to do some very hard, cold figuring. You can assess your needs only by asking *just where would the family stand if I died NOW?*

A realistic appraisal calls for drawing up two columns, for liabilities and assets. To begin with liabilities, your family would first face the high cost of death; ask yourself how you stand on medical/hospitalization insurance in case of prolonged illness or injury prior to death (Chapter 13). Would the house be sold? Would your wife earn? How long would your children be dependent? Note in your calculations that your wife would lose the advantage of filing joint income tax returns.

Check Chapter 16, from which you will get some guidance on estate matters, and also on your will.

Consider the funeral arrangements. Do you have a cemetery lot? Would the family have to purchase one or have you stated a preference for cremation? Common sense, not morbidity, dictates that you investigate and make decisions on final arrangements. Note, on the plus side, that Social Security pays toward the funeral costs of an insured worker. (On the subject of funeral cost, the Better Business Bureau of Metropolitan New York, 220 Church Street, New York, New York 10013, will send, free, *A Guide to Help You Arrange Funerals and Interments.* Supply a stamped, self-addressed envelope.)

Now, your death being paid for, where does your family stand financially? In your estimates, you can only use current figures. The net worth tabulation you worked out (Chapter 2) will help you here. You can write down the state of your assets, including any company or organization benefits payable at death, and also the family indebtedness.

From your budgeting experience (Chapter 1), you know basically what it would cost your dependents to live month by month. (For convenience, use a monthly basis in your calculations.) In so many years, some members of your family are likely to be self-supporting, but you may also have to reckon that others, because of incapacity or declining years, may not be. Write down as close an estimate as possible of your financial commitment. For example, a son, already a capable teenager, might be able to earn through his college years and only need your support for another five years. But the contribution you make toward the support of an incapacitated brother might go on for twenty-five years.

Consider the benefits available for your wife and family from Social Security (Chapter 14). Obtain a current record of your credits (see page 211) which will come with information on obtaining a provisional working figure for your present purpose. You have to cover the difference, either through your own assets or through insurance. Essentially, your calculations should take into account these areas exposed by your death:

Last expenses. Cash should be easily available in a joint savings account.

After-death period. If you can keep about half a year's income in savings you can provide adequately for the readjustment your family would be making.

The home. If you are repaying a mortgage, use insurance to cover it (see page 127).

Income for living expenses. In general, this is the main area to be covered by life insurance policies by the breadwinner who does not have other very substantial assets.

Education of children. You will use insurance, but the family will have to fend for itself, too.

Your wife. If you have children, your widow would receive Social Security benefits until each child reaches the age of 18. A child who is a full-time student receives benefits through the 21st year. During the so called "blackout" period, your widow would not be entitled to benefits on your Social Security record until reaching the age of 60. To cover her lifetime income needs through *insurance* would be exceedingly expensive. A wife's best insurance is her ability to earn for herself in case of necessity. Where this would not be possible, try to build up her assets such as investments.

Following, we give a rundown on some of the many types of life insurance available. Your agent will explain the combinations his company offers; you will, at that time, bear in mind the needs of your family you have just defined.

TERM INSURANCE

Term insurance offers coverage for a specific span of time, covering either a certain span of years or up to a certain age. Usually, term policies do not carry beyond age 70.

Because term insurance carries no cash value buildup it costs less than whole (straight) life. It has been argued that a breadwinner is better off with term insurance than with whole life *if* he puts the difference between the two premiums into a savings bank where it will earn interest (less taxes). A man who can establish this rigid program may well prefer never to convert to straight life. The nonsaver will combine insurance and savings in the more expensive cash value policy.

As mentioned earlier, *renewable* term insurance is the type to take, because renewal rates will be stated and guaranteed, even though rates may rise in the meantime, and because the insured person does not have to produce evidence of *insurability*. If health has failed and he would now be judged a poor insurance risk, he can still renew his policy.

If your preference is for straight life, but you cannot presently afford it, make sure that your term policy is *convertible*. This means that, still without giving evidence of insurability, you may convert to a straight life or endowment policy. However, you may have to inform the company that you intend to convert, and the policy may have a deadline for doing so. Be sure to check on this point. If you have 10-year term insurance, for instance, you may have to announce an intention to convert before the first 7 years have elapsed.

Term insurance is often used in addition to whole life insurance by people who have extra risks to cover at certain periods of time. Perhaps a man has covered his family's needs with straight life insurance, then, unexpectedly, he is burdened by helping a brother straighten out his debts or becomes responsible for an aged relative. He finds extra protection for his income in one-year or five-year term insurance.

When the insured breadwinner is handling a heavy debt, such as a mortgage, a decreasing term policy or rider is an extra safeguard. The death benefit decreases during the term of the insurance, but so, too, does the amount of the debt and the consequent financial responsibility.

A combination plan of gradually decreasing term insurance and straight life is often suggested by an insurance company's agent as the best means of protecting family income.

WHOLE LIFE INSURANCE

With whole life insurance (also referred to as straight or ordinary life), you pay a certain premium; you receive life coverage and other stated benefits. *The age at which you buy your policy decides the premium rate at which you will continue to pay.* Your policy acquires a "cash value" because the company invests part of the premiums. This cash value is an asset, useful in raising loans (Chapter 6), and can help you to cover your insurance if, at some time or other, you are unable to pay premiums.

If you eventually wish to discontinue premium payments altogether, several possibilities are open to you: You can receive less insurance protection throughout your life (based on the cash value); you can set an ending date to the full protection; you can obtain a cash settlement for your canceled policy; instead of life insurance, you elect to receive income for a certain period.

Note that your policy will automatically put some provision into effect if you fail to pay premiums. Check to find out what it is because, if you cannot pay, you may wish a different provision to be made and you will have to so notify the company.

Straight life carries with it the virtue of being an enforced savings program besides imparting protection to the breadwinner. The cash value accumulated amounts to around 60 percent of the face value. Note that cash value is not an additional sum payable to your beneficiary; it is payable only if the policy is discontinued.

The cost of substantial coverage by permanent insurance may pose a financing problem for a father with young children. Over the next 10 years, his family responsibilities will be greatest. There is still a sizable mortgage debt on the family residence. The cost of children's college education must also be met. After 10 years, though, his need to protect his family against his premature death will gradually lessen. Even so, over the succeeding 15 years, he will still want comparatively substantial insurance coverage. Such coverage under a permanent policy will carry a high premium. Nevertheless, he desires permanent insurance to provide his wife with income-tax-free recovery regardless of when he dies. In effect, he wants (1) highest coverage over the next 10 years, (2) somewhat reduced coverage gradually decreasing in amount over the succeeding 15 years, and (3) permanent insurance continuing thereafter, without any further reduction in amount, for the protection of his wife.

He can purchase a straight life policy with a rider that offers extra coverage against premature death. Under this rider, extra coverage continues in undiminished amount for an initial 10-year period. Thereafter, over the succeeding 15 years, extra insurance recovery in the event of the insured's death gradually decreases to zero. After 25 years, only the face amount of a straight life policy is payable to the insured's beneficiary. The insured here ties insurance protection to his actual insurance needs under a straight life policy with term rider. Moreover, he benefits from a reduction in premium expense because the extra insurance under the rider is lower-cost term. It is level term insurance for an initial 10-year period and then decreasing term over the succeeding 15 years.

LIMITED PAYMENT LIFE

This policy is actually straight life, but it is paid for within a stated time, say 20 or 30 years, or by a certain age, such as 65, instead of being payable annually over a whole lifetime. Because of the higher premiums, it has the advantage of building up cash value faster, but the cost might prove a burden to the young man who will not reach his highest earning capacity until middle life. For the person whose early years mark the high earning point (an athlete or actor, for example), a limited payment policy may prove useful. Note, however, that early death after completion of premium payments would make this a very expensive policy.

ENDOWMENT

In essence, an endowment policy is a combination insurance and savings program. If the holder of an endowment policy dies, the beneficiary named collects the stated amount; if the policyholder lives, he himself collects on the matured policy. But if before that time he fails to keep up the premiums, he is subject to a penalty and can only recover part of his investment, plus dividends.

Say a person decides against a 20-year endowment policy. Instead, he takes out term insurance for the same period. At the same time, he opens a savings account into which he regularly pays the *difference* between the term insurance and the endowment policy, which is one of the costlier forms of insurance. If he dies, the term insurance would be paid to his beneficiaries; they would also fall heir to the savings account. If the insured person lives more than 20 years, his term insurance will, of course, lapse, but his savings account plus dividends, less income tax, will amount to much more than the paid-up endowment policy. Had he taken the policy, he would still have to pay income tax on the difference between the lump sum received and his original premiums.

Since a combination of term insurance and savings produces better results, why do people buy endowment policies? Some undoubtedly do so because they would never save otherwise. The penalty feature forces them to mail their premiums on time; no such spur sends them to the savings bank. Some take endowments because the waiver of premium rider can be added to it. In the event of disability, the company would pay the premiums and still fulfill the terms of the contract, i.e., to pay out either a death benefit or a lump sum.

Endowment policies also carry the main features of straight life insurance, such as availability for loans and surrender value.

BASIC LIFE CONTRACTS NOW ARE COMBINED

On the purchase of life insurance, an individual's choice in the past might have been limited to three basic policies: (1) term insurance, (2) whole life insurance, either a straight life or a limited payment contract, and (3) the endowment. Choice has been widened now by the availability of combination insurance contracts. Selecting from the many types of straight life plus term coverage, an individual can more closely meet his insurance needs. Today, through computers, a company may be in a position to present a prospect with not two or three but, say, 23 possible combinations. The values, benefits, and protection offered by each policy can readily be reviewed.

A typical policy combines 50 percent straight life insurance with 50 percent term coverage in reducing premium cost for higher amount of insurance protection. It has appeal for the father with a growing family. He gets high coverage when his insurance needs are greatest. Term coverage can be converted to permanent insurance up to age 62, but such coverage is not required. Continued high coverage decreases at age 65 by 5 percent a year until age 75. However, permanent protection thereafter does not drop further.

In the case of a young husband, another policy available combines straight life insurance with maximum amount of convertible term. A 25-year-old individual who purchases $100,000 coverage initially gets 10 percent straight life coverage with 90 percent term insurance which decreases at age 31, 34, 37, 40, 43, and 46. At any of these ages, however, an insured can convert portion of lapsing term insurance into permanent coverage. True, on such conversion, premium costs would be increased, but increases in an initial low premium are geared to increases in insured's earnings.

A graded-premium policy is also available. It is permanent insurance which gears lower initial premiums to anticipated increase in insured's earnings and future ability to pay. There is a low initial premium which increases over a period (e.g., over first 5 years), but thereafter remains unchanged. For instance, an individual who currently finds it difficult to finance the permanent insurance coverage he wants at regular rates anticipates that his income will increase over the next 5 years. By purchase of graded-premium policy, he can fit his ability to pay premiums to actual premium cost.

One form of graded-premium uses decreasing term insurance with straight life after the first year until at the sixth year the policy becomes a full straight life contract. Under this contract, the low initial premium increases each year for the first 5 years, but thereafter remains unchanged. In total premium cost, this policy does not promise any premium savings. However, it allows an individual to start a permanent insurance program by matching premium outlay with increasing income.

A modified life policy offers somewhat similar advantages in offering a low initial premium. Under a typical modified life policy, the insured would pay an unchanging premium lower than regular rate for the first 5 years of coverage. Then in the sixth year, the premium would be increased, remaining level thereafter without any further increase.

Double life insurance protection until age 65 is available under combined coverage in a single policy. A father takes out a policy which will pay his family $60,000 if he dies before 65. However, coverage is halved after 65. Thus, if he dies after 65, his beneficiary gets $30,000. Presumably at age 65, his children will be self-supporting adults with the result that insurance needs will have lessened. The policy combines $30,000 permanent insurance with $30,000 term coverage. True, he might buy similar coverage by purchasing a separate $30,000 straight life contract and a $30,000 term policy, terminating at 65. However, under this double protection policy, an insured combines both permanent and term coverage in a single insurance contract. As a result, he benefits from a reduced premium.

FAMILY INCOME

With a separate policy or rider you may obtain term insurance running for a certain period (but not beyond a maximum age limit).

During the period of coverage, your beneficiary receives a monthly income from date of your death. If you survive the stated period, the policy pays nothing.

Say your wife is the beneficiary. Depending on the company issuing the policy, there will be a choice of ways in which she could benefit. She might receive your basic policy's benefits immediately with the above mentioned monthly income till the end of the period. She could reserve payment of the main benefit till after the monthly payments had run out. She could split the main benefit, having part paid when the monthly payments start, the rest when they end.

Note that if you take out this type of policy, say for 10 years, and you live for nine of them, your beneficiary would receive one year's monthly income. This may be suitable if you are, say, protecting a child who will be able to earn for himself by the time the term expires.

Examine the settlement options of your basic policy and consider if family income protection is more suitable than supplemental term insurance.

The appeal of family income policy is greatest for a husband concerned that, on his premature death, he would be survived by a comparatively young widow with minor children. Policy combines permanent insurance with *decreasing term* coverage. It can provide an extra in the form of monthly income which starts on the death of the insured and continues for a specified period, e.g., 10, 15 or 20 years from the date the policy was originally purchased. Monthly income might be 1 percent per $1,000 permanent insurance (e.g., $10 per $1,000), 2 percent or 3 percent (e.g., $20 or $30 monthly income per $1,000 permanent insurance). At the end of the monthly income period, face amount of permanent insurance is paid to beneficiary. Note that monthly income is paid only if the insured dies prematurely within the specified period. For instance, assume a man buys $10,000 twenty-year family income policy, paying $100 monthly income (i.e., 1 percent of $10,000 face). If he dies one year after purchase, his beneficiary would get $100 a month for 19 years and then $10,000 face. On the other hand, if he lived for 21 years after policy purchase, his beneficiary would not get any monthly income but would receive immediate payment of $10,000 face.

FAMILY MAINTENANCE

This policy is a combination of permanent insurance and level term insurance. Unlike the family income policy, the period over which monthly income payments will be made to the beneficiary starts at time of insured's death, if he dies within specified period. For instance, a husband is 30 years old. He buys 20-year, 1 percent family maintenance policy, $10,000 face. If he dies prior to age 50, his widow-beneficiary will receive $100 a month for 20 years and then payment of $10,000 face. However, if he dies after age 50, there will be no monthly income payments but $10,000 face amount will be paid immediately to the widow.

A portion of each monthly income payment will reflect interest return on permanent insurance part of policy left on deposit. This interest is taxable income to the beneficiary. The remaining portion of each monthly payment will reflect an installment settlement of term coverage, constituting a principal (tax-free) and interest return. The interest portion, though, can be freed from tax—up to $1,000 a year—where the surviving spouse is the beneficiary. A lump-sum payment when monthly income ceases is income tax free.

FAMILY PLAN

A family plan policy is combined permanent and term insurance covering all members of the family. The purchase of the family plan policy by younger men continues to increase. This is how such a policy operates. The young father is the primary insured, covered by permanent insurance in the largest amount. His wife and minor children are secondary insureds, covered by term insurance in small amounts. While it is true that secondary beneficiaries normally survive the primary beneficiary, premature deaths do take place. While insurance recovery on the death of a secondary beneficiary is comparatively small, it may provide the funds needed to meet bills resulting from the dependent's last illness or funeral cost. Or if the mother of the family dies, funds are available for child care while adjustments are made to new conditions.

Insurance on wife and children is offered by some companies as a rider to the husband's insurance.

Check what your company issues in this type of life insurance and consider if it is for your family. A common package would be $5,000 whole life protection for the father, and term coverage of $1,000 each on the lives of the mother and children. Variations of the family plan are favorites with the insurance agents who sell them, but do not necessarily offer worthwhile protection in many situations.

MAIL ORDER INSURANCE

You may be attracted by an advertisement in which an insurance company in a distant state offers life (or other) insurance. Answering such an advertisement may bring a salesman to your doorstep. Because of the distance, you will have little or no chance of checking on the reliability of the company. Maybe it is sound; maybe the salesman can give good advice, but your best move is to do business nearer home and on a direct basis. Too, you run the danger that the distant company is not licensed to sell in your state. You lose out on the protection your state law may provide, and perhaps open the door to legal complications at your death.

SAVINGS BANK INSURANCE

If you live or work in a state where savings bank life insurance is sold, you have an excellent opportunity. These banks offer advantageous rates. While state law limits the total amount of savings bank insurance an individual may buy, a broad range of straight life, term, endowments, and many variations can be obtained. All savings bank plans pay dividends, which further reduce the overall cost.

No salesman will call to urge savings bank life insurance upon you; a substantial reason for the low cost is the fact that you must take the initiative, applying for your policy by mail or in person at the bank.

At this writing, New York, Connecticut, and Massachusetts are the only states where the law permits savings bank life insurance. The rules of the system differ in the three states. In New York, savings bank life insurance is available in amounts from $1,000 to $30,000 to residents and those who work in the state. Members of the immediate family, husband, wife, children, parents, brothers, and sisters are also eligible.

GROUP LIFE

As a member of a union or a professional association, or simply as an employee, you may be able to participate in group life insurance coverage. You may have to contribute to the premium (some employers pay total cost), but your group *term* insurance will not cost as much as you would pay as an individual. Moreover, there will be no medical examination.

Usually, upon retirement or on leaving a group, the member can convert to individual whole life or endowment, but it will cost usual rates, and at 65, say, these would be extremely high. *Group Paid Up* is a plan which helps to overcome such objections. Your contributions go toward paid up whole life insurance; your employer's go toward term, which covers your life. Upon retirement or leaving the group, you have your paid up whole life insurance which you can use in one of several ways. It can remain in force, or be surrendered for cash or life income. You may also be able to buy additional whole life insurance which will make up for what your employer formerly paid in term coverage.

In few cases will group insurance provide all the protection a family needs, but it can prove a useful addition to other policies and lower the overall cost of life insurance.

If you live in a state offering savings bank insurance, your group may be able to enjoy the advantages of a plan offered to 10 or more employees at low administrative cost.

BENEFICIARIES

You intend the money you are spending annually on life insurance to benefit those financially dependent on you, in most cases, wife and children; sometimes parents. A widowed or divorced career woman may have as much responsibility in this area as a husband or father.

The question is: Have you named your beneficiaries correctly? If not, the people you plan to protect may not derive the benefits you intended. The situation may become particularly involved where divorce is concerned. Perhaps, after a financial settlement has been reached, a former wife and children of the marriage should not benefit from a policy already in force. A change would have to be made in the beneficiaries named.

A point to note here is that *when you first take out the policy you should reserve the right to change the beneficiaries.* If you do not make this proviso, you must have consent in writing from the person formerly named before the company will make the change.

Your insurance company has a legal staff and if your personal situation is complicated, you should have the agent refer the case to these lawyers. He himself should be able to advise you when no unusual difficulties are involved.

If you are consulting an attorney about your will and estate planning, discuss the question of insurance with him. As the years bring changes, you will undoubtedly find that you must alter the names or order of your life insurance beneficiaries.

GI INSURANCE

Veterans frequently fail to change the beneficiary's name in their National Service Life Insurance policy. Originally, the insurance may have been intended to benefit parents. Then the serviceman marries, but he neglects to rename his beneficiaries, leaving his widow to find out that she cannot receive the proceeds of the insurance. Renaming beneficiaries of GI insurance is not complicated; consult your local Veterans' Service Agency.

On leaving the service, you should act to replace GI coverage within the 120-day period following discharge. An explanation of policy conversion rights issued by the Veterans Administration is provided for servicemen. Further information is available from your VA office. There, or from the Office of Servicemen's Group Life Insurance, 212 Washington Street, Newark, New Jersey 07102, you can obtain a list of the companies which will issue you a new policy at their standard rates. If you reside or work where savings banks offer life insurance, their lower cost plans are available to service personnel who act within the time limit.

PAYING YOUR INSURANCE PREMIUMS

In Chapter 1, we mentioned the importance of saving for heavy commitments. It will certainly pay you to put money aside regularly to meet your life insurance premiums on an annual basis. If you pay every month, quarter, or half year, you will be liable for the carrying charges leveled for payments on the installment plan.

THE DECISION IS YOURS

As we have said, the insurance needs in your family will differ widely from another's. So, too, will your attitude. If you have the resolve to save regularly and to put aside the difference between renewable term and ordinary life, you may well find term insurance which covers the years of your greatest financial responsibility to your family to be the answer. In your later years, the need to protect others may have diminished, if not vanished, and you can avoid carrying high-priced coverage. A prudent investment or a savings program can roll up dividends on money that might have gone into cash value insurance.

On the other hand, you may prefer full insurance coverage until you are 65 and, at the same time, you feel safer with the prospect of the return you will get on the cash value of your policy than with a savings and investment program. Your personal temperament and circumstances will guide your decision.

The Consumers Union Report on Life Insurance, a valuable and objective analysis which can assist you in your preliminary investigations, is available for $1.50 from Consumers Union, Mount Vernon, New York 10550.

THE LANGUAGE OF LIFE INSURANCE

Since the terms used in life insurance are not familiar to all, we give definitions of some below:

Annuitant. A person during whose life an annuity is payable; the recipient of the annuity income.

Annuity. A contract which provides a guaranteed income for a certain number of years or for life.

Beneficiary. The person named in the policy to receive the insurance money upon death of the insured.

Cash value. The money a policyholder will get back if he gives up that policy.

Convertible term insurance. Term insurance giving the insured the right to exchange the policy for permanent insurance without evidence of insurability.

Disability benefit. A rider which provides for waiver of premium, sometimes monthly income also, when the insured is proven totally and permanently disabled.

Dividend. Amount returned to participating policyholders as a refund of overpaid premium. It is not taxable; but, being dependent on company operations, it is not guaranteed.

Double indemnity. A policy rider which provides for double the face amount of the policy if death should occur through accident.

Endowment insurance. Payment of a definite sum to a policyholder, or his beneficiary, after a stated number of years.

Face amount. The sum stated on the face of the policy to be paid on death of the insured or at maturity.

Grace period. The time allowed after the premium due date for payment during which period the policy does not lapse.

Insured. The person on whose life an insurance policy is issued.

Lapsed policy. A policy ended by nonpayment of premiums.

Limited payment life insurance. Whole life insurance paid for in a specified number of years.

Maturity. When the policy's face value is payable.

Nonparticipating policy. One that pays no dividends.

Ordinary life insurance, also called straight life, is payable by premiums until death.

Paid up insurance. All premiums have been paid.

Participating policy. Dividends are payable.

Policy. The terms of the insurance contract are set forth on this document which is issued to the insured.

Policy loan. A loan made by the insurance company to a policyholder and secured by the cash value of that policy.

Premium. The regular periodic payment made for the insurance.

Settlement options. Alternative ways in which the insured or beneficiary may have policy benefits paid.

Rider. An endorsement which changes the terms of an existing policy.

Term insurance. A policy payable at death if that event occurs during the term of the insurance.

Waiver of premium. A provision whereby an insurance company will keep a policy in force without payment of premiums. Usually operates as a disability benefit.

Whole life insurance. Includes ordinary or straight life insurance on which premiums are payable until death and limited payment life insurance on which premiums are paid for a certain number of years only.

ANNUITIES

An annuity is an investment that generally guarantees a fixed income for the remainder of a person's lifetime. Where life insurance assures funds to your dependents in case of untimely death, annuities assure you against outliving your financial resources. Life insurance covers the risk of dying too soon, while annuities assume the hazard of living too long.

The principle of annuities is simple, although policy combinations may tend to confuse you. In return for payment of premium, you are promised a guaranteed annual income beginning at a designated age and continuing for the rest of your life, no matter how long or short a time that might be. The amount of annuity income you will receive depends on the amount you invest in premiums, your age at the date of the contract and at the time payments are scheduled to begin.

Although annuity income is often referred to in annual terms, installments may be paid monthly, quarterly, semiannually, or annually, depending upon the arrangement you make with the company.

The price of an annuity can be figured in either of these ways: You can find the amount it would cost to buy an annuity paying the annual income you require. If you had a specific sum to invest, perhaps the cash value of life insurance policies or proceeds of a policy or from the sale of a home, you could find how much income you would receive by investing the sum in an annuity contract.

Annuities may be purchased either on an individual or a group basis. They are available on a group basis under tax-protected plans set up by employers. Some employers pay the full cost of the annuity in behalf of their covered employees. Under other plans, both employer and employee share the cost of the annuity; the employee's contribution may be deducted from his pay check.

TYPES OF ANNUITIES

There are several kinds of annuity contracts to choose from. All provide guaranteed payments for the life of the annuitant. Some annuities contain additional guarantees and coverage; these are more expensive and pay a lower income in relation to the premium paid.

A *straight life annuity* is a "pure" annuity paying regular installments of income to the purchaser for his entire life. At his death, all payments cease. An annuitant may receive only one installment, or he may receive hundreds, depending on how long he lives. He will, however, under the straight life annuity receive the largest amount of income for his investment. A straight life contract is the most economical annuity you can purchase, but it has this drawback: the possibility always exists that a person may not live long enough to recoup his investment. He may only just start receiving annuity installments when he dies. No further payments would be forthcoming to his heirs under a straight life annuity; the company would have completely fulfilled its obligation. This is a gamble many are reluctant to take. Other, more expensive, types of annuity contracts are available offering more liberal terms.

Life annuity with installments certain. This type of annuity specifies that if the annuitant dies within a certain time, such as 5, 10, or 20 years, a beneficiary would continue to receive the installments of income for the remainder of the guarantee period. If the annuitant survives the specified period, no payments would be made after his death. The longer the period of guarantee, the lower the annuity income would be.

Refund annuities promise that the amount invested in the contract will be returned to the annuitant or his beneficiary. If the annuitant recovers his investment during his lifetime, no further payments will be made.

Installment refund annuity. If the annuitant dies before collecting what he paid in, his beneficiary will continue to receive the installments from the company until the annuitant's investment has been refunded.

Cash refund annuity. Instead of installments after annuitant's death, the beneficiary will receive the balance of annuitant's investment in a lump-sum payment.

Refund annuities should not be considered a means of leaving an estate to one's heirs. If you, as the annuitant, live long enough to recover your investment, there will be nothing left for your beneficiary. Under an annuity contract promising payments for at least a certain number of years, once the annuitant survives the guarantee period, the heir has no expectancy.

Remember, these clauses in the annuity contract are not purchased cheaply. Per cash investment, annuities with guarantees give less income than a straight life annuity.

Joint and survivor annuity. An annuity contract may provide income for more than one person's lifetime. It may be based on the lives of two or more persons, usually a husband and wife. Where more than one life is covered under an annuity contract, it is a joint and survivor annuity.

Under a joint and survivor annuity, the income would be paid as long as one of the persons remained alive. Payments would cease after the death of the surviving annuitant. The contract may provide for a constant amount of income during the lives of the annuitants covered, or it may call for a reduction in the amount of the payments after the death of one.

Per cost investment, the joint and survivor annuity provides less income than a straight life annuity, particularly if there is a great disparity in the annuitants' ages.

BUYING ANNUITIES

Annuities may be bought with a single lump-sum payment or on the installment plan. An annuity can be purchased to start paying income immediately, or the contract may provide for installments to begin sometime in the future.

An immediate annuity provides for income to begin shortly after the contract date. Income payments may start one month from the date, if payments are to be made on a monthly basis, or one year from the purchase date, if payments are annual. Widows and persons who are retired or who are planning soon to retire are most likely to purchase immediate annuities.

Under a *deferred annuity* contract, payments begin at a future date. A deferred annuity may be purchased by a single premium. It is more likely to be bought over a period of years in annual or more frequent installments. Should the purchaser of a deferred annuity die before payments start, the amount invested or the cash value, whichever is higher, can be recovered by his beneficiary.

Many retirement plans that are referred to as deferred annuities actually are savings plans. Some include insurance coverage but contain no annuity element during the deferred period. Under these plans, a fund is accumulated which may be used to buy an immediate annuity at the end of the deferred period.

NEW TYPES OF ANNUITIES

Years of inflation have eaten into the fixed-dollar return and people who have counted on annuities to bolster retirement income have been hard hit. To eliminate the inflation drawback of the regular type of annuity, contracts providing a varying return are now being offered by insurance companies.

For an extra premium, you could now buy a cost-of-living annuity which provides a return geared to the cost-of-living index. The higher return you receive offsets the loss of dollar purchasing power.

Insurance companies have also developed the variable annuity which offers a return backed by investment values, the holder's payments being invested primarily in common stocks. Ultimately, the income payments he will receive will depend on the value of his accumulated investment at the time he retires and the performance of the stocks in the company's investment fund.

Variable annuities were originally planned for groups and not for the individual. One plan, intended for teachers, combined the variable annuity with the fixed-dollar annuity, thus protecting the participant during economic conditions that did not favor investment returns. The fixed-dollar segment of the plan would provide a guaranteed amount.

SHOULD YOU BUY AN ANNUITY?

Annuities are a conservative method of financing retirement. The chief advantage of the annuity is the assurance that you can never outlive your capital. You can depend on the annuity as a source of income during your entire lifetime and have complete freedom from investment management.

On the other hand, the type of financial security offered by the conventional annuity has the drawback of being vulnerable to inflation. Whereas the fixed-dollar payments are guaranteed, their purchasing power is not. As an investment, annuities earn a low rate of interest. Once payments begin, the annuity has no cash or loan value and cannot be used as a source of funds in an emergency.

Annuities should not be purchased if you seek a return on your investment, rather than a secure lifetime income. Finally, you should not consider refund annuities as a way of leaving an estate.

Chapter 11

INVESTING IN SECURITIES

Investing in the stock market is one of the largest economic activities in the world. Millions of investors who want to increase their capital and income at rates exceeding the return offered by savings banks or low-risk debt obligations turn to the market. However, the risks which accompany an investment are substantial. A few strike it rich, some do better than if they left their savings in the bank, others lose.

In your particular case, only you can judge whether to run the risks of investing in the market. To help you in your decision, we present basic information.

WHAT ARE SECURITIES?

If you are new to stock investment, read the following section. You need to know the difference between common stock and preferred stock and the difference between stocks and bonds.

Stock. When you buy stock of a corporation, you are investing money in the company and, in a sense, you become part owner of it. In return for your investment, the corporation generally pays you dividends out of its earnings and profits. If the corporation is successful, the value of your shares of stock may increase. Any increase in value of your shares is not taxable until you sell them. On the other hand, if the corporation does poorly, you may receive few or no dividends and your shares of stock may decline in value. Other factors, including general economic conditions, also affect your stock; your shares may decline in value even though the company itself is making money and growing.

There are two classes of stock, common and preferred. (For investment purposes, stock may also be graded according to the company's business reputation and dividend-paying record.) Holders of common stock participate in the concern's profits or losses. Preferred stock is the senior stock of a corporation and its dividend is usually set at a fixed amount. The claims of preferred stockholders come after company bondholders and take precedence over those of common stockholders. That is, if the company goes bankrupt or liquidates, bondholders' claims on the company's assets come before those of preferred stockholders. The interest due on the company's bonds takes precedence over the dividends on its preferred stock.

However, in terms of safety, the preferred stock of one company may be a "safer" investment from the point of view of assets and earnings than the bonds of another company. As between the common and preferred stock of a company, high-grade preferred stock usually provides a steadier dividend income than common stock. Common stock, on the other hand, offers greater opportunity for appreciation.

Convertible securities. Convertible securities are issued in preferred stock or bond form. They are called convertibles because the preferred stock or bonds can be converted into common stock of the issuing company at the election of the investor. Generally, the convertible privilege is included in the provision written into the bonds or preferred stock itself. There are some issues, however, which are convertible as the result of a detachable warrant issued with the security, usually a bond.

You will find conversion privileges and terms vary with the particular security. The convertible preferred of one company might be convertible into one share of its common stock, while that of another company might be convertible into three shares of its common stock. Also, the conversion privilege might continue indefinitely or be limited to a period of time ending on a specific date.

You might want to invest in convertible securities for capital gains and a hedge against market decline. As a convertible security is either a bond or preferred stock, it has a senior position in the company's capitalization before common stockholders are paid off. If the stock market drops, these securities are sometimes less vulnerable to the decline. Thus, danger of a large capital loss with tax limitations is lessened. Since the convertible can be converted into the common stock, its value moves up as the value of the common rises. In fact, once parity point is reached, its capital gain potential is enhanced over that of the common stock. A convertible preferred that can be exchanged for three shares of the common stock will jump three points on every one-point rise in the common once the parity point is reached.

A convertible generally will command a premium over and above its intrinsic worth. You must pay something for the conversion privilege.

Bonds. When you buy a bond, you are lending money to the issuer of the bonds. You do not become an owner; you are a creditor. The borrower pledges to pay you a specified amount of interest on specified dates, generally twice a year, and to repay the principal on the date of maturity stated on the bond.

You do not, however, have to wait until the bond matures to get your money. The bond may mature 10 years from now, but you are free to sell it on the open market at any time at the currently quoted price. The date of maturity means only that the company has promised to pay the face value of the bond on the day it comes due.

Your income from the bond is not affected by any change in interest rates. The issuing company pays the stated rate of interest until maturity. If interest rates decline, however, and the issuer is able to replace your loan at a lower interest cost, your bond may be called in and paid off before maturity.

Some bonds mature in a few months or years. These are short-term issues. Others mature after many years and are called long-term issues. They are normally issued in units of $1,000 par value. Bonds usually have two rates of interest; a stated rate and an effective rate. The stated rate, called the coupon or nominal rate, is printed on the bond. The effective rate depends upon the price you paid for the bond.

Marketability or liquidity (the ease with which you can convert your bonds into cash) is also important. If your bonds are bought and sold frequently, it is likely that you can get a fair price if you should have to sell in a hurry. Registered bonds, however, are safer, in case the bonds are lost or stolen, since payment of principal and interest will be made only to the registered owner.

What bonds should you buy? If the objective is a high degree of liquidity—meaning you may need your cash at a sudden notice—you should invest in top-grade, short-term bonds. If the objective is a steady income plus relative price stability, you may invest in high-to-medium-grade bonds with longer maturities.

Bonds with the highest yield may not be the safest investment. Higher yield generally means greater risk. For example, government bonds find willing buyers even though they carry relatively low interest rates. Bonds of new or unstable corporations are more speculative and the corporations must pay a high return to attract investors.

You should always be interested in the maturity date of the bond (that is, the year when the borrower has promised to repay the money borrowed). Long-term bonds generally have higher yields than short-term bonds. There are three main reasons: (1) A distant maturity date makes it difficult to predict the financial strength of the borrower at the time the bonds will fall due. This uncertainty makes it necessary to offer some bonds at a higher yield. (2) Where inflation exists, there is fear that bond values will continue to shrink. Since the rate of inflation is unpredictable, long-term bonds are a greater risk than short-term issues. Inflation could cut deep into the purchasing power of the proceeds by the time the bond matures. (3) When interest rates are on the rise, investors are unwilling to tie up funds in long-term, low-yield bonds. Issuers of long-term bonds must offer higher rates to attract buyers.

An example: If the stated interest rate is, say, 7 percent and you pay the full value of the bond, or par, the amount of interest you receive will be 7 percent of the amount paid. If you purchase the bond below par, it will return more than 7 percent of your investment.

On the other hand, if you purchase a bond at a premium above par value, the bond will yield less than 7 percent interest. Your net return on a bond investment, the amount you get to keep after income taxes, depends on the kind of bond you buy as well as the manner in which the income comes in.

Consider a 6 percent coupon bond that you buy 10 years before maturity at a cost of $800. If you hold the bond until maturity, you will enjoy, in addition to the $60 of interest you receive each year in cash, a profit of $200, i.e., the difference between the $1,000 par value paid on maturity and your $800 cost. Your total return comes to $800. If you think of this as earned over the 10-year period, at $80 per year, it appears at first glance, like a 10 percent annual yield on your $800 investment. But this is not correct; your investment grew from $800 to $1,000 over the 10 years, and you have thus tied up an average of about $900 over the entire period. The total return of $800 ($200 of which, since it is delayed for 10 years, is, of course, worth less than if it were received on a current basis) on your average investment of about $900, amounts, on a rough approximation, to under 9 percent per year.

Municipal bonds. The tax status of the bond is an important feature. Interest from corporate bonds is taxable. But income from state and municipal government bonds is exempt from Federal tax, which makes them particularly appealing to people in the higher income tax brackets.

There are two types of municipal bonds: General obligation bonds, which are backed by the "full faith and credit" of the issuing government, and revenue bonds, which are backed by the charges or tolls of the facility, e.g., turnpike, bridge, or tunnel financed by the bonds. General obligation bonds are the safer investment. While the interest paid on municipals is exempt from Federal income tax and from state income taxes in the state where issued, the interest may be subject to tax in other states. If a municipal bond is purchased at a discount and held to maturity or sold at a profit, the gain attributable to the discount is not tax exempt. It is taxed as a capital gain.

United States obligations. The main virtue of an investment in U.S. obligations is safety. You are certain that you will be repaid. Whether or not you are repaid in full depends on how much you paid for the bond. If you bought at a premium above par, you, of course, do not get all your money back. And, since inflation affects U.S. obligations as it does corporate bonds, the purchasing power of the dollars you get back may be diminished considerably. An important advantage, however, is that interest on U.S. obligations is not subject to tax by states or cities.

Treasury bills are short-term U.S. obligations sold at a discount. They are issued in terms ranging from three months to one year to maturity; minimum investment, $10,000. Treasury bills can be purchased through commercial banks or brokers. There is usually a charge made for this service. Or, with a little more effort, they can be bought directly from the Federal Reserve Bank without incurring any service charges. Write to your nearest Federal Reserve Bank for further information.

Gain on the sale or redemption of Treasury bills is ordinary income on your Federal tax return. Interest on Federal obligations is exempt, however, from state and local income taxes. If Treasury bills are sold prior to maturity, it is possible to realize a loss. Such a loss is deducted against ordinary income and does not offset capital gain.

RISKS OF INVESTMENT ON THE STOCK MARKET

You do not invest in the stock market as such, you invest in particular companies. There is no guarantee that the companies in which you invest will meet your investment objectives. The stock of the largest companies, as well as of lesser ones, has been known to fall out of favor and succumb to price erosion. When dealing with stocks you must keep in mind that it is impossible to avoid risk even in the seemingly safest of situations. Day-to-day fluctuations in the market or in the price of an individual stock are almost impossible to predict. These are only a few of the hazards of stock ownership, which cannot be stressed too strongly to the novice investor.

Unfortunately, there is no way to eliminate investment risk; no reliable means have been found to predict future economic trends. You must be prepared to see the value of your stock decline as well as rise. During critical periods, the atmosphere surrounding stock market investment is charged with fear and apprehension. Panic selling may take place, sending stock prices down sharply. A potential investor must consider his own emotional makeup. If he cannot operate under conditions of stress, then the stock market may not be for him.

The stock market, a highly complex field, demands patient study. Few stocks, if any, are so safe that they can be purchased and forgotten in the vault. You can only minimize risk by a constant supervision of your investments. Also, get the best advice you can. If you have a broker who has satisfied you in the past, rely on his judgment. If you have had no experience in security investment, read the literature published by the large investment houses and choose a broker you feel will best serve your purposes.

Because there is an element of risk in any investment transaction, you must be prepared to see the value of your stock decline as well as rise.

INFORMATION ABOUT INVESTMENTS

To reduce the element of risk, familiarize yourself with services available to the investor. Here are sources of important data on investing:

1. The Department of Public Information, New York Stock Exchange, Wall Street, New York 10005. Write for the free *Investor's Notebook—A Guide to the Working Language of Wall Street*. Request also the list of member firms.

Also, by sending $1 to the New York Stock Exchange's Department SU, Box 252, at the above address, you can obtain an "investor's kit," a useful compendium of elementary information.

2. The financial sections of newspapers and the publications of concerns specializing in financial developments. Several long-established, respected financial services operate throughout the country; they summarize basic news. These are available to any subscriber in any town or city. Many libraries have in their reference rooms copies of *The Wall Street Journal, The New York Times, Barron's, Forbes,* and other periodicals giving financial news.

3. The companies themselves. If you write to a company whose stock you may be interested in buying, you can obtain an annual report and prospectus which will give you information about the company.

4. The officers of a bank in your locality. Banks generally employ security experts to help invest their own deposits and guide their customers in investments. If you go to an officer in your bank and tell him your investment needs and objectives, you can usually get his counsel and advice.

5. Stockbrokers. Many brokerage firms maintain large research departments and many have branches throughout the country. They can provide a valuable source of information.

6. The investment advisory services. They charge fairly substantial fees for their week-to-week and month-to-month reports, however.

7. The investment counsel firms. These charge fixed fees for their advice and may completely manage the investment portfolio of a client. The larger investment counsel firms usually do not accept clients with small accounts and annual fees for personal supervisory service by an investment counselor may run from $500 up.

8. Most bonds are publicly rated by well-known financial and advisory services, such as Moody's or Standard & Poor's. You may get these ratings at your bank or library.

HOW MUCH CASH RESERVE DO YOU NEED BEFORE INVESTING IN STOCKS?

Before you start planning an investment program, you must decide how much of a cash reserve you will need to fall back on for emergencies and current obligations. For maximum protection, you should have a readily available cash reserve to carry you along for a definite period of incapacity. One suggestion: This reserve might approximate the total of your living costs for one year, overhead costs, and any other known obligations, plus an extra 10 percent, *less* insurance benefits and other supplemental income. Such a reserve would be in savings accounts, or in easily converted investments such as government bonds.

Of course, this yardstick may not cover your particular requirements. Just as you had to evolve your own budget to meet your individual circumstances, you will have to take into consideration your needs and concerns before you can decide how much you can afford to invest. Your answers to the following questions will guide you.

1. Have you income from other sources or will your investments be a major source of your funds for day-to-day living?

2. What is your need for the cash you are investing? Can you afford to keep it invested indefinitely? You may need the money at a fixed time, in which case you must restrict yourself to safe and marketable securities which can generally be converted to cash at any time.

If you plan to buy a house or furniture or an automobile on the installment plan, you have specified debts that must be met by specified dates. You should keep funds in the savings bank to meet these obligations as they arise.

Only when you have commitments fully covered and a sound savings bank account should you enter into stock market investment. The person who cannot afford loss should not venture.

WHAT TYPE OF INVESTOR ARE YOU?

In your investment planning, consider your investment goals and decide how you will reach them. First, ask which of these basic types of investor you consider yourself: The conservative or long-term investor, the aggressive investor, or the speculator. While each will measure safety against the risks involved in any investment, they will differ considerably in taking risks.

The conservative or long-term investor holds securities for a long time, seeks steady income together with long-term appreciation, and is more interested in safety of principal than anything else. He must minimize danger of capital loss by avoiding investment which carries higher risk.

The aggressive investor is more venturesome. He buys and sells more often and typically invests in securities bearing the label "businessman risk." He is willing to take more chances in seeking greater capital growth. He is willing to sacrifice some current return, accepting average or below-average income in the expectation of receiving greater return in the years to come.

The speculator often trades in and out for quick profits. He may buy securities with high risk of loss.

The safe investment which promises some capital appreciation but only over the long term will have investment appeal to the conservative investor but not to the speculator primarily concerned with quick profits. Regardless of investment goals, however, there is no hard-and-fast rule which requires that all funds be maintained in one type of security. For instance, the conservative investor might have the bulk of his funds in investments offering a high degree of safety, a portion in businessman risk investments, and even a small amount in a particular speculation. In other words, at any one time, an investor may have funds in different securities with different safety-risk factors, although the bulk of his funds will be invested in the type of security which best meets his investment goal.

Changes in circumstances may require changes in investment goals. A young person with no family responsibilities may be in the position to speculate. After marriage and assumption of new responsibilities, he may become more conservative. Again, a middle-aged investor must consider the number of years remaining before retirement—when he must look to his investments for retirement capital. An investor who finds that his earnings are rising will be in a higher tax bracket; investments suitable to a lower-bracket investor may not be suitable to one who is taxed at higher rates.

FIXING YOUR INVESTMENT OBJECTIVES

Before selecting the securities you buy, you must also decide what you want and need from your investments. Do you want stock that will return dividends every few months and that will be relatively stable in price and high quality? Do you want a high income security in the hope that the income may cover part of your living expenses? Is your objective the sale of the stock at a substantially higher price than what you paid for it? Are you mainly concerned with liquidity and marketability, because you will need cash suddenly for some business or personal purpose and you want to be sure you can turn in the issue at a price approximating your cost whenever the need arises?

If your objective is "trading" profits, you will generally have to deal in stocks that are fairly risky and which fluctuate widely in price. If liquidity is your aim, you will have to buy stocks of the highest grade that fluctuate only slightly in price. High income, high profits, high stability, and high liquidity do not come in one package.

Decide on your objective or objectives. As a guide, here are some suggestions to consider.

1. For investment, choose sound, essential industries. Food and utilities are basic industries and can more readily hold their values during economic declines than nonessential industries that provide services and luxuries. Of course, all essential industries must be watched and attention paid to any trend that might suggest a particular industry is becoming replaced or outmoded by new technological developments. But what is an essential today may not be one year from now. For example, the production of steam locomotives was an essential industry. Today, there is no such production.

2. Invest in companies that are recognized leaders in their in-

dustries. True, some analysts do not agree with this advice and hold that the only substantial profits are made in new, unknown companies. The answer to this that you are investing and not trying to "get rich quick." Some smaller companies may turn out to be more profitable than well-known firms, but your chance of choosing such a company is often a matter of luck. The advantages in selecting the recognized companies is that they have proven their ability, their management is experienced, they will have resources for research, and can finance their needs more easily than smaller companies.

3. Invest in several different companies, each in a different industry. Over a period of time you undoubtedly will make a bad investment. If you invest in only one company, an error may be costly; if you have, say, six different stocks, your good judgment on four of them may more than offset a bad decision on one or two. Of course, you may also "hedge" in the same way by investing in mutual funds (see next chapter).

4. Invest about the same amount in the shares of each company you select. Do not make a favorite of any one stock. There are many sound industries.

5. Invest in shares listed on a major securities exchange, preferably the New York Stock Exchange. Before its stock may be listed on a major exchange, a company must file information with both the private financial authorities and the Federal government. Specific standards must be met; regular reports must be published; transactions are under the constant check of the exchange, the Federal government, and expert investors and bankers. Furthermore, a listing on the exchange makes it easier to buy or sell stock. Listing, of course, is no guarantee of merit, but it is a fairly substantial guarantee that the company will operate according to current business standards.

6. Invest in shares that can show an unbroken earnings or a dividend record or both for the last 10 years. Such a record indicates that an enterprise is sound.

7. Buy shares that over the past 10 years have earned at least $5 dollars for every four paid out in dividends. A company should not pay out all it earns, but should build up a reserve to handle emergencies or to insure its ability to take advantage of future opportunities. A company that earns considerably more than its dividend is preferred to one that just about earns it.

8. During period of a year or two, sell at least one stock, choosing the weakest on your list without considering its original cost. Invest the proceeds in a more profitable security.

9. Do not buy on margin. Stocks can decline and you can lose your investment if it is financed by margin loans. Buying stock on margin is not advisable for the investor. Buying on margin is primarily for the trader who is shooting for short-term profits.

10. Choose an established brokerage firm. When you place an order to buy or sell, do not set a fixed price; buy or sell "at the market." Buying or selling at the market means your order will be filled at about the price of the next transaction in your stock on the exchange. This is a better approach than giving your broker a fixed price. You are a long-term investor, and even an expert cannot fix the value of a stock to within fractions of a point. Since you are investing for the long term, it will be completely unimportant over that period whether you paid $20 or $21 for a specific share of stock.

11. If you do buy on margin, you should check the fine print of your agreement and understand the rights retained by your broker. You may find you have to notify him if you want to prevent his taking certain buy-and-sell actions. The broker wants to save paperwork; his rights may not always suit your plans.

12. Brokers find it easier to hold the stock of small investors "in street name." You may prefer to insist that your stock is registered in your name. Customers are now insured to $50,000 against brokerage house insolvency.

WHEN TO BUY STOCKS

A review of the stock market's history indicates that there is a cyclical character to prices. The trouble, however, is that the low and high markets stand out clearly only in retrospect on charts already drawn, charts showing "where the market has been," not necessarily where it is going. True, the expert studies the current market to determine whether it is advisable to buy or sell at current market prices and to predict the future moves of a particular stock. But for the average investor, market analysts suggest, "Give up any idea of 'beating the market,'" and develop a program of paying current securities prices with current earnings.

Dollar cost-averaging. Under a program of dollar cost-averaging, you purchase stock with a fixed amount every month, or perhaps every quarter. Your money buys more shares when prices are low and fewer when prices are high.

The monthly investment plan. A monthly investment plan offered by many brokers provides a method of investing as little as $40 at a time. Or invest as much as $1,000 a month in any of the stocks listed on the New York Stock Exchange. The plan takes advantage of dollar cost-averaging and lets you invest on a pay-as-you-go basis. You pay the regular commission charged by members of the Exchange, plus the regular odd-lot differential.

The monthly investment plan is noncontractual. You can start and stop whenever you wish and there is no penalty if you skip a payment. Your stock is purchased for you whenever your periodic payment is received, and your account is credited with full shares plus any fractional interest in a share, figured to the fourth decimal point. Under the monthly investment plan, your dividends can be credited to your account and automatically applied to the purchase of additional shares of stock. This automatic reinvestment of dividends enables you to increase your holdings more rapidly than you might by buying stocks without benefit of the plan, an effect similar to the effect that compounding interest has on a savings account.

RETIREMENT INCOME

When retirement time approaches, an investor may switch from growth stocks to income stocks before the income is actually required. For tax purposes, this may be a costly step. Profit on the sale of stocks is then subject to tax while he is still working and may be in a high tax bracket. If he waits a full year after retirement before switching his stocks, his tax bracket may have dropped and, with the aid of double personal exemptions enjoyed by man and wife aged 65 or over, the gain may even escape tax altogether.

Moreover, since income stocks would presumably bring in larger dividends than growth stocks, anyone who makes the switch on such stocks, say, two years before retirement, would pay the higher tax on those dividends. Had the original growth stocks been held, the taxpayer would have enjoyed the remaining capital gain potential.

You should consider the tax angle carefully when planning the development of retirement income from investments. In addition, you should ascertain the months when dividends will be paid on your income stocks. Through a careful buying plan you can have dividends coming in each month of the year.

Chapter 12

INVESTING IN MUTUAL FUNDS— LETTING THE EXPERTS MANAGE YOUR INVESTMENTS

In the last chapter, we talked about investments in the stock market. The emphasis there was on your decision to plan and execute your own investment program. Perhaps you have come to the conclusion that you do not have the time, ability, or temperament for such a program. If so, you do not have to give up the idea of investing in securities. By investing in mutual funds you turn over the duties of investment management to the fund itself. Even if you do your own investing, you may want to set aside some of your capital in mutual funds.

Although you may invest in mutual funds to relieve yourself of the major burden of investment decisions, you must not and cannot avoid the responsibility of choosing a fund that meets your investment needs. As will be explained in the following pages, first, mutual funds differ widely in their objectives and in what they return to investors; second, you must periodically review the performance of any particular fund in comparison to the general market conditions and to the performance of other funds.

WHAT IS A MUTUAL FUND?

The mutual fund idea is a practical one. Many small investors (large ones, too) put their money into various companies which invest this mutual fund in common stock, preferred stock, bonds, or specialized investments. Such funds are professionally managed, so, in theory at least, a small investor, like a wealthy person, can have the benefit of diversified investments and expert portfolio management.

Mutual funds vary in size, ranging from a few million dollars in assets to well over two billion. They are divided according to their method of operation into the older (but far fewer) "closed-end" investment companies and the far larger group of "open-end" mutual funds which today control billions of dollars of investments for both small and large individual investors, pension funds, corporate groups, and institutions.

Whether they are large or small, open-end or closed-end, the basic appeals of all investment companies lie first in professional management and second in diversification—a spreading of risk among many types of securities.

Open-end companies. An open-end company is called "open-end" because its capitalization is open. Such companies create and sell shares whenever you want them, buy them back and retire the shares whenever you want to cash in your chips. In other words, you join by turning over your funds to the company and getting newly created shares which represent your pro rata share of the entire fund.

Today, the term "mutual funds" generally applies to open-end companies, and the main discussion in the chapter applies to such funds.

Closed-end companies. These companies issue a specific number of shares when formed and, since they do not intend to issue more, are "closed-end." Shares are traded on the stock exchange or over the counter and in buying or selling you act through a broker as you do in common stock transactions.

Whether buying or selling closed-end shares, you pay a broker's commission as well as an indirect fee each year for the management of the fund. You can use the monthly investment plan of the New York Stock Exchange (see page 184) for your purchases.

In individual cases, a point against closed-end shares might be a lack of the liquidity. The seller of closed-end shares may not find the right sale at the right price at the right time.

The dual purpose funds. The dual purpose fund, no longer being formed, came to market early in 1967. Dual funds are closed-end investment companies established with two classes of stock. One class is called the preferred or income stock. Its holders receive all dividend income after deduction of operating expenses. A minimal annual return is promised. If, because of variation of dividends, the promised amount is not paid out in a particular year, the shortage becomes a claim against future years. The funds have a specified life, frequently about 15 years. These preferred shares receive first claim against the assets of the fund up to the amount of the original purchase price, plus unpaid dividends, if any.

Capital shares, the other class of stock, receive no income dividends during the life of the fund. These shareholders have all capital gains reinvested and are entitled to all assets of the fund at termination after satisfaction of the preferred (income) shareholders' claims.

The dual purpose funds appeal to the investor looking for current income; he receives the dividend income earned by $2 of capital for every $1 he put into the fund though he gives up hope of growth. The investor interested in growth has no claim on current income but enjoys the efforts of $2 invested for every $1 he puts in.

Dual funds may satisfy your needs for growth or income. But you should have the advice of a reputable, experienced broker who knows your investment needs. He can tell you how the dual funds fared in the bear markets that developed when they were still newcomers, and if their current performance is promising.

These funds are closed-end companies so you buy and sell your shares on the exchanges or in the over-the-counter market. There is no fixed "bid" or "asked" price, as is determined daily by open-end mutuals.

Hedge funds. These are comparative newcomers that did not do well in bear markets. No evaluation is presently possible. However, hedge funds are not for the newcomer or, for that matter, for the average investor.

OBJECTIVES OF MUTUAL FUNDS

Mutual funds fall into three broad categories:

1. *Growth funds.* Their objective is to achieve a growth in the value of shares, which eventually leads to growth in income. Growth fund assets are usually invested in common stocks up to about 90 percent.

Star performers in bull markets, many growth funds have shown a tendency to sag when bears take over. This type of fund generally appeals to younger investors.

2. *Balanced funds.* Funds aiming for balance invest in common stock, preferred stock, and bonds. The idea is that these three kinds of investment provide defensive strength in a declining market. Investments are divided approximately into common stocks, 60 percent; bonds and preferred stocks together, 40 percent. In a rising market, balanced funds generally do not show the increase in value of a growth fund. Balanced funds appeal to conservative persons.

3. *Income funds.* Investments here are primarily in high-yield securities. There are differences even within this category, as some income funds will take slight risks in order to give shareholders a higher yield. Investments are in preferred stocks, bonds, and common stocks with a high yield.

In addition to the three basic types of mutual funds, there are funds which attempt to combine two or more of these basic objectives and others which may be described as specialty funds. Some of these funds are:

1. *Bond funds.* Securities purchased in this kind of fund generally provide a fixed income and do not increase substantially in growth. A mutual fund may specialize in investments in United States bonds and other government obligations.

2. *Industry funds.* Investments are concentrated in a single industry, including subsidiaries. On occasion, sponsors of industry funds offer funds from several industries. You may switch from one industry fund to another in the sponsor's portfolio at a small sales charge.

3. *Real estate investment funds.* These are designed to encourage small investors to participate in diversified real estate ventures. As an investor in the real estate fund, you may enjoy a slight tax ad-

vantage as you will have nontaxable distributions from depreciation reserves.

Most mutual funds pay quarterly dividends each year. These will, of course, vary in amount from time to time depending on fund earnings. The fund receives many dividend and interest checks from the investments made for its members and each member receives a proportionate share after management fees and operating expenses are deducted. In addition, you may receive capital gains distributions resulting from profitable security sales by the fund. If you invest in several of these funds with different dividend payment dates, it would be possible for you to receive a dividend check each month.

GETTING INFORMATION ON MUTUAL FUNDS

Mutual fund data is readily available. The public information center for the industry is The Investment Company Institute, 1775 K Street, N.W., Washington, D.C. 20006. Many no-load funds are represented by the No Load Mutual Fund Association, 475 Park Avenue South, New York, New York 10016.

The records of the closed-end companies are found in all the standard manuals. Most of them are traded on the stock exchanges and their day-to-day price fluctuations are easily followed in such publications as *The Wall Street Journal, The New York Times,* and *Barron's.*

Available from The American Institute for Economic Research, Great Barrington, Massachusetts 01230, is a $2 annual publication entitled *Investment Trusts and Funds from the Investor's Point of View.* Your library may carry this examination of both closed-end and open-end companies. Large libraries only are likely to have *Investment Companies,* data published annually by Wiesenberger Services Inc., 1 New York Plaza, New York, New York 10004. Where material is unavailable at a library, check stockbrokers' offices.

Also seek out the *Mutual Fund Directory,* published by the Investment Dealers' Digest, 150 Broadway, New York, New York 10038; *Pocket Summary of Mutual Funds,* from Kalb Voorhis & Company, 726 Woodward Building, Washington, D.C. 20005; Johnson's Investment Company's *Charts,* Rand Building, Buffalo,

New York 14203; information from Arthur Lipper Corp., 140 Broadway, New York, New York 10005.

A useful and informative monthly publication is *Fundscope,* Suite 700, 1900 Avenue of the Stars, Los Angeles, California 90067. The April issue each year is a comprehensive guide to mutual funds and their performance. This magazine does not sell funds but aims to state the facts concerning them for the guidance of investors.

Study the stock market quotations on mutual funds which are carried daily in many newspapers. While the past record of many funds has generally been good, like other investments they have slipped in bear markets. The newcomer to mutual fund investment has no guarantee that the funds that have consistently made a good showing will do so in the future, but he can avoid the more showy and speculative funds that tend to zoom and fizzle.

The funds themselves will, of course, be happy to mail you their literature. A broker will advise you. Through your reading and inquiries, you can enlarge your understanding of mutual funds so that, in deciding to buy, you do so from an informed background.

COST OF BUYING INTO MUTUAL FUNDS

If you buy the shares of a closed-end investment company through your broker, you will pay a commission computed in exactly the same way that your commission would be figured in buying shares of any industrial corporation. These range from 6 percent of total amount of money involved down to around 1 percent on larger purchases.

You buy most open-end mutual funds through brokerage offices or through selling organizations set up to handle a series of funds or one fund. Each fund has its own schedule of fees. Maximum commission costs may exceed 8½ percent of the total cost of the shares for small investments. When investments running into the tens of thousands of dollars are involved, commissions may be halved or even less.

You can tell at a glance what the maximum fee is by checking the price of the fund in the special list of mutual fund quotations carried by many newspapers and financial publications. The fund will be listed thus:

	Bid	Asked
XYZ Fund	$11.34	$12.26

The fund's asset value per share (its total assets divided by the number of shares outstanding) stood at $11.34 per share on this day. The asked price is the price you would pay per share. The 92-cent difference represents the commission cost per share which, in this case, comes to 8.1 percent. Another fund might be listed $13.12 bid, $14.00 asked, the 88-cent difference here representing a commission of about 6.7 percent.

A letter of intention is one means of reducing sales commissions. If you sign up, stating you will invest a large sum such as $10,000, $15,000, or $25,000 over the next 13 months, you receive the benefit of lower rates. However, the figures will be recalculated if your actual investment falls short of the promised amount.

The no-load funds. There are over 160 funds which charge no sales commission. That is because they have no salesmen or sales organization. Most of these funds grew out of investment advisory services which originally managed the investment of large sums for individuals, but were prevailed upon by smaller investors to open their services to them, also. While they charge no commission, they charge for management like other funds.

You can always identify a no-load (no commission) fund merely by running your finger down the mutual funds list in any financial publication: the "bid" and "asked" price will be identical. For example:

	Bid	Asked
ABC Fund	$16.94	$16.94

If you want to buy into a no-load fund, you must take the initiative. While these funds also do some of the modest, low-pressure advertising allowed the mutual fund industry, any inquiry on your part will not be followed up by a salesman.

Most people approach the no-load mutual funds by mail. However, at least one large brokerage house advertises that it will handle the no-loads.

Load versus no-load. You may wonder why people choose to pay the sales charges of a load fund when they could avoid them in a no-load. This is a matter for personal decision. There are more loads than no-loads and, on checking up on performance of a number of funds over a period of time, you may come to the conclusion that the loads are worth the cost. They do have the financial means to employ topflight management. However, many investors feel the no-loads fulfill their objectives. Judge for yourself by looking into current and past performance of the many such funds available. Some charge a redemption fee; others do not, while reserving the right to do so.

BUYING MUTUALS THROUGH VOLUNTARY OR CONTRACTUAL PLANS

You can buy a mutual fund by making a large single investment or you can invest fixed amounts over a set period of time. You can purchase through voluntary or contractual plans, which may differ from fund to fund.

Under a basic type of voluntary plan, you are not bound by contract to systematic payments though you may choose to adopt one. However, there will in most cases be a stated initial payment and a minimum on future purchases. For each transaction there is a sales charge unless you buy "no-loads" (see page 192). Capital gains may be reinvested at no charge. You do not have the privilege of replacing withdrawn funds without paying another commission.

A contractual plan involves "front-end load," that is, as much as half the commission payable over the total investment period may be deducted during the first year. Assuming you contract to invest $100 a month for 10 years, your first year's *investment* of $1,200 might be cut to almost half by the deduction of a 9 percent commission. The balance of the commission charge is spread over the rest of the 10-year investment period.

Some states, including California, Illinois, and Wisconsin, have regulations not met by front-end loads, so they cannot legally be sold there. The objection to these funds is not only the severe drop in the amount of money left for investment in the first year, but the loss sustained by any investor who fails to complete his contractual plan.

New law has cut down on the loss such an investor might sustain. Shortly after buying into a contractual plan, he or she receives a letter saying that if within 45 days an end to the plan is sought, a refund of all charges plus value of account will be returned. Some funds offer a 60-day grace period in which the investor may claim a refund. Beyond that point, there is now by law an 18-

month period during which an investor may opt out. He will still get back the value of his account, but he will lose 15 percent of the gross payments made. Only the 45-day refund right need be extended by mutual funds which deduct no more than 64 percent of the total sales charge over the first four years of the contractual plan. No more than 20 percent of the investment can be deducted in any year; a reasonable spread would be 16 percent a year.

Contractual plans offer certain bonus features. Dividends are invested at asset value, for example, whereas voluntary plans use offering price. The contractual plan can also be tied to a declining balance term insurance. (Some voluntary plans offer this feature, too.) Then, if the investor should die before the end of his 10- or 15-year commitment, the insurance pays for the remaining balance due.

Why would anyone commit themselves to a contractual plan when there are so many voluntary plans? In general, they appeal to the investor who needs a stick held over him to compel him to complete his plan. Also, he might like a particular fund that operates under the contractual plan. Mutual fund salesmen have every reason to push contractual funds in preference to voluntary. They know what commission they will earn—bar refunds. What are they going to get out of a voluntary-plan investor who puts down a minimum initial payment of $10, $20, $50, or $100, and is erratic in his subsequent minimum payments since he has no firm commitment? Some brokerage houses are just not interested in the small investor who wants to put as little as $25 a month into mutual funds—and may shortly fail in his intention.

It is difficult to calculate whether a voluntary or contractual plan is less expensive if both are completed over a fixed period of time. The contractual's commission charges may be offset by the reinvestment of dividends and gains at no charge. The lower commission of a voluntary plan may be offset by emergency withdrawal privileges and the fee for reinvestment of dividend income.

In making your decision, consider your ability to make regular payments and your other resources to meet emergencies. Above all, do not commit yourself to a plan unless you are aware of the privileges and charges involved.

CHOOSING INVESTMENT GOALS

There is always risk in investment, but it can be reduced by diversifying. Dollar cost-averaging, described on page 183, can be used for your mutual fund investments. Since some funds have low initial and minimum payments, you could split your planned amount—whether $100 a month or $50 every three months—among several, so as to spread loss and open up more areas for profit. Dollar cost-averaging is for the long run, so if you are not tied to a contractual plan of 10, 12, or 15 years, you should make such a commitment to yourself and keep it. Overnight results should not be expected.

Many experienced investors in mutual funds keep cash or other liquid assets ready so that they can buy during a market decline. They choose funds that have shown evidence of good management during the past 10 years and, particularly, during market declines.

Even if you are young and want to venture into the more risky growth funds, reserve some part of your investment for conservative balanced funds, or bond and preferred stock funds.

If you are only a few years from retirement, there is no advantage in initiating a 10-year monthly payment program, especially under a contractual plan whereby 50 percent of your first payments will be used to prepay part of the commissions for the entire 10-year period. Unless you have money to spare in retirement you may not be able to continue the investment, and unless you withdraw during the grace period (page 194), those prepaid commissions will be wasted.

Insurance with mutual fund investments. Do not confuse the life insurance provided by mutual funds on contractual plans and some voluntary plans with lifetime protection. This type of low-cost, declining balance term insurance is intended to cover your investment program should you die before completing it. It does not in any way replace your regular life insurance policy.

MEETING THE MUTUAL FUND SALESMAN

Many funds are sold through salesmen who may work for a distributing organization handling one or more funds, or who may represent a brokerage firm. In any event, the business of the salesman is to sell—often using high pressure techniques.

This means that you must be on your guard. When you go to your brokerage firm to discuss investment in a mutual fund, you must expect a salesman to try to sell you the fund, or one of the funds, handled by his brokerage firm.

Do not be rushed into buying. Resist any high-pressure sales tactics and take time to decide on the course that seems most likely to fulfill your investment goals.

MUTUAL FUND PLANS FOR RETIREMENT INCOME

Just as you can redeem your mutual fund shares at any time, so with most, though not all, funds you can set up an automatic withdrawal plan which would be payable monthly or quarterly for any purpose you wish. While often used as supplements to retirement income, mutual fund withdrawal plans can also serve to pay for education costs, cover mortgages or rents when due, pay alimony, insurance premiums, or other expenses.

A common investment amount before a withdrawal plan is possible is $10,000. Some funds set $5,000 or $7,500; a few state no minimum. There are several types of withdrawal systems you could set up, but the level withdrawal plan is the most popular. The widely accepted rule of thumb for this program is a $50-a-month check from a $10,000 investment. To make this payment, the fund will redeem enough of your shares every month to provide a payment of $50. Then, when it declares its dividends and capital gains, it will repurchase shares.

Mutual funds do not offer you an annuity—that is, a contract like those obtainable from insurance companies, religious and charitable organizations—that *guarantees* specified income at stated times. Given good management and good markets, a fund could pay $50 a month out of $10,000 forever—and even increase the value of the investment. Or, over a period of years, the $50 payments might wipe out the investment. Anything might happen because such a plan is not an annuity. It is a system for drawing a regular monthly check in the hope that the fund can generate enough earnings to keep the $10,000 intact, or even increase it. Remember, you draw $50 a month from an equity investment—and equities can go up or down. Participants in such mutual fund withdrawal plans do not always reckon with the fact that the payments may represent a loss of some of the capital formerly at work.

Instead of fixing withdrawals at a dollar figure, the withdrawals can be expressed in terms of shares. If, let us assume, your mutual fund asset value now stands at $10 a share, you might ask the fund to sell five shares a month and send the proceeds to you. If the price goes to $11, you will receive $55; if it falls to $9, you will get only $45. If you need exactly $50 a month, this type of withdrawal is not for you. But if your budget can stand some slight variation from month to month, then the share plan works out slightly better over the years since you will not find yourself having to sell more shares when the price is low and fewer when the price is up—the reverse of the dollar-averaging plan which is often so advantageous in buying mutual funds.

Chapter 13

YOUR HEALTH INSURANCE

Today, the anxiety over sickness or injury is not confined to the thoughts of pain and disability that may result. The fear of financial bankruptcy is almost equally oppressing. One hears of a lifetime of savings wiped out by sudden illness or accident. Widespread concern for this problem is slowly leading to forms of government-financed health plans. Whether you favor or oppose this development, government-financed medical protection is a fact for many. Federal medical insurance already covers the major medical costs of senior citizens 65 or over and medical programs cover the medical expenses of many families in the lower income brackets. One need not be a prophet to predict that, in time, almost all medical costs will be covered by governmental programs. However, at the present time if your needs are not covered under the senior citizens' program and you are not in a low income bracket, you personally will have the burden of protecting your family's security through some form of medical insurance.

Illness or injury can arrive with devastating suddenness, and when such misfortune occurs, you may have no inkling of what the ultimate financial cost will be. Facing the possibility that the worst can occur, that you and your family will be prone to accident and illness of varying seriousness, and that hospitalizations and operations are likely, you have to develop an insurance program around these possibilities, modified by what you can afford in insurance protection.

Ask yourself what expenses you would incur if illness or injury struck, and what income would be available to meet expenses. Directly flowing from the illness or injury would be doctor's and surgeon's fees, hospital care costs of various types, costs of treatments, appliances, drugs. In addition, if you are the breadwinner of the family, your prolonged absence from employment would lead to loss of income.

YOUR EMERGENCY RESERVE

One hundred percent insurance protection against all forms of sickness and accident is an impossibility. Moreover, insuring organizations and companies prefer that you carry part of the burden yourself. Almost all policies use "deductible" formulas and limits in paying medical expenses. Therefore, you must employ your own budgeting methods to help you to co-insure. By putting money aside to handle predictable expenses yourself, you will do better than by trying to buy expensive health insurance coverage against all eventualities.

How much health protection reserve money do you need in the bank? Individuals' and families' needs will vary with the size of the family and with basic health since, whatever is said about averages, some people go through life with far less need for medical care than others. Through budgeting, you should be able to work out the average annual sum necessary for your family, taking into consideration your usual type of bills. Above that amount, you will need to cover any deductible stated on your policy or policies, the premiums (unless handled through payroll deduction), and the unpredictable amount you would have to pay in excess of your insurance protection.

While it is impossible to foresee exactly how much you might be called upon to pay out of your own pocket for hospitalization resulting from any given sickness or accident, you have to bear in mind the limitations of the particular coverage you select. With a paid-in-full type of service you may have to pay half of the costs, then the whole, after specified periods of time have elapsed. Unless your income is below a stated level, the fee that would be paid for surgical care under your service-type surgical-medical plan will not cover all a surgeon may charge you; you carry the remainder of the cost. If you have an indemnity type of policy, you may have a limitation on room and board payments; you pay the excess. You are liable for a certain "deductible" amount, then 20 or 25 percent of the medical, surgical, and other charges. With this type of policy, you may have to make immediate payment of all bills; the insurance company reimburses you for its portion later.

Against this difficult-to-forecast area of financial responsibility, you have the comfort of knowing that the average period of hospitalization is seven or eight days, but you may well fear that your family might be one of those involved in sudden catastrophe, perhaps even long-term or permanent disability of the breadwinner.

For most families, the solution to this worry lies in major medical protection, as offered in policies available from reliable, well-known insurance companies. With most types of sickness and accident covered by your regular group or private health insurance, you would draw upon a major medical policy in case of disaster.

YOUR SOURCES OF PRIVATE INSURANCE PROTECTION

Three sources of private medical and health insurance are: (1) Insurance companies. (2) Blue Cross and Blue Shield insurance. (3) Independent group practice, generally organized and operated by communities, medical groups, or unions.

Source (3), not further discussed below, should not be confused with a group insurance policy. A group-practice plan usually offers the services of specific physicians and specialists under a prepayment system which covers the member and his family for most health care. While patients may not always see their favorite physician, the plan has much to recommend it. Write Group Health Association of America, 1321 Fourteenth Street, N.W., Washington, D.C. 20005, for information on group-practice plans in your vicinity and how the system operates.

Generally, it is advisable to seek health care coverage from an organization that has purchased a group insurance policy, because it can offer medical benefits at lower premium rates. Your employer may, of course, cover you in a group plan and pay all or part of the premium. If no coverage is available through a job, you may be eligible to join a plan offered by your professional or fraternal society, or alumni association.

TYPES OF HEALTH INSURANCE

The following types of insurance protection are available to offset these expenses and losses:

Hospitalization insurance. A hospital cost or hospitalization insurance policy pays the cost of a hospital room and board for a number of days and, generally, expenses such as drugs, operating room charges, and laboratory fees.

Surgical expense insurance. Here, the policy pays up to a specified amount for each type of operation, such as hysterectomy, hernia, removal of tonsils, and removal of gallbladder, etc. X-ray examinations and therapy may also be covered. The cost of physician's visits in the hospital may be covered, but at an extra premium charge. Surgical insurance is often combined with a hospital cost policy.

Major or catastrophic medical insurance. This type of policy is generally taken out after you have coverage under a basic hospitalization-surgical policy. A major medical policy is tailored to protect you against severe rather than ordinary illness. As such, a major medical policy will have deductibles, generally ranging from $100 to $1,000. Benefits are not paid until you or your basic hospital-surgical insurance pay medical costs up to the deductible amount. Above the deductible, the policy pays 75 percent or 80 percent of the costs up to a maximum amount, generally $15,000 to $20,000.

If you do not have basic medical insurance, you can get a comprehensive major medical policy, but this type is more expensive than a supplemental major policy where you have basic medical policy.

Disability insurance. Here, the policy compensates you for loss of income, not for medical expenses. Payments are set at a monthly rate for a period, during which you are totally disabled or partially disabled. The policy may cover disability arising from an accident or illness or both. Payments do not generally begin until after you have been disabled for a specified length of time.

You may already be protected by some form of disability insurance under an employer's plan, under the laws of your state, or under Social Security. Therefore, before buying a private policy, check the extent of your protection under such insurance programs.

Some forms of private income insurance apply only to hospitalization. Some pay when the policyholder suffers illness or accident; some apply only when hospitalization is necessary because of accident. When you consider buying income protection insurance, compare the cost of policies that pay out for both sickness and accident, whether in hospital or at home. In many cases, a disabled person may be discharged from hospital long before he or she can return to work. The limitations of these types of policies should be studied carefully. Some are widely advertised and sell by mail. Many people are tempted to sign up before they have thoroughly checked into the various income protection policies available.

Accidental death and dismemberment. The policy pays an amount for death or injury caused by an accident. For example, the policy may pay $25,000 for accidental death, with lesser amounts payable for the loss of both hands, or both feet, or the sight of both eyes or the loss of a hand and foot.

CHOOSING THE RIGHT POLICY

When you are faced with the actual task of selecting a policy among the many offered by competing services, you will have the task of screening the many details of each policy to see how they will or will not meet your objectives.

1. Do not be overimpressed by higher maximum benefits offered by a medical care policy. Check to see that it covers a larger proportion of usual expenses of common ailments. The chance of a catastrophic bill occurring is not as great as the chance of incurring usual hospital expenses ranging from $300 to $3,500.

Check the hospital rates for room and other services in your locality. If a policy does not cover a good proportion of these costs, it is not for you.

Remember that there are no bargain insurance rates, except for the lower rates of policies offered by group plans. If you are buying an individual policy, a lower premium may mean insufficient protection.

Study the method of payment also. A benefit may be paid in terms of services or indemnity. In a service-type policy, the insurance organization pays for the service. For example, if the policy states that it will pay the cost of a semiprivate room, the type of payment is a service type. An indemnity policy will state that the insurance company will pay a stated sum per day for the cost of a hospital room. In general, room and board payments are based on the average rate most commonly charged for a semiprivate room and board in your area's hospitals. Consequently, premiums and payable rates will differ from city to suburb and across the country. When you choose a private room, a policy of this type would pay its stated semiprivate amount *or the hospital's most common semiprivate room rate, if less;* you pay the difference.

2. When you take out additional health insurance to back up your present coverage which is, say, group insurance at your place of employment, you will have to check carefully on the regulations governing the payment of benefits. Health associations and insurance companies are combining to ensure that there is no overpayment of benefits. Consequently, if your second, personal policy duplicates the benefits payable under your group policy, you may be paying premiums for benefits you cannot collect. The insuring agencies will settle the matter between themselves. Take care that you supplement, not duplicate, benefits.

3. Check what the policy will not cover. Some usual exclusions are: Diseases or physical impairments contracted before the policy was taken out. Medical expense of care provided by a Veterans Administration hospital, state workmen's compensation plan, or other Federal or state program. Injuries received in a military action. Pregnancies that began before the effective date of the policy. Long-term care in a mental institution.

Some policies now cover part of the cost of psychiatric treatment or consultation.

"Pre-existing conditions" may be covered after a waiting period. When groups are enrolled, the insuring organization may agree to waive this time lapse and give immediate coverage. If you are already insured and transferring to another type of health insurance coverage, watch this point. A representative of the insurers may tell you the waiver will apply. Such an assurance given verbally carries no weight. The health plan association or company should give the waiver in writing before the members of the group can be certain that they will not be officially informed, they have to wait—perhaps almost a year—until pre-existing conditions are covered.

4. Do not buy mail order insurance unless you are sure of the company's reputation, that it will pay any benefits that meet your needs, and *that it is licensed by the insurance department of your state*. Mail order policies providing inexpensive premium come-ons, such as a first month premium of $1, offer little protection. Some of these companies carry names that are designed to be confused with the names of reputable firms.

If you wish to know more about an out-of-state insurance company before becoming involved, you can address an inquiry to the Insurance Department of the state in which that particular company is located. Such an Insurance Department will usually be with other government offices in the state capital.

5. Review the policy terms for renewability. They vary from policy to policy. A policy can be renewed only if the company accepts your election. This type of policy is usually called an optionally renewable or commercial policy. In addition, the company can change the premium rate on renewal. A guaranteed renewable policy is renewed at your election. The premium rate changes only if the company revises the rates for those in your classification. A "noncan" policy is a noncancelable, guaranteed policy that you can renew with no change in premium. For this privilege you are charged a higher premium. Paying the extra charge may be advisable if you are concerned about getting insurance protection in case you become seriously ill and thus become a "poor risk."

Blue Cross and Blue Shield insurance protection is generally renewable as long as you continue to pay premiums. (An older person wishing to supplement Medicare may have trouble *joining* the plan at a late date if he or she has a poor medical history.)

Note that, across the country, Blue Cross and Blue Shield organizations vary in the contracts and services they offer and in cost. State law or insurance company law may be operative over a particular organization. If you move from one state to another, and have this type of coverage, find out how it is affected in payments and benefits.

6. In choosing a policy providing disability income benefits, you must find out from your insurance agent exactly what you are buying. Ask these questions and get satisfactory answers before you buy a health, accident, or disability policy: (1) Are there any benefits for

accidental death, and, if so, how much would your beneficiary receive? (2) What would you receive and when if you become disabled? (3) How does the policy define accident and sickness disability? (4) Does this policy provide benefits only for total disability or will it pay for partial disability too? Does disability on the policy mean incapacity to engage in your usual work or incapacity to do work for which you are suited by education and training or incapacity to perform *any* work at all? Must you be confined to your home to receive benefits? (5) How long will you receive any benefits if you are disabled? (6) Is there provision for waiver of premium in the event of long total disability? (7) Are there any other benefits outside of payment for loss of time, such as payment of hospital bills, medical fees, nursing expenses, etc.?

Remember in buying disability insurance, to consider any disability income to which you may be entitled from your employer, the state law, and Social Security. Also check your life insurance policies, which may contain disability income provisions.

7. Premiums are most economical when you mail an annual check. Paying an agent or in monthly installments means added charges.

In conclusion, your doctor may be able to help you decide on the policy best suited to the family's needs.

MEETING MEDICAL EXPENSES AFTER MEDICAL CARE INSURANCE IS USED UP

Expenses can be reduced by following these economies:

Use semiprivate or even ward facilities instead of a private room unless there are medical reasons for a private room.

A private nurse at home may cost less than the cost of care at a hospital. Perhaps even the services of a visiting nurse might be adequate.

If recuperation will take time, a nursing home may offer adequate facilities at a cost considerably less than that of a hospital.

Diagnostic services or therapy may be obtained at a lower cost on an outpatient basis.

DENTAL INSURANCE

The inclusion of dental costs in health insurance plans is not yet widespread. The slow development of dental insurance coverage is unfortunate since the cost of treatment is a constant and heavy expense for most families. Insurance is generally still confined to certain group plans of unions, employers, and communities.

Chapter 14

SOCIAL SECURITY, A FEDERAL INSURANCE PROGRAM

Social Security is much more than a governmental system of providing senior citizens with retirement benefits. It provides insurance protection for the growing family if the breadwinner dies, disability benefits for the seriously ill, the injured or disabled, and, of course, pension benefits and medical care at retirement as well as death benefits.

Because the law on Social Security is often changed, you should inquire at the local office for details of current benefits and requirements. The information given below is general and intended to alert you to aspects of the Social Security program. Confirmation of your personal standing and current law that may be applicable must be sought.

ARE YOU WITHIN THE SOCIAL SECURITY SYSTEM?

You probably are. At one time coming within the Social Security system was a problem to many workers and their dependents. But current laws extend coverage to almost all citizens and resident aliens.

What is your Social Security status? You must work for a required period of time in covered employment to obtain an insured status. The required time depends on your age or the date of your retirement, death, or disability. If you have worked for at least 10 years in covered employment, you are fully insured, regardless of your age. If you have not, you may still qualify under one of several tests which give insured status even if you have less than 10 years in covered employment. There are two types of coverage, currently insured status and fully insured status.

Currently insured status protection is designed for the benefit of the families of those who die without having enough coverage to qualify for retirement benefits. Currently insured status is achieved when you have at least six quarters of coverage, generally during a period of over three years and one quarter before death.

If you have currently insured status, your children and the mother who cares for them receive the following insurance benefits on your death:

1. Children's benefits. On your death, Social Security pays survivor benefits to:

Your unmarried children under 18

Your unmarried children who are full-time students under 22

Your unmarried children 18 or over who are totally disabled because of a physical or mental impairment suffered before they became 22.

2. Mother's benefits. Your widow receives benefits if she cares for your child (except generally students over the age of 18 entitled to benefits on their own).

3. Lump-sum death benefits. Paid to your widow.

Fully insured status. If you have fully insured status, you and your family may receive retirement and disability benefits, and your family also receives protection in case of your death. Here, briefly, are the benefits available to fully insured workers and their families.

1. Your retirement benefit when you retire or reach the age of 62 or over.

2. Your wife's retirement benefit when she reaches 62. If she is under 62 when you retire, she can receive benefits only if she cares for your child who is under 18 or who was totally disabled before 22. But you must be 62 or over and receiving benefits in order for her to receive retirement benefits on your account.

3. Child's retirement benefits to any child of yours who is under 18 or who is a full-time student under 22, or who was totally disabled before 22.

4. If you die, benefits are paid to your widow when she reaches 60, or at age 50 if she is disabled.

5. Parent's survivor benefits at 62.

Disability protection. If you are unable to earn a living because of illness or injury after you are fully insured, you and your family receive the following benefits:

Disability benefits for you.

Wife's benefits to your wife if she is aged 62 or over or

Mother's benefits to your wife (of any age) if she is caring for your child under age 18 or for a disabled child of any age.

Child's benefits to your unmarried children who are under 18, and to those between 18 and 22 who continue in school or college, and to disabled children of any age while they remain disabled.

SOCIAL SECURITY AND YOUR PLANNING

For many, Social Security is a necessary mainstay of their income in their retirement years. But if you have been accustomed to more than the minimum needs in housing, food, recreation, and clothing, the benefits of Social Security cannot be the sole financial basis in your planning for retirement. They will be inadequate to meet a large part of your basic needs. Even though Social Security benefits may be increased periodically, the retired person cannot yet rely on this system for full financial support. At present, a substantial savings account and income from investments are a necessity for maintaining a good standard of living.

The Social Security law was set up in such a way that a person could receive any amount of income from sources other than work (from investments, for example), and not lose a cent of Social Security retirement benefits to which he or she was entitled. But if that person had so little other income that Social Security benefits at retirement were insufficient, earnings from a job might be necessary. Yet if earnings exceed a specified amount part or all of Social Security benefits would be lost.

You need to keep abreast with changes in respect to this earnings ceiling. New law has raised the amount that can be earned without loss of Social Security benefits; the ceiling may eventually be eliminated entirely. In the meantime, you have to reckon with the fact that the law favors the Social Security beneficiary who has investment income and discriminates against the retired person who has to make ends meet by working.

No reduction in benefits in made for earnings of those 72 or over. However, in the year a person becomes 72, he may lose benefits for excess earnings in the months in which he was under 72.

Benefit loss due to wages or self-employment income above a specified amount is not permanent. All or part of the payments are reinstated as soon as income earned through working drops below the current ceiling.

THE AMOUNT OF YOUR SOCIAL SECURITY BENEFITS

Benefits are calculated by averaging the amount of your earnings subject to Social Security taxes during a certain period. To get maximum benefits, you have to consistently earn the maximum amount subject to Social Security tax during the period for which wages are averaged. In this book, it is not practical to explain the somewhat complicated method of averaging benefits, which over the years has been subject to change. If you are interested in finding the amount of your benefits, we suggest you contact your local Social Security office for advice, and for the excellent pamphlets available that explain the Social Security system and its operation.

Do not overlook the importance of Social Security in planning your life insurance program if you have young children. Consider the fact that Social Security would provide benefits to your children if they are minors, disabled, or are attending school up to the age of 22. In addition, you wife would receive benefits as long as the children are under her care. Here, if you had been earning an amount equal to or exceeding the maximum amount subject to Social Security taxes, your family might be entitled to over $400 a month in benefits. Depending on your family's needs, you should plan to supplement Social Security income with funds coming from insurance, savings, and other investments. Also to be considered is the "blackout period" which is placed on a widow between the time her youngest child reaches the age limit when benefits for the child and herself cease and the time she reaches 60 years of age. During that time she would have to earn unless you otherwise provided for her.

KEEP A RECORD OF YOUR CREDITS

At least once every four years, you should mail Form OAR-7004 to the Social Security Administration, Baltimore, Maryland 21235, requesting a statement of the wages credited to you. You may secure this form at the local Social Security Agency (for address, look in your telephone book), or you may write a request for the form to headquarters in Baltimore.

YOU MUST ACT TO COLLECT YOUR SOCIAL SECURITY

You cannot collect Social Security without applying for it. The government is not obligated to remind you of your rights to benefits. All you have to do is write to, telephone, or go to your local Social Security office for information. Social Security personnel will try to help you. Their objective is to give you your full benefits under the law.

MEDICARE

Most Americans age 65 or over are eligible for Medicare. Medicare consists of two parts. Part A covers hospital insurance. If you are entitled to Social Security or Railroad Retirement benefits you are automatically eligible for Part A. The hospital insurance covers most of your hospital expenses for up to 90 days. You also have a "lifetime reserve" of 60 additional days after the 90-day coverage has been used up.

Medicare Part B covers medical insurance. It is voluntary. Before July 1973, the law called for enrollees to sign up for coverage within specified periods. Starting July 1973, those entitled to hospital benefits under Medicare are automatically enrolled for Part B unless they decline coverage. Others have to meet special provisions. Ask your local Social Security office about Part B coverage before you reach age 65. There is a monthly premium for Part B coverage which is deducted from your Social Security check.

Chapter 15

TAX PLANNING AIDS TO INCREASE
YOUR AFTER-TAX INCOME

Income taxes are inevitable, and for most taxpayers, a very heavy annual expense. Year after year, they cut deeply into income. Perhaps the regularity of income tax and the fact that its terms are couched in complicated legal language has made you fatalistic about your ability to reduce your tax burden.

"What can I really do?" you ask. "Taxes are withheld from my pay, tax rates are increasing without the prospect of significant reductions. The government utilizes data processing systems to check my return so that everything I receive is noted and reported. What can I do but prepare my tax return and pay the tax?" But your personal and economic life are not static. Income and family relationships do change. You can change your prospects and sources of income. As these events occur, you may have an opportunity to reduce your tax liability. And even if your income is fixed, your present approach to your tax liability may be inadequate. You may be failing to keep adequate records of tax reducing items and be unaware of tax law benefits you can apply to reduce your tax.

Only you can take the steps necessary to reduce your taxes. The

Internal Revenue Service has no obligation to tap you on the shoulder and say, "Mr. Taxpayer, you have been overpaying your taxes because you have not taken advantage of these provisions."

The complexities of the tax law require more than the space of this chapter for explanation; moreover, there are changes year by year. But here you will find basic approaches to income tax savings.

KEEP RECORDS

Record keeping is an essential part of your all-around tax planning. Your detailed records will help you figure your income and deductions at the end of the year. Do not trust to memory. With bills accumulating during a year, you are bound to overlook items. But more important, you will have no record to present to the IRS if they should call you down. Reprinted in this chapter is a sample of the type of record book you can keep to ease your tax-recording chores. It replaces your checkbook stubs and, as you write checks, allows you to list deductible items in addition to other major items that you may want to record.

Make a rule to keep a detailed record of any expense ordinary and necessary to the production of income. Keep bills for investment, legal, or tax counsel, or for rent of a safe deposit box. Legal or accounting fees paid for advice on investments are tax deductible. Also deductible are costs involved in the preparation of a tax return.

When you hold property as an investment, keep statements of expenses pertaining to maintenance, management, or conservation of the property. You may deduct these even if there is no probability that the property ever will be sold at a gain or produce income. Included in such expenses are: (1) Investment counsel fees or commissions. (2) Custodian fees paid to banks or others. (3) Auditors' and accountants' fees. (4) Traveling costs for trips away from home to look after investments, conferring with your attorney, accountant, trustee, or investment counsel about tax or income problems. (5) Maintenance costs of idle property where effort has been made to rent or sell.

Good record keeping applies particularly to rental property. Because there are many deductible expenses involved, record keeping is extremely important. You must have a complete record of the cost of the property, including legal fees, title insurance, the date the property was acquired, the date and cost of each material alteration or addition. The records you must keep during each year include:

1. Amount of rental income received.
2. Bills paid for utilities (heat, light, water, gas, telephone).
3. Bills paid for repairs (painting, cleaning, papering, redecoration).
4. Property taxes.
5. Management expenses.
6. Salaries and wages paid to janitors, elevator men, service men, maintenance men, etc., and Social Security taxes paid on their wages.
7. Legal expense for drawing short-term leases, dispossessing tenants, acquiring rentals.
8. Fire, liability, plate-glass insurance premiums.
9. Interest on mortgage or other indebtedness.

That you rent only one-half of your house, or one room out of eight, doesn't change the need for a record of every item. In renting part of your house, you may deduct a proportionate part of the expense of running the house against the rental income. You do not know what to deduct unless you have a record of all the expenses. On the same statement, you can keep an explanation of the basis of the apportionment you use for the tax return.

Even if you occupy the house you own and do not rent any part of it, you are entitled to certain of the deductions listed above. You should keep a record of taxes, interest, and casualty losses for your tax deduction list.

Canceled checks are adequate proof of contributions you make, which are deductible. But contributions may be in forms other than cash. Keep a record, therefore, of the cost of articles you purchase and give to charitable or religious organizations. This may include such items as donations of food baskets, contributions to bazaars, preparation of food for charitable dinners or picnics. Or if you give household or miscellaneous articles to recognized charitable, religious, educational, or similar organizations (such as Red Cross or a hospital), establish a fair-market value of the property you give and keep a list of the contributions.

If your work involves travel, you should keep a day-by-day record of expenses.

If you have purchased appliances, an auto, or other goods or services on the installment plan, keep a record of the interest portion of your payments.

For dividend and interest income from stocks and bonds or for trading investments, keep a record of: (1) Name of issuing company. (2) Number of shares or bonds owned and certificate or serial number of each. (3) Date of purchase. (4) Amount paid (including stamp taxes and broker's fees). (5) Date of sale. (6) Amount received (net after stamp taxes and broker's fees). (7) Broker's statements. (8) Each dividend or interest payment received.

You may hold a number of shares of stock of the same company purchased at different times at varying prices. If you wish to sell some of them the question of whether you have a gain or a loss and whether short-term or long-term depends on which particular securities you sell. If you cannot identify each particular lot and its cost, the law will assume that the shares you are selling are those you first acquired. This may be contrary to what you really wish. Consider the case of an investor who didn't bother to keep the certificate numbers of the various shares he bought from time to time. When he sold some of the stock in a declining market, he thought he was selling shares he had bought at a high price and was therefore taking a tax loss, but when an agent of the Internal Revenue Service questioned the deduction, he couldn't prove which shares he had sold; he didn't have any records. The result was that the agent ruled he had sold shares that had been bought cheaply. Instead of taking a tax loss that he needed to offset other income, he realized a taxable gain in a top tax year.

Here are some pointers to help you avoid this trouble:

1. Keep a record of each certificate registered in your name. The date it was acquired, the certificate number, and any other identification should be recorded. How it was acquired should be shown. Then, when it is sold, you can identify the particular certificate number sold. You need not sell the earliest acquired shares first.

2. If the certificate numbers are unknown, you should inform your broker (and have him confirm) that you wish to sell particular lots. The broker should be told the date of purchase. If possible, the original purchase memorandum should be referred to, giving date and number.

3. If the certificates were received as a stock dividend or in the exercise of rights, the date they were issued should be recorded. The date the option was exercised, the numbers, and other information

| | | | RECORD OF DEPOSITS | | | | | | RECORD OF CHECKS |

Date	Source of Items Deposited	Amount of Each Deposit Item	Amount of Total Deposit	Amount	Check No.	Date	To Whom Paid	Explanation
	Opening Balance		$	$				
		$						
1	TOTAL OF OPENING BALANCE PLUS DEPOSITS	$						
2	LESS: TOTAL EXPENDITURES						BANK CHARGES	
3	BALANCE CARRIED FORWARD	$		$			TOTAL MONTHLY EXPENDITURES	

xes	Interest	Medical & Drugs	Contri-butions	Other: Job Costs Tax Help, etc.	Insurance	Savings & Invest.	Home: Utilities, Repairs, etc.	Personal: Food, Clothing, etc.	Auto & Trans-portation		
$	$	$	$	$	$	$	$	$	$	$	$
	$	$	$	$	$	$	$	$	$	$	$

should be noted. When a sale is ordered, this data should be referred to precisely and the dealer given the facts.

4. When new certificates for old are received in a recapitalization or in a reorganization, each particular certificate should be identified with the old certificate. This is done by taking the lowest numbered certificate of the new and identifying it with the lowest numbered certificate of the old. Then the next higher numbers are correlated. When finished, all the new certificates should be correlated with the old certificate numbers.

5. All brokers' and dealers' purchase and sales memoranda should be kept, together with all notices or slips from the corporation whose securities are held.

Your records should be kept for a minimum of three years after the year to which they are applicable. Some authorities advise keeping them for six years, since in some cases the IRS may go back as far as six years to question a tax return. In cases of suspected tax fraud, there is no time limitation at all.

BASIC PRINCIPLES

You should know the answers to these basic questions about income tax: What income is taxable? What is not taxable? What expenses or other items are deductible from your taxable income? What are the effects of graduated income tax rates? What is capital gain income?

Income. Your common-sense idea of what constitutes income probably approximates the tax law definition of income. Income is the payment made for labor (wages, salaries, commissions), for capital investments (dividends, interest), and for business or partnership profits. Income also includes gain on the sale of property. Most of what you receive for your work or from investment is taxed. But the following type of receipts are generally not taxed: Gifts and inheritances, Social Security benefits, employee death benefits up to $5,000, scholarships, accident and health benefits, certain employee fringe benefits, sick pay up to certain limits, most life insurance proceeds, and interest from state and local government obligations and bonds.

Everyone is allowed to reduce this income total by exemptions for his dependents and for himself.

Deductions. A deduction is an item that reduces income subject to tax. Deductions may be divided into two types: (1) Money spent in order to earn your income. (2) Money spent for personal reasons (not connected with earning income), but which the law allows as deductions.

The first class of expenses are such costs as business travel and entertainment, management fees, depreciation of equipment used to produce income, etc.

The second class includes a mixed group of items: Charitable contributions up to a certain amount, medical expenses, alimony paid, interest, taxes, loss of personal possessions by casualty or theft.

Credits are somewhat like deductions, but they are more advantageous. A credit is deducted from your tax, dollar for dollar, whereas a deduction reduces income subject to tax. Credits are available for certain retirement income, political contributions, income taxes paid to foreign countries, and purchases of assets used in business.

Income tax rates. Income tax rates are based on a graduated scale. As your income increases, your tax increases. Tax planning attempts to avoid the effect of graduated rates in several ways: (1) A taxpayer may try to split his income among family members instead of reporting all his income on his own return, thus subjecting it to lower rates. He may give a family member some of his investments so that income from the investments is reported in a lower tax rate bracket of the family member. Income splitting requires the complete transfer of the investment property. You cannot split income by just assigning your wage, interest, or dividend income. For example, if you wanted to split dividend income with your son, you would have to give him the stock on which the dividend income is earned or place the stock in trust for a number of years.

(2) A taxpayer may try to postpone income to a time when his income from other sources decreases or he may want to accelerate certain income in a year when income from other sources may drop. For example, you may be due a large bonus in a year when your income is high. It would be tax-wise to defer the payment of the bonus to a year when your income is lower. Such deferment requires careful planning.

(3) A taxpayer may try to increase his deductions in a year his income is high. Conversely, if his income is low in a particular year,

he may try to postpone deductions to another year when his income will be higher.

Capital gains. Profits from sales of property (securities, real estate, land, etc.) held for more than six months are generally taxed at one-half of regular tax rates. For capital gain treatment, you generally have to show:

1. You have a capital asset or the kind of asset on which the gain qualifies as capital gain. For example, securities which you hold for investment are capital assets.

2. You sold or exchanged the property or the transaction was the kind that is treated as a sale or exchange. This presents no problem when you sell your property, for example, securities, real estate, etc. However, other kinds of dispositions that may not be sales may also qualify for capital gain treatment. For example, receipt of a lump-sum payment from a qualified pension or profit-sharing plan can be capital gain.

3. You have held the asset for longer than six months. Capital gains and losses are either short-term or long-term. This is an important distinction. Short-term capital gains do not qualify for capital gain treatment. Only long-term capital gains do. A short-term gain results from the sale or exchange of property held for six months or less; long-term gain after a holding period of more than six months. The line between long-term and short-term gain may be a matter of a day. One day past the six-month holding period gives long-term gain. Do not make a mistake and sell a day too early.

TAX RETURNS FOR YOUR CHILDREN

Your minor child is a separate taxpayer. His income is not included in your tax return. When he files a return, he has the same exemptions and deductions as any taxpayer, including the standard deduction, which is, however, subject to a restriction discussed below. If his withholdings are not equal to his tax, he is required to pay the difference. If withholdings are in excess of his tax, he gets a refund. He is entitled to the benefit of a personal exemption on his own return even if he actually received more than half his support from you and you also claim him as an exemption.

This is the restriction on your minor child's right to use the standard deduction: If you are entitled to claim a dependency exemption for your minor child (or a child who is a full-time student), he may apply the standard deduction (or the low income allowance) only to his earned income such as salary or wages. He cannot use the deduction to set off unearned or investment income such as interest, dividends, trust earnings, and capital gains. Further, if you are entitled to claim a dependency exemption for him, he must file his own return if his gross income is $750 or more. Otherwise, an unmarried minor child would not have to file a return until his gross income reached $2,050.

In figuring a minor's gross income, long-term capital gains are included in full—at 100 percent. For example, if the minor has no other income except a long-term capital gain of $750, he must file a return. But he would owe no tax. Here are some important points to consider:

You can claim an exemption for a child earning any amount if he is under 19—or a full-time student of any age—and you furnish more than half of his support. In addition, the child gets an exemption for himself on his own return, if he has to file one.

Pay for work done by a child is included on his separate return— not that of his parent or guardian. This is so even though the parent makes the contract of employment and gets the wage, and regardless of the local state law governing the earnings of a minor.

You may employ your minor child in your business or income-producing activity and pay him a reasonable salary for services actually rendered. That gives you a deduction for the fair pay you give him, plus the exemption you get for supporting him if he is under 19 or a student. On top of that, he gets a personal exemption and is taxed in a very low bracket. Although your child may not be required to file a return, he may want to file to get a refund of any taxes withheld on his pay.

Keep records of the payments to your children who work for you. Family relationship is no excuse for not keeping records. A lack of records may jeopardize the wage deduction.

If your child pays you for board and lodging, the payments probably are not income to you. The amount contributed by the child is usually less than the cost of his board. If the child worked for you, you cannot take a deduction for board and lodging you provide— unless the child has been freed from your parental control.

A child may be self-employed (a newsboy over 18, for example) and have income of $400 or more. He must pay self-employment

Social Security tax even though no income tax is due. For that purpose only he must file a return. You may still claim him as a dependent if he is under 19 or a full-time student and you meet the support test. If he is over 19 and not a student, you claim him as a dependent only if he earns less than $750.

When a child owes income tax but is unable to file a required return, the law makes his parent or guardian responsible. If necessary, he may sign the return for the child. Furthermore, a parent is liable for tax due on pay earned by the child for services, but not on investment income.

TAX SAVINGS FOR MARRIED COUPLES WHO FILE JOINT RETURNS

A married couple filing a joint return pays less tax than a single person who reports the same amount of income. Joint return tax rates are based on the assumption that a married couple shares equally the income reported on the joint return. However, you do not have to give your spouse any income to file a joint return. You merely prepare one tax return reporting the income and deductions belonging to both of you. If your spouse has no income or deductible expenses, you report your income and deductions. You then figure your tax using the joint return rates and both you and your spouse sign the return.

However, note that joint returns do not always reduce taxes. Separate returns may be advisable when both of you have separate and comparatively equal incomes and one of you incurs and pays medical expenses. By filing separate returns, you can deduct a larger amount of the medical expenses.

TAX SAVINGS IN FAMILY INCOME PLANNING

Family income can be increased by the tax technique known as income splitting. You split income by spreading income now taxed in your top tax bracket among the lower tax brackets of your children or other relatives.

Assignment of income alone does not shift tax liability. You must give away the property that produced the income, such as stocks, United States bonds, mutual fund shares, and rental property. For example, an owner of a service station made a gift to his parents of the right to collect rent from the station and notified the tenant to pay the rent directly to them. But he retained title to the property, paid the property taxes, and deducted depreciation. He did not report the rent income on his tax return, claiming the income belonged to his parents. A court held he had to pay tax on the income since he did not transfer the property.

How to give securities to a child. Purchase of securities through custodian accounts provides a practical method for making a gift of securities to a child, eliminating the need for a trust. Gifts of securities to children under 21 can be made through a custodian account. The mechanics of opening a custodian account are simple. A parent can open a stock account for his child in a few minutes at a broker's office. He registers the securities in the name of a custodian for the benefit of the child. The custodian may be a parent, a child's guardian, grandparent, brother, sister, uncle, or aunt. In some states, the custodian may be any adult individual or a bank or trust company. The custodian has the right to sell securities in the account for the child, collect sale proceeds and investment income, and to use them for the child's benefit or reinvestment.

There are some limitations placed on the custodian. He cannot take proceeds from the sale of investments or income from investments to buy additional securities on margin. While he should prudently seek reasonable income and capital preservation, he generally is not liable for losses unless they result from bad faith, intentional wrongdoing, or gross negligence.

When the minor reaches 21 and property in the custodian account is turned over to him, no formal accounting is required. The child, now an adult, can sign a simple release freeing the custodian from any liability. But on reaching majority, the child can require a formal accounting if he has any doubts as to the propriety of the custodian's actions while acting as custodian. For this reason, and also for tax record keeping purposes, a separate bank account should be opened in which proceeds from sale of investment and investment income are deposited pending reinvestment on behalf of the child. Such an account will furnish a convenient record showing receipt of sales proceeds, investment income and reinvestment of the same.

As long as income from the custodian account is not used to support the child, income realized through the custodian account is taxed to the child, if taxed at all.

There is still an added income tax advantage. Even though the custodian accumulates a substantial amount of income for the ultimate benefit of the minor child, the child remains a dependent of the parent for tax purposes. On his Federal income tax return, the parent is still allowed a tax exemption for the child. That is so even if the giver of the securities is both the custodian and the parent of the child.

When setting up a custodian account you may have to pay a gift tax. The Treasury says a transfer of securities to a custodian account is a completed gift. But you are not subject to a gift tax if you properly plan the purchase of securities for your children's accounts. Each year, you can make gifts up to $3,000 to one person and be free of any gift tax. This $3,000 is called your *annual exclusion* and it is applied each year to as many people as you make gifts to. If your wife consents to join with you in the gift, you can give taxfree up to $6,000 to one person. All you need do is add her annual exclusion to yours. And even if your gift to one person is over the $3,000 or $6,000 limit, you may still avoid a gift tax. You can do this by applying part or all of your lifetime exemption of $30,000 against the excess of the gift over the annual exclusion. Here again, if your wife consents to the gift, you can apply a $60,000 lifetime exemption by adding her lifetime exemption to yours. By combining the annual exclusion and lifetime exemption, this year you can give up to $66,-000 taxfree to one person, as long as you have made no prior gifts which have been applied against the two lifetime exemptions.

If the custodian account is set up at the end of a calendar year, for example in December, another taxfree transfer of $6,000 can be made in the first days of January of the following year. In this way, a total of $72,000 is shifted within the period of one month. From this brief discussion, you can see that you have room in which to make gifts without running afoul of the gift tax.

As for the estate tax, the value of a custodian account will be taxed to your estate if you die while acting as custodian of an account before your child reaches 21. But remember, no estate tax is incurred if an estate is under $60,000 because of the $60,000 exemption. And if an estate is between $60,000 and $120,000 and the maximum advantage of the marital reduction is taken, the estate tax liability is eliminated. Furthermore, if there's a chance the custodian account will be taxed to your estate, you may avoid the problem by not naming yourself custodian but by naming someone else, for example, your wife.

SETTING UP A TRUST FOR YOUR CHILDREN'S COLLEGE YEARS

A trust can be set up to provide funds for your child's college education. In setting up the trust for your child, make sure that you will not be taxed on income used by the trust to pay for educational expenses. Under the tax law, where your legal obligation to support your minor child is discharged by a trust which you set up, you are taxed on income so applied by the trust to your child's support. Whether you are legally obligated to send your child to college is determined by the law of the state in which you live. The current trend of law recognizes that a father who is financially able to provide a college education for his children has an obligation to do so. This, however, does not mean that the law in your state has reached this conclusion. You will have to review this point with your attorney.

The issue of whether you are obligated to send your child to college might be avoided by setting up the trust when your child is young, say seven or under. You transfer property to a trust which is to continue until the child reaches college age—a period of at least 10 years. You also set up a bank account in the child's name to which trust income is paid, or invest the income in government bonds in the child's name. Before the child reaches college age, the trust ends and you receive back the trust property. When your child starts college, he begins to withdraw funds from the bank account or to cash in the bonds to pay his college expenses. Under this approach, the trust has not been used to pay the college costs directly, as it no longer exists. In setting up the trust, see that the trust deed does not state that income is for educational purposes if there is a danger that you may be held legally obligated to provide a college education.

TAX SAVINGS FOR INVESTORS IN SECURITIES

As an investor, you have a major tax advantage. Appreciation on investments you hold for more than six months is subject to low capital gains rates when you finally liquidate your holdings. This advantage alone would be sufficient to encourage investments. But certain types of investments bring additional advantages. Investments in tax-exempt bonds, for example, permit you to receive income without a tax cost. Tax on dividend income from domestic companies is reduced by the dividend exclusion, and is even taxfree from some companies under certain conditions.

Planning year-end tax saving strategy. First find your gain and loss position for the year. Then study how to minimize your tax liability or improve your investment position.

Any substantial change in the market during December may require fast action on your part to get the best tax break.

In organizing your survey, review the records of earlier years to find any capital loss to be carried over against this year's gains or ordinary income. Include nonbusiness bad debts as short-term capital losses. After you know the gains and losses already realized during this year from completed securities transactions, go over your paper gains and losses. What transactions might now be completed to:

Offset actual gains?
Utilize potential losses?
Step up the tax cost of your securities?
Improve your tax position for future years?

The following check list provides suggestions for deciding which securities to sell. If your completed security transactions show:

Long-term gain. You might avoid taking any losses this year and pay capital gains tax on these gains. If you want to realize losses, sell securities giving long-term losses.

Short-term gain. You might realize losses to offset these gains that would be taxed at ordinary income tax rates. Sell securities giving long-term losses to offset these gains.

Long-term loss. You might consider realizing gains which would be offset by these losses. Sell securities giving short-term gain. Net long-term capital losses in excess of short-term capital gains are subject to this limitation: Only 50 percent of the net long-term loss is deductible from up to $1,000 of ordinary income. Therefore, to take full advantage of the loss, it is advisable to realize short-term gains.

Short-term loss. You might consider realizing short-term gains to offset these losses. In planning the extent of your sales, note that short-term losses up to $1,000 may be deducted in full from ordinary income.

Net long-term gain and net short-term loss. You might sell securities giving short-term gain up to the amount of short-term loss.

Net short-term gain and net long-term loss. If the long-term loss is equal to the short-term gain, you might consider no further transactions, as the loss eliminates the gain. If short-term gain exceeds the net long-term loss, you might sell securities to realize long-term loss to the extent of the excess. If the long-term loss exceeds the short-term gain, you might sell securities to realize short-term gain up to the extent of the excess loss.

Remember, these guides consider only the tax consequences of your security planning. You must weigh also the investment value of your stock and general market and economic conditions. If you are interested in a security because of its long-term potential, you might hold off buying until late in December or perhaps in January of the following year for possible lower price purchase at the later date due to year-end selling.

Realizing losses may pose a problem if you believe the security is due to increase in value sometime in the near future. The wash sale rule prevents you from taking the loss if you buy 30 days before or after the sale. If you believe the security will go up, but not immediately, you can sell now, realize your loss, wait 31 days, then recover your position by repurchasing before the rise. You can hedge by repurchasing similar securities immediately after the sale provided they are not substantially identical. They can be in the same industry, of the same quality, etc. Check with your broker for advice.

In planning year-end sales, watch the deadline for recording sales. The deadline depends upon whether you have a gain or loss and are on the cash or accrual basis. When you buy and sell securities through a registered stock exchange, the holding period starts on the day after the "trade date" although you do not pay for and receive the securities until the "settlement date" several days later.

The reason for the intervening days is that stock exchanges do not require delivery and payment to be made until the third or fourth full business day after the day on which a sale or purchase is ordered. Often the period may be longer because of intervening holidays.

Although this stock exchange practice does not affect the tax consequences of security transactions made during the year, it can seriously alter the timing of gain taken at the end of the year. Because of the holiday season, the settlement date of a sale ordered a week before the end of the year may occur in the next year with this result: A gain which you wanted to report this year is taxable next year. The reason: As a cash basis taxpayer you do not realize gain until you actually or constructively receive payment, that is, on the settlement date. Generally, stock exchanges give advance notice of the last trading date on which profit-seeking sales can be made for the year. In December, look for the date so that you can properly time your profitable sale orders. As for losses, you need not be concerned with this particular timing problem. You can sell until the last business day of the year and realize your losses regardless of the settlement date.

WAYS TO SAVE TAXES

1. Claim all your exemptions. The more exemptions you have, the less tax you pay as each exemption reduces your taxable income. Exemptions are not divided or prorated, so even if you got married on the last day of the year, you claim your wife as a full exemption. There is no limit on the number of dependents you can have on your tax return as long as they meet these tests: (a) Your dependent is a close relative such as a child or parent, or a person who has made your home his principal residence for the entire year as a member of your household. (b) You contribute more than one-half of the dependent's support. (c) Your dependent's gross income for the year is less than $750. However, if the dependent is your child under 19 years of age, or a full-time student, then the amount of his income doesn't matter.

2. If you receive payments from an employer of a deceased parent, relative, or friend who made you his beneficiary, these sums are taxfree up to $5,000 if they were paid because of the deceased's death and he did not have a nonforfeitable right to the payment while he was alive. Check these two points with the company paying you the benefit.

3. Claim the dividend exclusion on dividend income you received. You get a dividend exclusion by reducing the dividend income by $100. If your wife also earns dividend income, she has her own $100 exclusion, so on a joint return your exclusion can be as high as $200.

4. Distinguish between the different types of dividend payments

you get from your mutual fund investments. Mutual funds generally pay their shareholders three kinds of dividends: (a) Ordinary dividends which are fully taxed but entitled to the dividend exclusion. (b) Capital gain dividends which are taxed at low capital gain rates. (c) Return of capital proceeds which are not taxable. Check your mutual funds annual statement; it will tell you what percentage of your receipts fits into each of these three categories.

5. Generally, you do not report as taxed income common-stock dividends or stock rights received on common stock. You pay no tax unless shareholders had a choice of taking either cash or stock, or some common stockholders received a dividend in preferred and others in common stock. In other words, you include the common stock dividend in income where there was a cash election or where others received a dividend in preferred stock. Usually, the company's statement will tell you whether the dividend is taxfree.

6. Investments in securities offered by state and local governments give you an opportunity to receive tax-free income. You can compare the value of tax-exempt interest to taxable interest for your tax bracket by using this formula:

Tax-exempt interest return $= E$
Taxable interest (to be found) $= T$
Your tax bracket $= B$

$$T = \frac{E}{1 - B}$$

Example:

You are deciding between a tax-exempt bond and a taxable bond. You want to find which will give you more income after taxes. You have a choice between a tax-exempt bond paying 5 percent and a taxable bond paying 6 percent. Your tax bracket is 36 percent.

Using the above formula, you find that the tax exempt is a better buy in your tax bracket as it is the equivalent of a taxable bond paying 7.8 percent.

$$T = \frac{.05}{1 - .36}$$
$$T = 7.8\%$$

Despite the income tax shelter offered by tax-exempt bonds, you should carefully weigh these disadvantages of tax exempts. The market for tax exempts is not as large as the market for stock. If you buy a small lot, you may be unable to find an immediate purchaser for your holdings if and when you want to liquidate. And, too, prices of tax exempts vary with the fluctuation of the basic interest rates and the supply and demand of tax exempts. In other words, there is the possibility that at the time you might be forced to sell a bond for current funds, you may not receive the full amount you paid for the bond.

7. You have a tax saving election with United States savings bonds. You can report the annual interest by merely including it on your tax return each year, or you can wait to report the interest in the year you finally redeem the bonds. The latter method can help you build up the value of E bonds during your lifetime without tax.

8. Apportion home expenses if you use part of your residence as an office. Then deduct the household expenses apportioned to your business. Any reasonable plan of apportionment will be approved, allowing you to deduct the cost of heat, light, telephone, insurance, and depreciation fairly apportioned to the office. Your apportionment might be based on the ratio of the number of rooms devoted to your office to the total number of rooms in the house.

9. Installment reporting of a sale of property can cut the immediate tax due on the profit made on the sale. It can also help you spread the tax payment over future years. You can use the installment sale method whenever you sell personal property for a price of more than $1,000 or real estate for any price. You do not have to receive payments in the year of sale. But if you do, they must be 30 percent or less of the sale price.

10. Make sure you deduct debts due you in the year they become worthless. Unless you deduct them in that year, you lose the deduction. In fixing the year a debt became worthless, you must show that the debt had no value because, for example, the debtor went bankrupt or disappeared in that year.

11. If you have an endowment policy that is going to mature in the near future, you have a tax-saving election. If you take an annuity option before the policy matures or within 60 days after maturity, you pay no tax on the matured policy. You pay tax only during the years you receive annuity payments. If you wait more than 60 days after maturity to make the election, you pay tax on the matured policy.

12. You do not report gifts or bequests you have received. Gifts,

bequests, and inheritances are taxfree. However, income you receive from such property after you own it is taxable.

13. You do not report as income any insurance proceeds you receive as beneficiary of a deceased relative or friend. However, if you receive the proceeds in installments, you may have to pay tax on the interest paid on the principal. A surviving spouse receiving installments has an annual exemption for interest up to $1,000.

14. You can deduct donations to religious, charitable, and educational institutions. A contribution need not be in cash. You may deduct up to 30 or 50 percent of your adjusted gross income, depending on the type of donation and the type of charity you give to. Giving a charity appreciated real estate or securities held long-term permits you to get a deduction of up to 30 percent of your adjusted gross income for the full market value of the donation while avoiding tax on unrealized profit (the difference between the cost basis of the property and its market value).

If you do voluntary work for a charitable organization without pay, you can deduct as charitable contributions your unreimbursed commutation expenses to and from the charity's place of operation. As a measure of your auto costs, you can use a rate of 6 cents a mile. However, you cannot deduct the value of your services.

15. If you receive a large amount of income in one year, see if you can reduce your tax by averaging your income. You may even be entitled to average if your income has steadily increased over the last five years or if your wife has gone back to work, thereby raising your joint income. More specifically, you may average if your taxable income in a current year exceeds by more than $3,000 an amount that is ⅕ greater than the average of your taxable income in the four preceding years.

Averaging can apply to almost all types of income such as salary, dividends, interest, short-term and long-term capital gains, rental income, business or professional income, gambling winnings, and income received on gifts during the past four years and current year.

16. Deduct all interest you pay on your borrowings including all business, personal, and family debts. Interest on money borrowed to defray personal expenses, or money borrowed to purchase property is deductible. The debt need not be evidenced by a note or mortgage. But there are limitations on deductions for interest paid to carry investments.

17. "Finance charges" paid on revolving charge accounts and bank credit card plans are fully deductible. The Treasury now treats such charges as deductible interest. A separately stated interest charge on an installment purchase is also deductible. However, if the interest is not separately stated, and there is a fixed finance charge, you deduct as interest 6 percent of the average balance you owe during the year.

18. In figuring your medical expenses, be sure to include the medical bills which you have paid for your wife, children, and other dependents. You can deduct medical expenses of your children and other dependents even though they are not exemptions on your tax return. All you have to show is that you paid the expense and contributed more than one-half of their support.

19. You can deduct as medical costs the expenses of a trip prescribed to relieve a specific chronic ailment; for example, to remedy arthritis; or the cost of a trip to visit a specialist in another city. However, the costs of board and lodging incurred on an out-of-town trip are not deductible. The deduction is limited to the actual cost of transportation.

20. You might deduct some home improvements as medical expenses. An ailment may require you to install special facilities or equipment in your home such as an air conditioner, or an elevator to carry a heart patient upstairs. To get this deduction you must show that the equipment alleviates the illness and does not increase the value of your home.

21. Deduct as medical expense the cost of sending a mentally or physically handicapped person to a special school or institution that is designed to overcome or alleviate such a handicap. Such costs can cover teaching in Braille or lip-reading and the training and care of a mentally retarded person, including the cost of meals and lodging.

22. Deduct one-half of the insurance premiums paid for a medical care policy covering yourself, your wife, or your dependents. The maximum deduction cannot exceed $150. Premium costs exceeding $150 are deductible as a medical expense subject to the 3 percent of adjusted gross income limit.

Premiums are deductible if the insurance contract covers the payment of deductible medical care expenses. If it pays for other than medical care (such as for loss of income, or for loss of life, limb or sight), premiums are not deductible unless (1) the contract or a separate statement from the insurance company specifies what part of the premium is allocated to medical care, and (2) the premium allocated to medical care is reasonable in relation to the total premium.

23. Deduct the cost of courses you take to maintain your job skills. Include in this deduction not only the cost of courses you take but also travel expenses to and from a school which is away from your home city. Living expenses such as food and lodging while at school away from home can also be deducted. A regular course of study leading to a degree may be deductible if it does not prepare you for a different occupation or profession.

24. Deduct expenses incurred to produce or collect income. For example, you have investments in securities. You can deduct investment counsel fees, the rental fees of a safe deposit box to hold your securities, or the salary of an accountant you employ to keep track of your investment income.

25. Deduct the costs for preparing your Federal, state or local tax returns. This deduction covers not only the expenses of preparing your income tax return but also the expenses of defending your return in a Treasury examination.

26. You can recoup losses suffered from storms, fire, accident, or other casualties by claiming casualty loss deductions on your return. Your loss is generally the difference between the value of the property before and after the casualty. However, if you received any insurance, you must reduce your loss by any insurance received and also a $100 limitation for each casualty.

27. Deduct losses of property stolen from you. To insure the deduction you should get statements from witnesses who saw the theft, or police reports of persons breaking into your house or your car. When you suspect a theft, make sure you make a report to the police. Even though your report doesn't prove that a theft was committed, your failure to report is evidence that you are not sure that your property was stolen.

28. Use the correct tax rate schedule in figuring your tax. If you are married and file a joint return, use the joint return rates which give you the advantage of splitting income between yourself and your spouse. If you are unmarried and support dependents in your home, see if you are able to take advantage of the head of household rates. These rates give you about half the advantage that a married couple gets on a joint return. If your spouse died within the last two years,

you may still be able to use joint return rates as a surviving spouse if you have dependent children.

29. If you earned income from foreign investments, don't forget to take a tax credit for any foreign taxes that have been paid on your income. Generally, you will save money by claiming a credit rather than a deduction. A deduction is only partially offset against your United States tax, whereas a credit is deducted in full from your tax.

30. If you sold your residence for a profit, you do not have to pay tax if you buy or build another house (or acquire a cooperative apartment) at a cost at least equal to the sales price of the old house. However, make sure you buy and use your house within one year before or after you sell your old house. Or, if you build a new house, build and use the house within one year before or 18 months after you sell your old house.

31. If you are 65 or older and you sell your house at a gain, you may elect to avoid tax on gain attributed to the first $20,000 of the sales price of your house. To get the tax break, you must have used the house as a residence (and owned it) five out of the eight years preceding the sale.

32. Losses on the sale of a personal residence are not deductible. However, you might get a deduction by renting the house before you sell it. Rental usually converts the house to business property on which a deduction is available if you have to sell at a loss.

33. Convert dividend income into capital gain by selling the stock when the dividend is declared but not yet paid. The selling price reflects the dividend which becomes part of your profit. Be sure you make this sale before the record date of the dividend. If you still hold the stock on the record date of the dividend, you will not get tax savings when you sell the securities.

34. You can sometimes control the year of real estate income. Generally, the tax is due in the year that title to the property sold passes to the buyer. However, often you can control the year the title passes. For example, you intend to sell property this year but you figure that by reporting the profit next year it will cost you less in tax because you expect lower income next year. Plan to have title pass next year. But make sure you do not give the buyer possession this year. If you do, you will be taxed this year even though title doesn't pass until next year.

35. Don't lose a loss deduction on the sale of property to a relative such as a child or parent. The law disallows losses on sales to

close relatives even though the sale is in good faith or occurs through a public stock exchange and a family member buys equivalent property on the exchange.

36. If property you own has been condemned by a government authority to make way for a highway or for public works, you can avoid tax on profit realized on the condemnation. Do this by investing the condemnation award in other real estate. Be sure you make your investment within two years after the end of the year in which you realized the profit. If you cannot buy a replacement within the required time, ask your local District Director for an extension of time.

37. If you pay a maid or sitter to watch children or other dependents while you work, you may be able to deduct all or part of the wages you pay. You can claim up to $400 a month as an itemized deduction for home care of a child or children under 15, an incapacitated spouse, or incapacitated dependent relative. An unrelated dependent would also qualify if he lived with you for the entire year. The deduction also covers the expense of ordinary household service, not merely direct care of the child or dependent. But you must maintain a household which includes a child or incapacitated dependent in order to claim the deduction. The expenses of caring for children outside the home, as in a day care center, are included to the extent of $200 for one child, $300 for two, or $400 for three or more. Deductible expenses, including day care costs, cannot exceed $400 in any month. You claim the deduction whether you are married or single. If married, both spouses must work, unless one is disabled. Generally, the deduction is reduced by one dollar for each two dollars of income in excess of $18,000, and is eliminated when income reaches $27,600.

Expenses of caring for a disabled spouse must be set off by any tax-free disability payments he or she receives. Remaining expenses are deductible up to $400 a month. Similarly, care costs for a disabled dependent are reduced by the dependent's gross income (including tax-free disability pay) in excess of $750.

Note that you cannot deduct payments made to a dependent who makes his or her home with you, whether or not related, or payments made to the following relatives: (1) Child, stepchild, or grandchildren; (2) parent, stepparent, or grandparents; (3) nieces, nephews, aunts, uncles, related by blood; (4) brother, sister, stepbrother or -sister; (5) son- or daughter-in-law, father- or mother-in-law, brother- or sister-in-law.

38. Deduct expenses of moving to a new job location if you meet these tests: (1) Your new job location is at least 50 miles farther from your former home than your old job was. (2) You remain in the new locality as a full-time employee for at least 39 weeks during the 12 months immediately following your arrival. The time periods are measured from the date you arrive at the new location to begin work on a regular basis. If your employer reimburses you for expenses, you must include this amount in your income and then deduct your actual moving expenses. You may also deduct within certain limits the cost of househunting, temporary living quarters at the new location, and certain costs connected with the sale of your old home, the purchase of your new residence, or the breaking or acquiring of a lease. The ceiling on the deduction for these additional costs is $2,500 of which only $1,000 may be claimed for househunting and temporary living expenses.

You take the deduction whether you are starting a new position, being transferred, or beginning your first job. You also take the deduction if you are self-employed, but you must remain in the new locality for at least 78 weeks during the 24-month period following your arrival.

39. Costs for work clothes may be deductible, and the cost of cleaning and repairing them if: (1) They are specially required for your job and (2) they cannot be worn as ordinary streetwear. Tools and equipment you use on the job are also deductible. If the items last only one year, you can deduct their full cost in the year you buy them. Otherwise, you must depreciate them over their useful lives.

Chapter 16

DECIDE THE FUTURE OF YOUR
ESTATE NOW

We have been discussing money management and the current expenses of living. The eventuality of death and its effect on the finances of your family have been considered in the chapter on life insurance. Now we come to plans for the distribution of your estate. Many people tend to push this question aside—as if death itself can so be avoided; their failure to face the problem squarely often causes pain and expense to members of the family who should have been protected.

In this chapter, we will discuss your estate and the plans you can make, including the making of a will, followed by guidance on estate taxes. First, we will take up the question of joint property, which is sometimes used indiscriminately as a substitute for a will.

JOINT OWNERSHIP OF PROPERTY—
ADVANTAGES AND DISADVANTAGES

There are some sound reasons for joint ownership of property by married couples and relatives. Joint ownership is easy to arrange; title to the property is simply put into two (or more) names, jointly with a right of survivorship. Upon the death of the first to die, title immediately passes to the surviving owner without expense, delay, or legal entanglements; he or she has the right to immediate possession and control of the property. On the other hand, if the property is to pass on death by will, the will has to be proved valid by a court, and the individual named as executor in the will has to qualify to handle the estate and transfer title. Where there is no will, the deceased is said to have died intestate. In this case, to pass title from the deceased, a court has to appoint an individual as administrator of his estate. Property not in joint ownership passes from either the executor or administrator of the estate as the case may be, to the person entitled to take it. In joint ownership, title passes outside of the estate.

Some people, trying to avoid the costs of probate, think that arranging joint property ownership eliminates the need for a will altogether. But this maneuver may result in most unfortunate results because joint ownership does not adequately meet all the eventualities that take place after a death. In certain circumstances jointly owned property may pass to people the deceased did not intend to have the property.

Here is an example. A childless couple put all their property in joint names; neither made a will. The husband died in an automobile accident that left the wife seriously injured. A few weeks later, she, too, died. Because she was sole owner of the property for those weeks, all of it went to her brothers and sisters. Her husband's parents received nothing. Had the couple made a will they would have been able to distribute the property fairly between both families.

The popular notion that joint ownership frees property from estate tax is incorrect. *Under Federal estate tax law, it is presumed that all property held in joint names belongs to the owner who dies first.* Say the survivor in fact paid for, inherited or acquired, by gift or otherwise, the property which was held as joint property. Since the law presumes that the property belonged to the person who died, the estate will have to establish that no part of the value should be included in the deceased's estate for tax purposes.

For example, a husband buys property and puts title in his name and his wife's name as joint owners. On his death, the *full property,* not half, will be included in his taxable estate. But say the wife died first. The Federal government would probably claim that she was the owner of the property and consequently it is taxable in her estate. Her estate would have to establish that the husband alone bought and paid for the property out of his funds, and no part of the value of the property is taxable in the wife's estate.

That jointly owned property is liable to *increased* estate tax liability can be seen dramatically in this case: Over a period of years, the wife received over $40,000 from her parents. She turned all the money over to her husband so that he could invest it for her. He bought municipal "bearer" bonds on which the owner's name does not appear and placed them, together with his own securities, in a safe deposit box. This box was rented in the joint names of husband and wife.

The husband died and, as required by state law, a representative of the state tax commission was present when the safe deposit box was opened. The tax commission included the bonds in the husband's estate. The wife had no records to show that she was the true owner. Because she was the sole beneficiary, she ultimately recovered the bonds, but only after tax in her husband's estate had been paid on them.

We suggest that complete and accurate records should be kept of the contributions made from the personal funds of each owner when property is purchased or put into joint names.

Here is another danger which arises because jointly owned property automatically passes to the survivor. The executor or administrator of the estate generally cannot use that property to pay the taxes or debts of the deceased person. To raise needed cash, other estate assets may have to be sold, perhaps at sacrifice prices, to satisfy obligations.

Certain tax alternatives can be used to reduce estate taxes, but joint ownership may prevent their use. For example, a husband wisely sets up trust arrangements for the benefit of his wife and, ultimately, the children or other relatives. Estate tax in the husband's estate is avoided on the property so passing. Had the property been jointly owned it might have been subject to tax. Setting up joint ownership may make the property involved subject to Federal gift tax. But for most individuals, gift tax is not a problem because the tax is not imposed until gifts reach certain limits and, through proper planning, the gift tax can usually be avoided.

MAKING A WILL

Through a will you can direct who is to take your property and the amounts your beneficiaries are to receive. Without a will, state law will determine who should take your estate and the shares for each. Thus, people you did not intend to benefit may inherit; others whom you wished to share in the estate might receive a smaller share or none at all.

To prevent such an occurrence—and the ill feeling likely to arise, to say nothing of possible lawsuits—you need your own written will. Here, we have some very direct advice. Do not draw your own will! Have an attorney prepare it. If you do not have a regular attorney, contact a local bar association for recommendations. The fee for drawing a will is not large, and the experienced attorney charges no more than the inexperienced.

The purpose of the following discussion is to help you consider and decide what you want to achieve with your will. Once you have reviewed the extent of your property and your objectives, you can intelligently discuss your will with an attorney.

WHO ARE YOUR BENEFICIARIES?
WHAT DO YOU HAVE TO LEAVE?

Your first step is to *list your beneficiaries.* Write the names of your immediate family, your wife, your children (and their ages), your brothers and sisters, your parents. List other beneficiaries you may wish to remember such as a trusted friend, employees, your place of worship, your college, a medical, educational, or other philanthropic organization.

Many charitable organizations have similar names. Be careful that the correct titles go into your will. If you misname a charitable beneficiary, its identity may have to be decided by a court and the legal expenses involved will be a charge against your estate. List alternative charities in case those you name cease to function or cannot take your bequest.

Next, *list your assets*. Here, your review of your net worth and your household inventory (Chapter 2) will help you. Be sure that you have not overlooked a bank account or a bond bought many years ago. This is a common occurrence. Each year banks and other financial institutions list names of persons who have forgotten their accounts. You might also forget small jewelry or heirlooms, a valuable collection of stamps or coins laid aside many years ago.

What of the shares of stock you purchased years ago and put away? An investment or property not producing income now may seem of little value but in time it may become valuable. A business that you consider a sideline may become an asset which will put your estate into a high tax bracket. (See page 244 for further comments on listing assets.)

When you list properties, be sure they are really yours to give. Note that title to certain properties passes outside your will. Examples are property held with your wife either as joint tenants or as tenants by the entirety; insurance payable to a named beneficiary, even though for tax purposes it may be part of your gross estate; United States savings bonds held in your name but payable to another at your death; estates in which you had a life interest, after your death the remainder goes to another.

Do you have two residences, say, one in New York, the other in Florida? If so, list your possessions in the two states involved for your attorney. He will draw your will in accordance with the laws of the state in which the will must be probated. Generally, dispositions of personal property are controlled by laws of the state of your principal residence; real property, according to the laws of the state in which it is located. The laws of one state may be more beneficial for your estate than the other. Ask your attorney now what steps you can take to ensure that the disposition of your estate will be made in accordance with the laws of the state that gives the best treatment.

In making a will, your marital status must be considered. Some states, in certain circumstances, allow widows to elect to take the share of a husband's estate under the laws of intestacy in place of the bequest left under a will. In many states, the law protects the rights of adopted children and after-born children not named in a will to share in a parent's estate.

Your state's laws may provide your widow or children with homestead rights or give your widow the right to remain in your home for a certain length of time, with a sustenance allowance from your estate. If the laws of dower or curtesy are in force, they, too, limit your right of disposition over property. In most community property states, each spouse is limited in the portion of property that can be left by will to others.

There should be provision covering the possibility of death of both spouses in, for example, a plane or automobile crash. Your will could provide that if you and your wife die in a common disaster under such circumstances as to make it doubtful which died first, it should be presumed for purposes of the will that your wife survived. Such a provision could save the marital deduction. (See page 251.)

THE EXECUTOR OF YOUR ESTATE

If you leave no will, the court will appoint someone to administer your estate. He may not be acquainted with your family or sympathetic to their interests. With a will, you can select the person or persons you feel qualified to administer your estate. You may appoint your spouse, an adult child, or both to serve jointly as executors.

If the administration of your estate requires business or professional training and experience, consider appointing an attorney or a business associate as executor. It is possible that the person you name will become unable to perform his function as an executor. You may provide alternative names.

The executor may serve without bond if you so stipulate. This is usually the case when you name a member of your family as your executor.

Your executor is entitled to commissions for his services, generally computed on a percentage basis of the value of all your property and income that passes through his hands. The amount he receives is a deductible expense in computing your taxable estate. Commissions are fixed by local law, but you can provide in your will that your executor shall act without compensation or that he should have a specified allowance in place of statutory commissions. Your attorney will advise you how to handle your executor's commissions.

GUARDIANS FOR YOUR CHILDREN

Will you leave property to a child who is a minor? If so, name in your will a guardian of his property. If you do not, the court will appoint one. Although a parent is considered the natural guardian of the person of a minor, he is not the guardian of his property unless so named. If you name your widow as guardian of your child's property, provide an alternate in case she dies, or does not qualify to act. The duty of a guardian of property is to hold, manage, and conserve the property for the minor until he reaches the age of majority according to local law. You can name one guardian, or two or more persons to act jointly in this capacity.

REVIEWING YOUR WILL

Review your will periodically, especially when these events occur: Your family relationships change; you marry, separate, are divorced; your spouse dies; a child is born, dies or is adopted; a grandchild is born, dies or is adopted; your estate increases or decreases substantially; you acquire property in another state or abroad; you move to another state; you retire; inheritance and estate tax laws are changed.

Some changes in your will may only require a codicil; others may require a new will entirely. When executing a codicil, remember it must, like your will, be legally drawn and witnessed. Any handwritten or typed changes in your will or codicil will invalidate it. So, if you have a good will, do not spoil it. When you make a new will, follow your attorney's instructions on how to destroy the old one and any codicils to it.

In Chapter 2, we suggested the keeping of a record book that would show where important family papers are to be found. Once you have a will, you should certainly write down where it is kept. It is not recommended that the will be kept in your safe deposit box because the bank will seal the box as soon as it learns of your death. Yet immediate access to the will may be vital, especially if you have expressed wishes for certain funeral arrangements. It is suggested that the original will should be retained by your family lawyer who is always accessible. Alternatively, if you keep the original in the safe deposit box, a family member should know where a copy is placed. The copy may be sealed and marked "To be opened only on death" if you do not want the provisions known to anyone.

YOUR ESTATE AND FEDERAL TAXES

The estate of every deceased citizen or resident in this country is allowed an exemption of $60,000. If your estate does not amount to more than $60,000, Federal estate taxes will not be due, and no return need be filed. However (unless you live in Nevada and have no property elsewhere), your estate will probably be liable to a state death tax. (See page 246.)

Understand what the word estate means in the Federal estate tax law so that you do not underestimate the value of your taxable estate. The estate includes not only your real estate (foreign and domestic), bank deposits, securities, personal property and other more obvious signs of wealth, but can also include insurance, your interest in trusts, and jointly held property.

The estate tax is a tax on the act of transferring property at death. It is not a tax on the right of a beneficiary to receive the property; the estate and the estate alone pays the tax.

You cannot intelligently estimate what will remain for your family unless you consider estate taxes. To help you make an estimate of what will remain for your heirs, we offer this guide to Federal estate taxation. It will alert you to the cost of the estate tax, if any, and if you find that you have an estate subject to tax, to plans for estate tax savings that you may discuss with your attorney.

The listing of your assets was briefly discussed on page 241 in regard to making your will. If those assets are substantial, you will have to give a considerable amount of time and thought to estimate the value of your estate.

The first step in estate planning follows a simple business custom of taking inventory of everything you own.

Listing all belongings is admittedly an involved process. You must go over records of purchases, fire and theft insurance inventories, deeds, mortgages, bank books, brokers' statements, etc. You need to include your cash, real estate (here and abroad), securities, mortgages, rights in property, trust accounts, life insurance payable to your estate or payable to others if you have kept a certain measure of ownership, personal effects, collections and art works. (Life insurance is includable in your estate if it names your estate as beneficiary or, where payable to others, you have retained a certain interest in it that amounts to ownership under the law.) You should also list property you gave away recently. This is necessary since gifts made within three years of death may be subject to estate tax as having been made, under the law, "in contemplation of death."

If you own property jointly with your wife, list the entire value of the property unless you can establish that she invested her own funds in the property.

If you have had appraisals made of unusual or specially treasured items or those of substantial value, file such appraisals with your estate papers and enter the value on your inventory.

There are some assets that you might not ordinarily consider as part of your taxable estate. Nevertheless, include them in your inventory. For example, list trust arrangements in which you have kept (1) a life estate (the income or other use of property for life); (2) income that is to be used to pay your legal obligations (support of a child, for example); (3) the right to change the beneficiary or his interest (a power of appointment); (4) the right to revoke a trust transfer or gift; or (5) a reversionary interest (possibility that the property can come back to you).

FINDING THE VALUE OF YOUR ESTATE

When you have completed your inventory, assign to each asset what you consider to be its fair market value. This may be difficult to do for some assets. We all tend to overvalue articles which arouse feelings of pride or sentiment, and undervalue some articles of greater intrinsic worth. For purposes of your initial estimate, it is better to err on the side of overvaluation.

If you have a family business, your idea of its value and that of the Treasury may greatly vary. Many well-made estate plans have been upset by the higher value placed on such a business by the Treasury. You can protect your estate by anticipating and solving this problem with your business associates, accountant, and legal counsel.

If your business is owned by a close corporation, and there is no ready or open market in which the stock can be valued, get some factual basis for a figure that can be reported on the estate tax return. One of the ways to do this is by arranging a buy-sell agreement with a potential purchaser. This agreement must fix the value of the stock. Generally, an agreement that binds both the estate and the purchaser and restricts lifetime sales of the stock will effectively fix the value of the stock for estate tax purposes. Another way would be to make a gift of some shares to a family member, and have value established in gift tax proceedings. Unless there is a drastic change, the valuation thus established will have considerable weight in later estate tax proceedings.

You can list ordinary personal effects at nominal value.

A life insurance trust can serve two purposes: a tax-free transfer of wealth and liquidity of assets. Say your estate will consist principally of nonliquid assets. You effectively transfer the insurance on your life to an insurance trust. The proceeds are not taxed to your estate, but they provide the cash necessary to meet the estate tax liability. A forced sale of your nonliquid assets at a sacrifice price is avoided. Insurance funding combined with the stock purchase agreement above mentioned can provide the money with which the purchasers will buy the stock.

In addition to the $60,000 exemption, credit is allowed for state death taxes, for gift taxes paid on property includable in the estate, for taxes paid on prior transfers of property includable in the estate, and for foreign death taxes paid.

STATE DEATH TAXES

State death taxes are levied in all states but one, Nevada. Generally, they are levied against the estates of residents and on the property of nonresidents that is located within the state. Federal estate tax laws allow a limited credit for state death taxes paid, and states generally allow credit for taxes paid to other states having reciprocal taxing arrangements.

Intangible personal property, such as securities, is generally taxable by the state in which the decedent was domiciled at the time of his death, regardless of where the intangible property is located. Real estate and tangible property is usually taxed in the state wherein it is located.

Some states levy an estate tax, similar to the Federal tax, on the entire estate. Others levy a tax on the shares received by the beneficiaries, called an inheritance tax. Still others use both types and may also levy additional taxes on residents; some levy taxes on residents and nonresidents alike.

YOU ARE NOW READY TO ESTIMATE THE FEDERAL ESTATE TAX

Once the value of the estate has been determined, the next step is to compute the itemized allowable deductions against the gross estate. The balance will be your taxable estate. Follow these steps:

Gross estate (put in the value you estimated in your
　　inventory)　　　　　　　　　　　　　　　$＿＿＿＿＿＿

Less:

　　Administration expenses (executor's
　　　commissions, attorney's fees, etc.
　　　Estimate about 5% of your
　　　estate.)　　　　　　　　　　$＿＿＿＿

　　Debts, mortgages, liens　　　　＿＿＿＿

　　Funeral expenses　　　　　　　＿＿＿＿

Total deductions from gross estate　　　　　$＿＿＿＿＿＿

Adjusted gross estate　　　　　　　　　　　$＿＿＿＿＿＿

Less:

　　Marital deduction (put here property
　　　going to your wife. But the deduction
　　　cannot be more than 50% of adjusted
　　　gross estate.)　　　　　　　$＿＿＿＿

　　Charitable deduction (gifts to tax-
　　　exempt charities.)　　　　　＿＿＿＿

　　Exemption　　　　　　　　　$60,000

Total deductions from adjusted gross estate　$＿＿＿＿＿＿

Your taxable estate　　　　　　　　　　　$＿＿＿＿＿＿

Your estimated estate tax. (See estimated estate
　　tax rates below.)　　　　　　　　　　　$＿＿＿＿＿＿

RATES FOR ESTIMATING THE ESTATE TAX

| TAXABLE ESTATE | | | *Plus Following* | |
Over	But Not Over	Tax*	Percentage	Over
$ 0	$ 5,000	$ 0	3.%	$ 0
5,000	10,000	150	7.	5,000
10,000	20,000	500	11.	10,000
20,000	30,000	1,600	14.	20,000
30,000	40,000	3,000	18.	30,000
40,000	50,000	4,800	21.2	40,000
50,000	60,000	6,920	24.2	50,000
60,000	90,000	9,340	27.2	60,000
90,000	100,000	17,500	26.4	90,000
100,000	140,000	20,140	28.4	100,000
140,000	240,000	31,500	27.6	140,000
240,000	250,000	59,100	26.8	240,000
250,000	440,000	61,780	28.8	250,000
440,000	500,000	116,500	28.	440,000
500,000	640,000	133,300	31.	500,000
640,000	750,000	176,700	30.2	640,000
750,000	840,000	209,920	32.2	750,000
840,000	1,000,000	238,900	31.4	840,000
1,000,000	—	289,140	33.4	—

* The tax here is computed on the assumption that the state death or estate tax is equal to or more than the credit allowed by the Federal estate tax law. The net tax rate on estates exceeding $1,000,000 ranges from 33.4 to 61%.

© J. K. Lasser Tax Institute

To give you an idea of how an estate tax is computed, here is a simplified illustration: Assume the gross estate of an unmarried person is $200,000. There are debts, administration, and funeral expenses totaling $10,000, and charitable contributions of $10,000.

Gross Estate		$200,000
Less:		
Funeral and administration expenses, debts, etc.		10,000
Adjusted gross estate		$190,000
Less:		
Charitable deduction	$10,000	
Exemption	60,000	70,000
Taxable estate		$120,000
Estate tax due		$ 25,820

But see the difference in estate taxes when the person is married and leaves half his estate to his wife—all other figures being the same:

Gross Estate		$200,000
Less:		
Funeral and administration expenses, debts, etc.		10,000
Adjusted gross estate		$190,000
Less:		
Marital deduction	$95,000	
Charitable deduction	10,000	
Exemption	60,000	$165,000
Taxable estate		$ 25,000
Estate tax due		$ 2,300

REDUCING OR ELIMINATING A POTENTIAL TAX

Use these general approaches to eliminating or reducing a potential estate tax: Make direct lifetime gifts to remove property from your estate before it becomes subject to tax. Make a will in which you leave your property in such a way that will provide maximum tax savings for your estate, such as providing for the marital and charitable deductions.

ESTABLISHING A TRUST

Trusts are legal devices that have commonly been used by well-to-do people to protect certain money from high taxation or to safeguard the financial interests of members of the family. You can set up a trust to take effect during your lifetime or upon your death. It could be part of your will. Since a trust is generally treated as a separate taxpayer, it can serve as an income-splitting device. That is, if you are a high-income person who is heavily taxed, you can, through a trust, spread income from your property among several beneficiaries in lower tax brackets. A trust can also serve to delay the passing of title to property for a stated period, or for the lifetime of one or more income beneficiaries.

Trusts have been popularly recommended as a means to avoid probate. While it may be feasible in specific situations to use a lifetime trust in place of a will to pass property, this course should not be pursued without advice of a lawyer. Trusts are creatures of law, and the laws governing them are complex. You might believe that by establishing a trust you have saved money for your estate and at the same time arranged for property to pass safely to your beneficiaries. But if that trust was not properly drafted and used, it might not be valid to pass property. In consequence, costs you never anticipated might be charged against your estate. Possibly, too, beneficiaries might not receive the property you intended for them.

GIFT PLANNING

If you have a substantial estate that is subject to estate tax, your attorney may suggest you make gifts during your lifetime rather than leave your beneficiaries property for distribution at your death. Gift tax rates are about 25 percent lower than estate tax rates. This cost may be reduced even more through the offsets provided by the lifetime exemption of $30,000 and the yearly exclusion of $3,000 for each recipient. In fact, giving which coordinates timing and amounts with the special gift-splitting advantages allowed to married couples may avoid the gift tax altogether.

A well-planned gift program produces not only estate tax savings but also income tax savings. Gifts of income producing property that shift income from your higher tax brackets to the lower tax brackets of the recipient (whether an individual or a trust) bring about considerable tax advantage.

It may sound like a simple matter to give property away during your lifetime so that it is not included in your estate. But note these problems that arise when a gift-planning program is contemplated:

1. You may not want to give up control of your property during your lifetime. (You have to equate your reluctance to give up control with an estate tax rule which states that when you make a gift and still keep some control over it, the gift is part of your estate for tax purposes.)

2. You have to provide for future needs during your life.

3. The recipients of your gifts may be minors or persons otherwise not competent to manage property. (Gifts in trust can usually overcome this problem.)

4. The person you plan to benefit may already have large personal resources that will eventually be taxed in his own estate. (A gift

from you might reduce the tax in your estate but only at the expense of increasing his tax burden. Transferring the gift to a trust might avoid this possibility. For example, you could put the property into a trust giving one person the income during his life, with the principal passing to his children at his death. No Federal estate tax is paid on your death or at the death of the lifetime beneficiary, provided the lifetime beneficiary does not have the right to take any of the principal of the trust, or to revoke it or name other beneficiaries.)

After you have resolved these problems, time your gift-planning program with the gift tax law in mind. The gift tax law permits you to make tax-free gifts up to $3,000 to any number of individuals in any tax year ($6,000, when made together with your spouse), and in addition grants a lifetime exemption of gifts up to $30,000 ($60,000, husband and wife). The lifetime exemption may be used in any one year or spread over many years. When more than $3,000 is given to one individual in a tax year, a gift tax return must be filed. If gift tax is due, you pay at this time. Since gift tax rates are considerably lower than estate tax rates, it might prove to your advantage to discuss a program of lifetime gifts with your attorney in planning your estate.

THE MARITAL DEDUCTION

If you are married, the tax on your estate can be greatly reduced or even eliminated by the marital deduction. The law allows you to give your surviving spouse on your death up to one-half the value of your adjusted gross estate, taxfree.

To qualify for the marital deduction, the property must be given to the spouse outright or by other legal arrangements that are equivalent to outright ownership in law.

When a husband plans property arrangements for a marital deduction, he should ask himself the following questions:

1. How much property does your wife own? The marital deduction gives best tax results when a wife has less property than her husband. When she has an equal or greater amount, the husband's estate tax saving may be at the expense of her estate; the surviving children may be the losers.

2. What kind of property do you intend to leave your wife? To qualify for the marital deduction, property you leave your wife must

be left outright or in an equivalent manner. Where you leave a fractional share of your estate to her outright with no restrictions, few problems should arise. However, as a safety measure, your will and marital deduction plans should be periodically reviewed for technical disqualifications of which you are not aware. For example, when you plan to use the proceeds of life insurance as marital deduction property, your wife must be the unconditional beneficiary of the proceeds and also have unrestricted control over any unpaid proceeds. If these rights to the insurance are not given to her, the proceeds remaining unpaid at her death should be made payable to her estate. Otherwise, your estate will not have the marital deduction for the insurance proceeds. If the settlement terms of your policies do not meet these requirements, have them changed now to make the marital deduction secure.

3. What should be done if you do not believe your wife can manage the property you leave her? You will not want to give her complete and personal control. The law permits you to put the property in certain trust arrangements that are considered equivalent to complete ownership. Your attorney can explain how you can protect your wife's interest and qualify the trust property for the marital deduction.

THE CHARITABLE DEDUCTION

When you draw your will, you may wish to remember favorite charities. The estate tax deduction for charitable bequests is unlimited, except in the few instances where state law otherwise provides. Generally, bequests are deductible when made to tax-exempt nonprofit organizations devoted to educational, religious, charitable, and other philanthropic purposes. You are probably now deducting your charitable contributions on your income tax return; bequests to similar institutions in your will would generally be eligible for the estate tax deduction.

Charitable bequests can be of several types. They can be outright bequests, payable immediately. They can be in trust form, providing either for payments of income annually from the trust fund, or payment of the whole fund at a future time. (The latter type is generally referred to as a "remainder" trust and payment is usually deferred until after the life of a surviving wife or a child.)

The charitable deduction is often helpful to people of means whose estates would be liable to heavy estate tax. With advice of counsel, tax-saving plans involving the charitable deduction can be worked out.

LIFE INSURANCE PROCEEDS

Life insurance is one of your most important aids to estate planning. With care, it can be used to provide an almost tax-free transfer of wealth. Life insurance proceeds are subject to estate tax only if they are payable either to:

1. Your estate, regardless of who owned the policy; or
2. Other beneficiaries, if you kept certain incidents of ownership in the policy.

What are these incidents of ownership that make the policy part of your gross estate? The right to sell the policy or pledge it for a loan. Or the right to change the beneficiary, or to revoke an assignment already made. Your payment of premiums alone will not of itself make the proceeds includable in your estate. Thus, the cue to removing life insurance proceeds from your taxable estate is to give away the ownership rights in policies made payable to beneficiaries other than your estate.

However, if you are married, the retention of a minor incident of ownership in an insurance policy that you have assigned to a charitable organization can increase the marital deduction and reduce your estate tax. Say that when you assigned the policy to the charity you reserved the right to choose the settlement option. The retention of such minor right will make the policy includable in your gross estate. This will, it is true, increase your gross estate. But at the same time it will increase the marital share to go to your wife tax-free. And since the policy is payable to a charity, your estate will have a charitable deduction to offset the amount by which the estate was increased.

PROVIDING LIQUID FUNDS
FOR PAYMENT OF ESTATE TAXES

An estate may have substantial assets but no cash with which to pay estate taxes. This can be a pressing problem for the executor. The assets might be close-corporation stock, art collections, or large

personal residences which the family does not want sold to outsiders
—or for which there is no ready market. You will want to guard
against the necessity of a forced sale of assets to obtain cash for
taxes. Careful planning can anticipate the difficulties your estate will
have to face in raising the cash necessary for taxes. For example,
lifetime gifts of shares of stock to family members can reduce your
taxable estate and keep control of the business in the family.

It is not too difficult to estimate the estate tax that may be levied
by a state. But inheritance taxes are more difficult to estimate since
they are levied against the shares of the beneficiaries and each class
may have a different exemption allowance.

From this you can see why it is necessary when planning your
estate to tell your attorney where each item of your property is
located. All applicable state laws must be considered when your
will is drawn.

FUNERAL ARRANGEMENTS

When planning your estate, you should consider all aspects of
funeral arrangements. If there is no family burial plot, you would
consider whether or not to buy one, or to state your preference for
cremation. Though it may be disturbing to some to think specifically
about a funeral, others find comfort in making preparations that will
save surviving loved ones additional stress.

On the practical side, a grief-stricken husband, wife, or child
may be unable to make the best financial decisions. For years, the
inevitability of death has been exploited by certain unethical segments of the funeral and cemetery industries. Even where you deal
with a good funeral establishment, costs are liable to be unexpectedly
high. It is not morbid but a commonsense financial precaution to
make inquiries now. If a family is generally well informed about
death costs, as well as the practices of local funeral directors and
cemeteries, there is less risk of their falling victim to any high-pressure tactics at a time of sorrow.

In the family record book, there should be a reminder that Social
Security provides death payments, and a note of any help that might
be provided by a club or union to which members of the family
belong.

Because quotations on basic costs of a funeral are likely to apply only to the coffin and a few of the services that will actually be necessary, the funeral director should be asked to supply a written statement of costs before arrangements are concluded. Such costs are generally based on the type of coffin selected. Sometimes bereaved relatives will feel guilty if they choose a simple coffin so they order a more expensive one, not aware that other costs rise accordingly. An understanding within a family, and written preferences on the type of funeral and burial arrangements can save much emotional turmoil and provide a prop at time of need. "I am doing what John (or Mary, Mother, or Father) wished," is a solace—as well as a protection against plans advocated by too-busy relatives and friends.

Funeral costs have risen drastically within recent years. Where dollars are a consideration, the family breadwinner will keep an eye on death's bill in order to better provide for the needs of the living.

A FINAL WORD

You are now aware of the costs of transferring an estate and of the amount of tax that may be levied. But no estate plan is ever really final. Economic conditions and inflation steadily change values. As suggested on page 243, your estate plan must be reviewed periodically as changes occur in personal, family, and business affairs. Do not forget, too, that estate and gift tax laws may be revised. Such reform has indeed been pending for several years.

From what you have read in this chapter, you will realize that estate tax planning is not a do-it-yourself activity. Many people who have made out a will on a stationery store form think they have saved a legal fee. Instead, they may have left a tangle of affairs which will cost their beneficiaries dear in terms of time, money, and distress. Whether your estate is large or modest, we suggest you contact an experienced attorney to help you in your plans.

Chapter 17

PLANNING AHEAD FOR RETIREMENT

Though retirement may lie many years ahead of you, you would do well to start planning for it early so that the after-65 years are free of the cares that beset so many retired people. Your basic considerations are:

What will my (or, more usually, our) income be?

How will my net worth stand?

Where will I live?

How shall I occupy my time?

Will health affect my plans?

Each of these points is discussed below.

WHAT WILL YOUR INCOME BE?

Here are usual sources of retirement income:

Social Security

Pension from employment or union; profit-sharing plan

Annuity or other insurance payments

Investments

Interest from savings

United States savings bonds

Rents, royalties, personal business

How many of these sources will you have when you retire? If you are fairly young, you may not have thought much about the subject. You know you will be entitled to Social Security benefits; you may also be relying on a company pension plan. But the declining power of the dollar over recent decades should warn even the young that various sources of income should be developed—the earlier the better. Today, most aged people are estimated to be poor; inflation has seriously diminished fixed-dollar incomes. To have a financially secure retirement, begin planning early.

From earlier chapters in this book, you will have noted the retirement income possibilities from life insurance, endowment, annuities, investment, interest from savings; the earlier you can start developing some of these potential sources the better. A percentage of earnings regularly put into savings (see Chapter 9) is an essential bulwark for retirement.

The amount of your Social Security pension will depend on how many years you have paid on a maximum amount of earning (see Chapter 14), and that maximum is rising. If the salary range you are on does not reach the Social Security maximum, your retirement benefits will be correspondingly lower.

Are you with a company or in the type of employment which will provide retirement benefits through pension or profit-sharing plans? Many people who started young with a company are handed a booklet on the company retirement plan, then they promptly forget all about it even though they may contribute to the plan through salary deduction. Asked to state the benefit they will enjoy eventually, they do not know if the plan will pay off a percentage of their salary at retirement, a fixed sum, a lump sum, benefits to dependents if they die before retirement, or a widow's pension if the employee dies early in retirement.

Private pension plans became the subject of congressional investigation which found that over 90 percent of workers who had paid into pension plans did not receive the anticipated benefits. Some received less, some none. Stricter Federal control was sought. Regardless of any change in the law, you should acquaint yourself fully with the fine print of your company's pension plan.

Some people have had rude awakenings. Where workers had "vested" rights in a pension plan, they assumed they would collect upon retirement. But fine print might state the worker had a right to a pension when 55 years old and after 15 years of service. The person who claims that pension at age 45 after 20 years of service may not be able to collect. Where workers had no "vested" rights, they could lose all upon a company merger or if discharged in an economy move.

New law may require the transfer of pension rights with the worker so that he or she does not lose out on leaving one company for another.

Provision for a widow is of particular importance since the average woman starts out with life expectancy seven years greater than the average man. The gap decreases in time, but at 65 it is still over three years. Too, a wife is likely to be younger than her husband. The husband planning for retirement must take into consideration the possibility of his earlier death. Whether or not his widow can benefit from his company's retirement plan is a major factor in his planning. In face of little or no provision for a widow, the husband may wish to plan an annuity (see Chapter 10).

SAVINGS PAYOUT PLANS

Many savings banks and savings and loan associations offer payout plans to the retired. Say you have $5,000 in such an institution when you retire. You can draw $20.83 a month indefinitely without reducing the principal. (Figures are projected at 5 percent a year, compounded quarterly.) Again, you may have $50,000 in your account. The bank would then mail you a check for $208.33 a month, while you still retained the principal.

You might adopt a program over 15 years of depositing $100 a month, a total of $1,200 a year. At the end of the period, with the 5 percent interest, you would have $26,793.79. If you then began withdrawals on the same scale, $1,200 a year for 15 years, your principal in the account would not be diminished. It would in fact stand at $29,553.74.

But remember two points: These figures do not take into account the Federal and state income tax which is levied on the interest at ordinary income rates. Moreover, the quoted amounts represent fixed-dollar income. The $100 a month you put in is likely to be worth more than the $100 a month that you draw out 15, 20, or 30 years later. The loss of purchasing power on a fixed-dollar return will continue to be a problem in an inflationary economy.

REAL ESTATE INVESTMENT

The specialized field of real estate has proven highly profitable to investors who study its cycles and move in at the right time. Too, alert couples have developed a personal business by buying homes, furnishing them tastefully, living in them a time, and then selling, complete to the last picture on the wall. Others, more modestly, derive a useful income from seasonal renting of a second home in a summer or winter resort area. You may be one of those who can profitably invest in real estate. But there are many pitfalls. You may know of senior citizens who have been deceived by glib advertising of swamp or desert areas as "Your Retirement Home in Paradise" or "Profitable Real Estate Investment."

You may not realize that fine property desirably located can result in years of anxiety and financial loss to an older person, as the following example illustrates: Martha Jay, a well-to-do widow in her seventies now, owns a home in Connecticut. Some ten years ago, she bought two houses in Florida, one for winter living, the other for renting. Early, she found it difficult to secure reliable tenants; some were destructive; some simply did not pay the rent. She put the rental property up for sale. Though excellently situated, the house has not sold. It is constantly the victim of hurricanes and vandals, and its tenants—when it rents. Continually, the owner has to draw upon her resources to support it. She tried to sell the other Florida home. It, too, has stuck on the market.

Gladly, Mrs. Jay would sell *both* Florida properties; she would then rent her own living quarters each winter. She has tried to sell her Connecticut home so she could move into one of the Florida houses permanently. Neither of these possibilities has worked out. All the properties are good, but still the right buyers have not appeared. Mrs. Jay, harassed by worry, continues to spend money where she had hoped to receive income.

Though another person of retirement age might not experience the same misfortunes as Mrs. Jay, the warning is plain: avoid tying up capital in investments that lack liquidity and immediate marketability; avoid investments that require the personal attention which becomes burdensome to older people. (True, an agent will handle real estate problems, but his services will add to the cost of unprofitable ventures.)

On the other hand, you may already have enjoyed success in real estate investment. With knowledge of the field, you can count on income from sales and rentals in your retirement years. Others who, like Mrs. Jay, have no more experience in real estate than home ownership, should be wary in their later years of channeling money into investment property.

If you are interested in real estate for profit, an early start during your high-earning years makes good sense. Though some inexperienced retirees may have struck the jackpot with investment in motel, apartment house, or new development, many more have lost their savings. Begin young with a thorough study of this lucrative field, and you may well derive a handsome income from it in retirement.

YOUR NET WORTH AT RETIREMENT

If you are years from retirement, any estimate of your net worth at that time would be speculative. But you can assess your net worth annually as recommended in Chapter 2, so that you know the general trend of your finances. If you are projecting plans annually to better your long-term situation, preparing adequately for major expenses looming ahead such as the costs of children's college education, and aiming for a gain each year over the last, you are laying the groundwork for protected retirement years.

When your family is grown and no longer dependent upon you, you can more easily make a rough estimate of what your financial standing will be at retirement. Your investments will receive your attention, but, as is noted in Chapter 11, you should avoid switching from growth stocks to income stocks before retirement. Your lower tax bracket then will provide savings on your transactions.

RETIREMENT RESIDENCE

A surprising number of people let themselves in for considerable expense, upheaval, and mental anguish because they fail to work out the question of where to live upon retirement. On the basis of a few visits to Florida, say, a couple decide they will retire there. They dispose of the family home, say goodbye to their friends and depart to a small house or an apartment they have quickly located. Before long, even within a year or two, they are back in the friendly old home area looking for somewhere to live.

This kind of unhappy experience and financial loss can certainly be avoided. Some people should never move away from familiar scenes, good friends, relatives, and attachments to a place of worship, volunteer interests, and social life. Others, whose working life neighborhood is unsuited to retirement, will have their eye on distant places, but they should become reasonably well acquainted with them, and perhaps make some friends in one before making the physical move. If business commitments make it impossible to study an area before retirement, take time afterward to do the research; meanwhile, keep the home intact. Money set aside in advance for this type of vacation is well worthwhile and can save a far greater, vain outlay.

If you have, during working years, purchased a summer home, it, or other housing in the same location, may be ideal for retirement. You know the area, the opportunities, and the people; you are not taking a leap in the dark in moving there.

Throughout the country, many communities for retired people are springing up. In some, small houses are available at modest prices; in others, condominiums and apartments are specially geared to the living requirements of old people. Retirement villages, where recreation, entertainment, social life, and medical care are offered, find high favor with those who wish to avoid the inactive, lonely life often associated with retirement. Such surroundings speedily bring new friends, and they offer the retiree a sense of security and belonging instead of being a cast-off from former business and family responsibilities and ties.

While the retirement village can solve many problems, it may bring others, particularly unwelcome financial involvements. These instances arise where builders failed to carry out promised amenities because they ran out of funds, or where new residents were not fully advised that maintenance costs might rise steeply, or a hitherto private village with a lodge at the entrance might become part of the local township with the roads open to all. Such risks and possibilities are not usually part of the sales talk given to prospective residents, and specific questions may be glossed over. While there may not be any sure protection against shock of one kind or another, people whose financial resources are limited should be particularly wary. If they believe they can "just afford" a certain retirement village, it might be wiser to look elsewhere. Unless there is a drastic reversal to inflationary trends, the retirement village resident must be ready to meet demands for more money. "Don't live up to your income," warn the recent purchasers of a home in a retirement village. Though the couple's attorney approved the contracts, loopholes for additional charges and reduced facilities have developed. The resident who does not husband his financial resources against this type of situation may be in trouble.

Looking at other alternatives for the retired, in the vast majority of cases, it is a mistake for older people to have their married children set up housekeeping in part of the family home or, as is more often the case, for a widow or widower to go to live with the younger people. Better for the parents with too much space to rent to strangers so that the relationship is strictly business. A solution for an elderly widow who cannot keep up with the expenses of her house is to sell and join with a congenial friend in similar circumstances. By setting up housekeeping together, the two older women can cut expenses and gain companionship.

MEANINGFUL OCCUPATION OF RETIREMENT TIME

A fortunate number of people know exactly what they want to do upon retirement, they carry out their plan, and they thrive on what they do. These people have a goal; for them, retirement time is not a vacuum to be filled by whatever turns up, by happy chance or the good offices of another person. They made their own plans in accordance with their own interests and disposition; they did not lean upon others. All enjoy their leisure because they have struck a balance between work and play. Few find all leisure to be completely satisfying; the majority of retired persons need active participation in the workaday world. Many engage themselves in volunteer work for church, hospital, charity, or civic organization; others will seek out full or part-time employment, or will develop a profitable hobby into a personal business.

It is a fact that many people who have avidly looked forward to quitting the job at age 65 find themselves at a total loss when they no longer report for a working day. Even with adequate finances the retired person is likely to tire quickly of travel, sports, bridge, friendly gossiping, watching television, or whatever it was he thought would absorb his time and interest—if he had thought the matter through at all, and many don't. Doctors' offices are filled with older people whose aches and pains miraculously vanish at those times when the patient's mind is diverted, whether happily or by an emergency. When called by illness or accident to take over duties in a child's home, or to fill in temporarily at a job, they are suddenly well. Again, they feel wanted and useful.

Useful is the key word. The person whose work in plant, shop, or office, or in the home made him or her a necessary link in a chain of well-being to others cannot abide being left on perpetual vacation or occupied by nonpurposeful activities. Since this is a book on money management, we address ourselves to the retired, and soon-to-retire, people who need a supplemental income. The necessity to earn can be a spur to activity to those who might otherwise become bogged down in a lonely routine.

The loss of Social Security benefits when earnings rose above a certain level has deterred many retired persons from working as much as they wished. The level of benefit before loss has now risen. It is to be hoped that future changes will enable the person who earns after retirement to enjoy the same advantages as the person whose retirement income comes from unearned sources, and who suffers no loss of benefit.

Whether you are prepared to face loss of Social Security benefits (see Chapter 14) or simply wish to earn up to the maximum permitted, you will find there are many opportunities open to the forward-looking retiree; some, such as renting part of your home or seasonal work, may not involve benefit loss. Turn to Chapter 5 for a general discussion of profitable sidelines, personal businesses, and part-time work.

As an older person, you may not want to tax your health and strength by long hours, high pressure work, or too much physical activity. Also, being retired, you want to enjoy leisure, and not tie yourself down to a 50-weeks-in-the-year commitment. You will find many small businesses or professional offices will accept the part-timer on his own terms for a busy season, or for regular hours so many days a week. You may not see the particular opportunity you want advertised, but you may well make a niche for yourself by sending a résumé and covering letter to prospective employers, or by having a notice posted on a church or club bulletin board. Note that a number of employment agencies handling temporary office personnel are happy to offer part-time assignments to older men and women.

In some areas, there are nonprofit, no-fee, personnel placement bureaus which specialize in jobs for older people. In one city suburban area, the local newspaper daily reports job opportunities for senior citizens. Examples of openings are companion, payroll-bookkeeper, hotel desk clerk, alteration tailor. The news item also reports applicants available, such as a secretary, bookkeeper, carpenter, and taxicab dispatcher. Where jobs and personnel do not match, an older person may enjoy the excitement of breaking into a new type of work.

Throughout the country, the interests and needs of the older people are receiving the attention of government and community. If you are retired and find that in your area older people and suitable jobs are not being brought together, you may be able to initiate this valuable service yourself.

YOUR HEALTH IN RETIREMENT

Obviously, good health is a major factor in a happy retirement. Good health not only means having the strength and energy to enjoy life and participate actively, but it means money saved. Though the Medicare program covers a large proportion of expense, the person over 65 still needs his own financial resources or additional insurance to cover the gap. Since the risk of higher medical expenses usually comes in the later years, the maintenance of good health is of prime importance. Begin early with safeguards. Go to your physician for regular physical checkups, and also go periodically to your dentist and oculist. Excessive exertion, such as snow shoveling, is generally inadvisable for the older person.

Watch diet and nutrition. You may send to the U. S. Government Printing Office, Washington, D.C. 20402, for a listing of useful booklets available at low cost. The food needs of older people, nutrition, and various problems of the retirement years is discussed.

The government also has publications on fakes and swindles in the health field. While everyone is vulnerable to the health quack, older people are more often the target. Fraudulent schemes are legion, so be cautious. You will save dollars and grief by adopting commonsense measures to maintain health and energy rather than seeking them through nostrums and devices that often keep people from visiting their doctors when they should do so.

CONCLUSION

We hope this book, *Managing Your Family Finances,* has presented to you techniques through which you can program, protect, and increase your income; that it has offered many suggestions for the more effective use of income to enhance the lives and extend the interests of yourself and your family.

The basic ideas in this book will remain current for many years, but, of course, there will be changes in certain areas because of economic and political events. When you read of new developments and of Federal or state legislation that affects this book, you can provide yourself with useful reference material by clipping and filing each news item. If you send for pamphlets suggested in the text, put them into folders with other relevant data. This personal supplement will be of immeasurable help to you in achieving the objectives of this book.

You can manage money successfully! We wish you luck in your personal endeavor.

INDEX

O.